THE THEOLOGY OF
JÜRGEN MOLTMANN

THE THEOLOGY OF
JÜRGEN MOLTMANN

Richard Bauckham

T&T CLARK
EDINBURGH

T&T CLARK LTD
59 GEORGE STREET
EDINBURGH EH2 2LQ
SCOTLAND

First published 1995

ISBN 0 567 29277 0

British Library Cataloguing-in-Publication Data
A catalogue record for this book is available from the British Library

Typeset by Waverley Typesetters, Galashiels
Printed and bound in Great Britain by The Cromwell Press, Wiltshire

To Jürgen Moltmann

from whose work I have learned
rather less than I think
and a lot more than I realize

Contents

Preface

In 1987 I published a book[1] which traced the development of the theology of Jürgen Moltmann over the two decades 1960–79. This was the period in which Moltmann published his great trilogy of early works: *Theology of Hope* (1964), *The Crucified God* (1972), and *The Church in the Power of the Spirit* (1975). That study aimed to explain the influences on Moltmann's earlier work, to analyse the development of his thought in that period, and to expound systematically the central ideas of his theology both in the trilogy and in the minor works of the same period. It took 1979 as its concluding date, because from about that time Moltmann embarked on a second series of major works, a series of 'systematic contributions to theology', projected in six volumes, of which four have so far been published. The volume of important work Moltmann has published since 1979 already exceeds the work which was the subject of my earlier study. Readers of Moltmann's theology have come to expect each major work to embody highly creative and innovative developments and to take in aspects of the theological tradition and the contemporary world hitherto untouched in his theology, while at the same time continuing the characteristic structures and insights of his earlier work. A fully comprehensive and systematic study of Moltmann's whole *oeuvre* is a task which probably should not now be attempted before the completion of his current series of major works.

The present book is comprehensive in the sense that it covers the whole of Moltmann's work up to 1993, but it does

[1] R. Bauckham, *Moltmann: Messianic Theology in the Making* (Basingstoke: Marshall Pickering, 1987).

not aim to treat everything in the same systematic detail as my earlier study provided for the first two decades of Moltmann's theology. Instead, it offers, in the first chapter, a survey of his theology, which will introduce the reader to the nature and themes of Moltmann's work and provide a preliminary orientation to and contextualization of the topics which are taken up in more detail in subsequent chapters. The rest of the book deals, in a variety of ways, with most of the major aspects of Moltmann's work. Some chapters focus on specific major books, others trace an important theological theme through Moltmann's work. Some chapters concentrate on careful exposition of Moltmann's thought, an enterprise which is of great importance, because too many criticisms of Moltmann are based on careless reading and misunderstanding of his work. Other chapters combine exposition and analysis with critical evaluation and discussion. Whereas in my previous book I deliberately confined myself largely to exposition and analysis, in this book I also engage in evaluation and criticism.

It will soon be clear to readers that my overall evaluation of Moltmann's massive contribution to contemporary theology is strongly positive. I hope that, where it will also be clear that I find some developments in his theology problematic and some arguments open to serious criticism, my dissent, even at its sharpest, is offered in the context of my considerable sympathy for the nature and directions of Moltmann's theological enterprise. Moltmann has always aimed to write a kind of theology which is open to dialogue, and the development of his theology has demonstrated an outstanding ability to appreciate and to integrate insights from the most varied sources, theological and otherwise. Just as his theology develops in open dialogue, so he expects readers to engage with his thought in a dialogical way. It is not a finished and finalized achievement which the reader must either admire and slavishly reproduce or else criticize and reject. It is an unfinished project, like all theology necessarily provisional, finding its way as it seeks the way Jesus Christ and the Spirit take to the messianic future. The reader can therefore engage with it in dialogue and on a shared theological journey on the way to the kingdom of God. In the present book I give some results of my own dialogue with Moltmann's work over the past twenty years, not in the sense of writing my own theology, because this is a book about Moltmann's theology, but with the hope of stimulating readers in their own critical engagement with Moltmann's work. A book of this kind is successful only if it constantly sends readers back to Moltmann's own books, to reread, to wrestle, to argue, to find what they never noticed before, to find themselves at constantly fresh starting points for that kind of theological reflection which is inseparable from Christian life.

Among those to whom I owe thanks I should especially mention my students. Many undergraduates in the Faculty of Theology in the University of Manchester discussed Moltmann's theology with me in seminars. I have also been stimulated and informed by the work of those who have written postgraduate theses on Moltmann's work under my supervision: Margaret Bristow, Celia Deane-Drummond, Siu-Kwong Tang, Deborah Wilson (née Lyon), Mark Woods.

RICHARD BAUCKHAM
St Mary's College,
University of St Andrews
Pentecost 1994

1

Moltmann's Theology: An Overview*

1. Introduction

Jürgen Moltmann, born in 1926, and from 1967 to 1994 professor of systematic theology at Tübingen, first became widely known for his *Theology of Hope* (1964). This and his subsequent works have made him one of the most influential of contemporary German Protestant theologians, in the non-Western as well as the Western world, and in wider church circles as well as in academic theology.

Moltmann himself finds the initial source of his theology in his first experience of the reality of God when he was a prisoner of war in the period 1945–8. This was an experience both of God as the power of hope and of God's presence in suffering: the two themes which were to form the two complementary sides of his theology in the 1960s and early 1970s. Moreover, his sense of involvement, during and after the war, in the collective suffering and guilt of the German nation, set him on the road to his later theological involvement with public and political issues, not least the legacy of Auschwitz.

As a student at Göttingen after the war, Moltmann imbibed the theology of Karl Barth and it was some time before he saw any need to move beyond it. The new directions in which he was to move, while remaining indebted to Barth, were inspired in the first place by his teachers at Göttingen: Otto Weber, Ernst Wolf, Hans Joachim Iwand,

* This chapter is a considerably expanded version of chapter 14 ('Jürgen Moltmann') in D. F. Ford (ed.), *The Modern Theologians: An Introduction to Christian Theology of the Twentieth Century*, vol. 1 (Oxford: Blackwell, 1989), pp. 293–310.

Gerhard von Rad, and Ernst Käsemann. From Weber and the Dutch 'apostolate theology' of A. A. van Ruler and J. C. Hoekendijk, to which Weber introduced him, he gained the eschatological perspective of the church's universal mission towards the coming kingdom of God. Moltmann was one of the first theologians seriously to study Bonhoeffer's work, from which, as well as from Ernst Wolf, he developed his concern for social ethics and the church's involvement in secular society. The influence of Hegel reached Moltmann in the first place through Iwand: both Hegel and Iwand contributed significantly to the development of Moltmann's dialectical interpretation of the cross and the resurrection. Finally, von Rad and Käsemann helped to give his early theology its solid grounding in current thinking about biblical theology.[1]

The catalyst which finally brought together these converging influences and concerns in Moltmann's theology of hope was the work of the Jewish Marxist philosopher Ernst Bloch, whom Moltmann first read, with great excitement, in 1959. He conceived his *Theology of Hope* as a kind of theological parallel to Bloch's philosophy of hope,[2] and has kept up a continuing dialogue with Bloch throughout his career. Since it was possible for Moltmann to see Bloch's work as, from one point of view, a kind of Marxist inheritance of Jewish messianism, it is not surprising that the most important subsequent influences on Moltmann's thought from outside Christian theology were Marxist and Jewish. In the 1960s he was involved in the Christian–Marxist dialogue[3] and, especially in the early 1970s, he took up important concepts from the critical theory of the Frankfurt School. The influence of Jewish theologians such as Franz Rosenzweig and Abraham Heschel can be found at many points in his work.

[1] For these theological influences on Moltmann, see especially M. D. Meeks, *Origins of the Theology of Hope* (Philadelphia: Fortress Press, 1974), chapter 1. Note also Moltmann's own brief account in HTG 168–9. (For abbreviations used in this book for Moltmann's works, see section A of the Bibliography.)

[2] For Bloch's influence on Moltmann, see R. Bauckham, *Moltmann: Messianic Theology in the Making* (Basingstoke: Marshall Pickering, 1987), chapter 1.

[3] See his own accounts in EG 12–13; HTG 176–7.

While Moltmann remains a recognizably Protestant theologian writing in the German context, his work has become increasingly open to other traditions and movements: Roman Catholic theology, Orthodox theology, and the liberation theologies of the Third World. His experience of the world-wide church – including the sufferings, the charismatic worship and the political commitment of churches in many parts of the world – has also affected his ecclesiology in particular.

2. Survey

Moltmann's major works comprise two distinct series. In the first place, there is the trilogy for which he is probably still best known: *Theology of Hope* (*Theologie der Hoffnung*, 1964), *The Crucified God* (*Der gekreuzigte Gott*, 1972), and *The Church in the Power of the Spirit* (*Kirche in der Kraft des Geistes*, 1975). These represent three complementary perspectives on Christian theology. *Theology of Hope*, probably Moltmann's most original and most influential work, is not a study of eschatology so much as a study of the eschatological orientation of the whole of theology. *The Crucified God* is not simply one of the most important modern studies of the cross, but a 'theology of the cross' in Luther's sense, an attempt to see the crucified Christ as the criterion of Christian theology. *The Church in the Power of the Spirit* complements these two angles of approach with an ecclesiological and pneumatological perspective. The three volumes can be read as complementary perspectives in a single theological vision. Moltmann himself says of them:

> Though I had not planned it from the start, in retrospect I found that these three books belonged together. . . . If one looks at them together one can see that I have been evidently led from Easter and hope to Good Friday and suffering and then to Pentecost and the Spirit. The focal points for theological light changed, and changed in such a way as to supplement one another and correct the onesidedness in each instance which I found unavoidable (HTG 176).

Moltmann now regards this trilogy as preparatory studies for the second series of major works which is now in progress.

This comprises studies of particular Christian doctrines in a planned order, which will resemble a 'dogmatics', but which Moltmann prefers to call a series of 'contributions' to theological discussion:

> The expression 'contributions to theology' . . . is intended to avoid the seductions of the theological system and the coercion of the dogmatic thesis. . . . By using the word 'contributions', the writer recognizes the conditions and limitations of his own position, and the relativity of his own particular environment. He makes no claim to say everything, or to cover the whole of theology. He rather understands his own 'whole' as part of a 'whole' that is much greater. . . . Behind all this is the conviction that, humanly speaking, truth is to be found in unhindered dialogue (TKG xii–xiii).

This does not mean, however, that the series is unsystematic. Unlike the earlier trilogy, it has been planned in advance, though the initial plan for five volumes (see GC xv) has subsequently been expanded to six, by the addition of *The Spirit of Life* as the fourth of the series. Four volumes have so far appeared: *The Trinity and the Kingdom of God* (*Trinität und Reich Gottes,* 1980); *God in Creation* (*Gott in der Schöpfung,* 1985); *The Way of Jesus Christ* (*Der Weg Jesu Christi,* 1989); and *The Spirit of Life* (*Der Geist des Lebens,* 1991). Moltmann plans to complete the series with two further volumes on eschatology and on the foundations and methods of Christian theology.

The most important controlling theological idea in Moltmann's early work is his dialectical interpretation of the cross and the resurrection of Jesus, which is then subsumed into the particular form of trinitarianism which becomes the over-arching theological principle of his later work. Moltmann's dialectic of cross and resurrection is an interpretation of the cross and resurrection together which underlies the arguments of both *Theology of Hope* and *The Crucified God,* though the former book focuses on the resurrection and the latter on the cross. The cross and the resurrection of Jesus are taken to represent complete opposites: death and life, the absence of God and the presence of God. Yet the crucified and risen Jesus is the same

Jesus in this total contradiction. By raising the crucified Jesus to new life, God created continuity in this radical discontinuity. Furthermore, the contradiction of cross and resurrection corresponds to the contradiction between what reality is now and what God promises to make it. In his cross Jesus was identified with the present reality of the world in all its negativity: its subjection to sin, suffering and death, or what Moltmann calls its godlessness, godforsakenness and transitoriness. But since the same Jesus was raised, his resurrection constitutes God's promise of new creation for the whole of the reality which the crucified Jesus represents. Moltmann's first two major books work in two complementary directions from this fundamental concept. In *Theology of Hope* the *resurrection* of the crucified Christ is understood in eschatological perspective and interpreted by the themes of dialectical promise, hope and mission, while in *The Crucified God* the *cross* of the risen Christ is understood from the perspective of the theodicy problem and interpreted by the themes of dialectical love, suffering and solidarity. (These themes will be explained in section 3 below.) Finally, it is possible to see *The Church in the Power of the Spirit* as completing this scheme: the Spirit, whose mission derives from the event of the cross and resurrection, moves reality towards the resolution of the dialectic, filling the godforsaken world with God's presence and preparing for the coming kingdom in which the whole world will be transformed in correspondence to the resurrection of Jesus.

The dialectic of cross and resurrection gives Moltmann's theology a strongly christological centre in the particular history of Jesus and at the same time a universal direction. The resurrection as eschatological promise opens theology and the church to the whole world and to its future, while the cross as God's identification in love with the godless and the godforsaken requires solidarity with them on the part of theology and the church.

In *The Crucified God* Moltmann's theology became strongly trinitarian, since he interpreted the cross as a trinitarian event between the Father and the Son. From this point he developed an understanding of the *trinitarian history* of God with the world, in which the mutual involvement of God and the world is increasingly stressed. God experiences a history with the world in which he both affects and is affected by the world, and which is also the history of his own trinitarian relationships as a community of divine Persons who include the world within their love. This trinitarian doctrine dominates Moltmann's later work, in which the mutual relationships of the three Persons as a perichoretic, social Trinity are the context for understanding the reciprocal relationships of God and the world. The dialectic of cross and resurrection, now developed in a fully trinitarian way, now becomes the decisive moment within this broader trinitarian history, which retains the eschatological direction of *Theology of Hope* and the crucified God's suffering solidarity with the world but also goes further in taking the whole of creation and history within the divine experience. Increasingly, Moltmann has sought to overcome the subordination of pneumatology to Christology, and instead to develop both Christology and pneumatology in mutual relationship within a trinitarian framework.

In addition to these controlling theological ideas, two methodological principles of Moltmann's theology can be mentioned. The first is that it is orientated both to praxis and to doxology. From the beginning a strongly practical thrust was inherent in Moltmann's theology, expressed in *Theology of Hope* in terms of the church's mission to transform the world in anticipation of its promised eschatological transformation by God. From this sense of theology's task not merely to interpret but to change the world, to keep society on the move towards the coming kingdom, derived Moltmann's political theology. But already with *Theology and Joy* (1971) Moltmann became dissatisfied with seeing theology purely as 'a theory of a practice', and began to inject elements of contemplation, celebration and doxology into his work. Praxis itself is distorted into activism unless there is also enjoyment of being and praise of God not only for what he has done but also for what he is. And if praxis is inspired and required by the eschatological hope of new creation, contemplation anticipates the goal of new creation: enjoyment of God and participation in his pleasure in his creation. This rejection of the *exclusive* claims of praxis in theology enables Moltmann also, in his later work, to distinguish theological knowledge from the pragmatic thinking of the modern world in which the knowing subject masters its object in order to dominate it, and to reinstate, by contrast, that participatory knowledge in which one opens oneself to the other in wonder and love, perceives oneself in mutual relationship with the other, and so can be changed. Such an emphasis fits easily within Moltmann's later trinitarianism, in which reality is characterized by mutual, non-hierarchical relationships – within the Trinity, between the Trinity and creation, and within creation.

Secondly, Moltmann's theology is characterized by its openness to dialogue. He resists the idea of creating a theological 'system', as a finished achievement of one theologian, and stresses the provisionality of all theological work and the ability of one theologian only to contribute to the continuing discussion within an ecumenical community of theologians, which itself must be in touch with the wider life and thinking of the churches and the sufferings and hopes of the world. His theology is also in principle open to dialogue with and input from other academic disciplines. This openness is a *structural* openness inherent in his theology from the beginning, since it results from the eschatological perspective of his theology of hope. Theology is in the service of the church's mission as, from its starting-point in the cross and resurrection of Jesus, it relates to the world for the sake of the future of the world. The genuine openness of this future ensures that theology does not already know all the answers but can learn from others and from other approaches to reality. At the same time the christological starting-point, in the light of which the future is the future of Jesus Christ, keeps Christian theology faithful to its own truth and so allows it to question other approaches and enter *critical* dialogue with them. Later, from *The Church in the Power of the Spirit* onwards, this structural openness is reinforced by the principle of relationality which becomes increasingly important to Moltmann: to recognize that one's own standpoint is *relative* to others need not lead to relativism but to productive relationship.

Of the general character of his theology Moltmann himself writes:

> If I were to attempt to sum up the outline of my theology in a few key phrases, I would have at the least to say that I am attempting to reflect on a theology which has:
> – a biblical foundation,
> – an eschatological orientation,
> – a political responsibility (HTG 182).

What is surprising in that summary is the lack of reference to the trinitarian dimension which is so deliberately dominant in his work.

3. Content

(1) *Eschatology*

One of the most important achievements of Moltmann's theology has been to rehabilitate future eschatology. This was in part a response to the demonstration by modern biblical scholarship that future eschatology is of determinative significance for biblical faith. Whereas Schweitzer, Dodd, Bultmann and many others had thought biblical eschatology unacceptable to the modern mind unless stripped of its reference to the real temporal future of the world, Moltmann, along with some other German theologians in the 1960s, saw in future eschatology precisely the way to make Christian faith credible and relevant in the modern world. He wished to show how the modern experience of history as a process of constant and radical change, in hopeful search of a new future, need not be rejected by the church, as though Christianity stood for reactionary traditionalism, nor ignored, as though Christianity represented a withdrawal from history into purely subjective authenticity. Rather, the eschatological orientation of biblical Christian faith towards the future of the world requires the church to engage with the possibilities for change in the modern world, to promote them against all

tendencies to stagnation, and to give them eschatological
direction towards the future kingdom of God. The Gospel
proves relevant and credible today precisely through the
eschatological faith that truth lies in the future and proves
itself in changing the present in the direction of the future.

Christian hope, for Moltmann, is thoroughly christological since it arises from the resurrection of Jesus. His
famous claim that 'from first to last, and not merely in the
epilogue, Christianity is eschatology, is hope' (TH 16) was
possible only because it was a claim about the meaning of the
resurrection of Jesus. It also depends on setting the
resurrection of Jesus against its Old Testament and Jewish
theological background – a recovery of the Jewish roots of
Christian theology which is very characteristic of Moltmann's
work. The God of Israel revealed himself to Israel by making
promises which opened up the future: against this
background God's act of raising the crucified Jesus to new
life is to be understood as the culminating and definitive
event of divine promise. In it God promises the resurrection
of all the dead, the new creation of all reality, and the coming
of his kingdom of righteousness and glory, and he guaran-
tees this promise by enacting it in Jesus' person. Jesus' resurrection entails the eschatological future of all reality.

When this concept of the resurrection as promise is
related to Moltmann's dialectic of cross and resurrection
(see section 2), important aspects of his eschatology emerge.
In the first place, the *contradiction* between the cross and the
resurrection creates a *dialectical* eschatology, in which the
promise contradicts present reality. The eschatological kingdom is no mere fulfilment of the immanent possibilities of
the present, but represents a radically new future: life for the
dead, righteousness for the unrighteous, new creation for a
creation subject to evil and death. But secondly, the *identity*
of Jesus in the total contradiction of cross and resurrection is
also important. The resurrection was not the survival of some
aspect of Jesus which was not subject to death: Jesus was
wholly dead and *wholly* raised by God. The continuity was
given in God's act of new creation. Similarly God's promise is
not for *another* world, but for the new creation of *this* world,

in all its material and worldly reality. The whole of creation, subject as it is to sin and suffering and death, will be transformed in God's new creation.

Christian eschatology is therefore the hope that the world will be different. It is aroused by a promise whose fulfilment can come only from God's eschatological action transcending all the possibilities of history, since it involves the end of all evil, suffering and death in the glory of the divine presence indwelling all things. But it is certainly not therefore without effect in the present. On the contrary, the resurrection set in motion a historical process in which the promise already affects the world and moves it in the direction of its future transformation. This process is the universal mission of the church. This is the point at which Moltmann's *Theology of Hope* opened the church to the world as well as to the future. Authentic Christian hope is not that purely other-worldly expectation which is resigned to the inalterability of affairs in this world. Rather, because it is hope for the future of this world, its effect is to show present reality to be *not yet* what it can be and will be. The world is seen as transformable in the direction of the promised future. In this way believers are liberated from accommodation to the *status quo* and set critically against it. They suffer the contradiction between what is and what is promised. But this critical distance also enables them to seek and to activate those present possibilities of world history which lead in the direction of the eschatological future. Thus, by arousing *active* hope the promise creates anticipations of the future kingdom within history. The transcendence of the kingdom itself beyond all its anticipations keeps believers always unreconciled to present conditions, the source of continual new impulses for change.

(2) *Theodicy*

It was characteristic of Moltmann's theology from the beginning to give prominence to the question of God's righteousness in the face of the suffering and evil of the world. In the first phase of his response to the problem, in *Theology of Hope,* he proposes an eschatological theodicy.

Innocent and involuntary suffering must not be justified, as it would be if it were explained as contributing to the divine purpose. The promise given in the resurrection of Jesus gives no explanation of suffering, but it does provide hope for God's final triumph over all evil and suffering, and thereby also an initiative for Christian praxis in overcoming suffering now.

This approach to the theodicy problem in terms of the hope for God's future righteousness is by no means abandoned, but in *The Crucified God* it is deepened by the additional theme of God's loving solidarity with the world in its suffering. When Moltmann turned from his focus on the resurrection to a complementary focus on the cross, he was concerned to extend the traditional soteriological interest in the cross to embrace 'both the question of human guilt and man's liberation from it, and also the question of human suffering and man's liberation from it' (CG 134). He uses the double expression 'the godless and the godforsaken' to refer to the plight both of sinners who suffer their own turning away from God and of those who are the innocent victims of pointless suffering. This is the plight of the world, in the absence of divine righteousness, with which Jesus was identified on the cross.

In *The Crucified God* Moltmann's thinking moved back from the resurrection as the event of divine promise to the cross as the event of divine love. In this movement he was asking the question: how does the divine promise, established in Jesus' resurrection, reach those to whom it is addressed, the godless and the godforsaken? His answer is that it reaches them through Jesus' *identification* with them, in their condition, on the cross. His resurrection represents salvation *for them* only because he dies for them, identified with them in their suffering of God's absence. The central concept of *The Crucified God* is love which suffers in solidarity with those who suffer. This is love which meets the involuntary suffering of the godforsaken with another kind of suffering: voluntary fellowsuffering.

To see the cross as God's act of loving solidarity with all who suffer apparently abandoned by God requires an incarna-

tional and trinitarian theology of the cross. By recognizing
God's presence, as the incarnate Son of God, in the
abandonment of the cross, Moltmann brings the dialectic of
cross and resurrection within God's own experience. The
cross and resurrection represent the opposition between a
reality which does not correspond to God – the world subject
to sin, suffering and death – and the promise of a reality which
does correspond to him – the new creation which will reflect
his glory. But if God is present in the godlessness and
godforsakenness of the cross, then he is present in his own
contradiction. His love is such that it embraces the
godforsaken reality which does not correspond to him, and so
he suffers. His love is not simply active benevolence which acts
on humanity. It is dialectical love which in embracing its own
contradiction must suffer. Of course it does so in order to
overcome the contradiction: to deliver from sin, suffering and
death.

If Jesus the divine Son suffers the abandonment of the
godforsaken, as the cry of desolation shows, the cross must
be a trinitarian event between the incarnate Son and his
Father who leaves him to die. Moltmann interprets it as an
event of divine suffering in which Jesus suffers dying in
abandonment by his Father and the Father suffers in grief
the death of his Son. As such it is the act of divine solidarity
with the godforsaken world, in which the Son willingly
surrenders himself in love for the world and the Father
willingly surrenders his Son in love for the world. Because at
the point of their deepest separation, the Father and the Son
are united in their love for the world, the event which
separates them overcomes the godforsakenness of the world.
The love between them now spans the gulf which separates
the godless and the godforsaken from God. The trinitarian
being of God includes this gulf within it and overcomes it.

In Moltmann's understanding, the cross does not solve the
problem of suffering, but meets it with the voluntary fellow-
suffering of love. Solidarity in suffering – in the first place,
the crucified God's solidarity with all who suffer, and, in
consequence, also his followers' identification with the
suffering – does not abolish suffering, but it does overcome

what Moltmann calls 'the suffering in suffering': the lack of love, the abandonment in suffering. Moreover, such solidarity, so far from promoting fatalistic submission to suffering, necessarily includes love's protest against the infliction of suffering on those it loves. It leads believers through their solidarity with the suffering into liberating praxis on their behalf.

(3) *Ecclesiology*

Moltmann describes his ecclesiology alternatively as 'messianic ecclesiology' or 'relational ecclesiology'. Both terms serve to situate the church within God's trinitarian history with the world, more specifically within the missions of the Son and the Spirit on their way to the eschatological kingdom. In the first place, Moltmann's ecclesiology is rooted in his eschatological Christology. The church lives between the past history of Jesus and the universal future in which that history will reach its fulfilment: the former directs it in mission towards the latter. But this also means that Moltmann's ecclesiology is strongly pneumatological. For, in Moltmann's understanding of the trinitarian history, it is the Holy Spirit who now, between the history of Jesus and the coming of the kingdom, mediates the eschatological future to the world. If the church is an anticipation of the messianic kingdom, it is so because it is created by and participates in the mission of the Spirit. Its defining characteristics are not therefore its own, but those of the presence and activity of Christ and the Spirit. At every point ecclesiology must be determined by the church's role as a movement within the trinitarian history of God with the world.

If 'messianic ecclesiology' characterizes the church as orientated by the missions of Christ and the Spirit towards their eschatological goal, 'relational ecclesiology' indicates that, because of its place within the trinitarian history, the church does not exist in, of or for itself, but only in relationship and can only be understood in its relationships. It participates in the messianic history of Jesus, it lives in the presence and powers of the Spirit, and it exists as a provisional reality for the sake of the universal kingdom of the future. Since the mission of the Spirit on the way to the kingdom includes but is not confined to the church, the church cannot absolutize itself, but must fulfil its own messianic role in open and critical relationship with other realities, its partners in history, notably Israel, the other world religions, and the secular order.

Within this context, the church can only adequately fulfil its vocation if it becomes a 'messianic fellowship' of mature and responsible disciples. Here Moltmann, with his eye especially on the German Protestant scene, proposes radical reform and renewal of the church. His criticism is of the extent to which the church is still the civil religion of society, a pastoral church *for* all the people, unable to take up a critical stance in relation to society, unable to foster real community and active Christian commitment. The ideal is a church *of* the people, a fellowship of committed disciples called to responsible participation in messianic mission. Membership of the church must therefore be voluntary (from this follows Moltmann's critique of infant baptism) and characterized not only by faith but by discipleship and a distinctive lifestyle. The messianic fellowship will also be a free society of equals, since the Spirit frees and empowers all Christians for messianic service (from this follows Moltmann's critique of traditional doctrines of the ministry). Its life of loving acceptance of the other, however different, Moltmann is fond of characterizing as 'open friendship', since friendship is a relationship of freedom and the church's life of friendly relationships is always essentially open to others (from this follow Moltmann's proposals on the meaning and practice of the eucharist). Finally, the church's open friendship must be modelled on that of Jesus and therefore take the form especially of solidarity with the poor: not simply charitable activity for them, but fellowship with them. Unlike the pastoral church, with its inevitable tendency to accept the *status quo* in society, the church as a voluntary fellowship of committed disciples is free to be a socially critical church, identified with the most marginalized and the most needy.

(4) *Doctrine of God*

Moltmann's mature doctrine of God, as it developed from *The Crucified God* onwards, could be said to hinge on a concept of dynamic relationality. It understands the trinitarian God as three divine subjects in mutual loving relationship, and God's relationship to the world as a reciprocal relationship in which God in his love for the world not only affects the world but is also affected by it. He relates to the world as Trinity, experiencing the world within his own trinitarian experience, and so his changing experience of the world is also a changing experience of himself. The trinitarian history of God's relationship with the world is thus a real history for God as well as for the world: it is the history in which God includes the world within his own trinitarian relationships. All this Moltmann takes to be the meaning of the Christian claim that God is love.

Moltmann's distinctive development of the doctrine of God really began, in *The Crucified God*, from the principle that the doctrine of the Trinity is the theological interpretation of the history of Jesus. His interpretation of the cross as the event of God's suffering solidarity with the world required him to take three crucial steps in developing the doctrine of God. In the first place, as an event between the Father and the Son, in which God suffers the godforsakenness that separates the Son from the Father, the cross required trinitarian language of a kind which emphasized inter-subjective relationship between the divine persons. (The Spirit, however, is less clearly personal at this stage.) Secondly, it also necessitated a doctrine of divine passibility, not only in the narrow sense that God can suffer pain, but in the broader sense that he can be affected by his creation. In rejecting the traditional doctrine of divine impassibility, Moltmann is careful to make clear that not every kind of suffering can be attributed, even analogically, to God. But suffering which is freely undertaken in love for those who suffer Moltmann claims to be required by God's nature as love. Divine love is not merely the one-way relationship of active benevolence, but a genuinely two-way relationship in which God is so involved with his creation as to be affected by it. Moreover, because his experience of the world, on the cross, is an experience between the Father and the Son, it is in his own trinitarian relationships that God is affected by the world.

The third consequence follows: that Moltmann abandons the traditional distinction between the immanent and the economic trinities, between what God eternally is in himself and how he acts outside himself in the world. The cross (and, by extension, the rest of God's history with the world) is *internal* to the divine trinitarian experience. Because God is love, what he is for us he is also for himself. The doctrine of the Trinity is thus not an extrapolation from the history of Jesus and the Spirit: it actually is the history of Jesus and the Spirit in its theological interpretation. It can really only take narrative form as a history of God's changing trinitarian relationships in himself and simultaneously with the world. In his later work Moltmann elaborates this narrative in various forms, eventually including creation.

In all this, Moltmann found himself talking of God's experience. If it is as love that we experience God, then in some sense in experiencing God we also experience his experience of us, and if it is as trinitarian love that we experience God, then in some sense we experience even his threefold experience of himself in our history. On this basis, especially in *The Trinity and the Kingdom of God,* Moltmann develops his fully social doctrine of the Trinity. Significantly, for this to be possible, Moltmann had to recognize an activity of the Spirit in which he acts as subject in relation to the Father and the Son: his work of glorifying the Father and the Son. This makes it clear that the divine Persons are all subjects in relation to each other. It also makes clear that there is no fixed order in the Trinity: the traditional, 'descending' order Father–Son–Spirit is only one of the changing patterns of trinitarian relationship in God's history with the world. Behind and within these changing relationships is the enduring trinitarian fellowship, in which there is no subordination, only mutual love in freedom.

Moltmann constantly opposes any 'monotheistic' or 'monarchical' doctrine of God which would reduce the real subjectivity of the three persons. Instead he insists that the unity of God is the unity of persons in relationship. Three points can be made about this. First, it is in their relationships to each other that the three are persons. They are both three and one in their mutual indwelling (*perichoresis*). Secondly, since the unity of God is thus defined in terms of love, as perichoresis, it is a unity which can open itself to and include the world within itself. The goal of the trinitarian history of God is the uniting of all things with God and in God: a trinitarian and eschatological panentheism. Thirdly, Moltmann sees 'monotheism' as legitimating 'monarchical' relationships of domination and subjection, whereas social trinitarianism grounds relationships of freedom and equality. In himself God is not rule but a fellowship of love; in his relationship with the world it is not so much lordship as loving fellowship which he seeks; and in his kingdom (where 'kingdom' needs to be redefined in relation to the social Trinity) it is relationships of free friendship which most adequately reflect and participate in the trinitarian life.

(5) Creation

The doctrine of creation, relatively neglected in Moltmann's earlier work, receives full attention in *God in Creation*. This book's explicit context is the ecological crisis, which, as a crisis in the human relationship to nature, requires, in Moltmann's view, a renewed theological understanding of nature and human beings as God's creation and of God's relationship to the world as his creation.

The kind of human relationship to nature which has created the crisis and must be superseded is that of exploitative domination. In its place, Moltmann advocates a sense of human community with nature, respecting nature's independence and participating in mutual relationships with it. Human beings, as the image of God, have a distinctive place within nature, but they are not the owners or rulers of nature: they belong with nature in a community of creation which, as *creation,* is not anthropocentric but theocentric. But in order to ground theologically this emphasis on mutual relationships in nature, Moltmann appeals to his doctrine of

God, whose own trinitarian community provides the model for the life of his creation as an intricate community of reciprocal relationships.

Not only is the trinitarian God a perichoretic community and his creation a perichoretic community, but also God's relationship to his creation is one of mutual indwelling. Because God is transcendent beyond the world it dwells in him, but because, as the Spirit, he is also immanent within the world, he dwells in it. With this dominant notion of the Spirit in creation, Moltmann is able also to take the non-human creation into his general concept of the trinitarian history of God. The whole of creation from the beginning has a messianic orientation towards a future goal: its glorification through divine indwelling. The Spirit in creation co-suffers with creation in its bondage to decay, keeping it open to God and to its future with God. Humanity's eschatological goal does not lift us out of the material creation but confirms our solidarity and relatedness with it. In all of this Moltmann achieves a strong continuity between creation and redemption, and between the creative and salvific activities of the Spirit.

(6) *Political theology*

Moltmann has never reduced the Gospel to its political aspect, but he has consistently emphasized it. It was in the years immediately after *Theology of Hope* that he developed his thought into an explicitly political theology, in the sense in which that term came into use in Germany at that time, i.e. in the sense of a politically critical theology aiming at radical change in society. Moltmann's praxis-orientated dialectical eschatology was not difficult to translate into an imperative for radical political change, but Moltmann's political writings in the late 1960s tend towards a rather generalized rhetoric of revolution. What appealed to him in Marxism at this stage was its vision of a new society of freedom, rather than its economic analysis or its strategy for revolution.

Moltmann's turn to the cross brought with it the requirement of a political praxis of solidarity with the victims, which deepens the praxis of hope. The latter was rescued from the danger of a rather romantic vision of revolution or of confusion with the ideological optimism of the affluent by the requirement that desire for radical change must result from real solidarity with the victims of society and be rooted in their actual interests.

Political concerns continue to feature in, though not to dominate his later theology. His social trinitarianism in *The Trinity and the Kingdom of God,* for example, provides a theological basis for democratic freedom in society. But probably the most important later development in his political theology has been the prominence of the notion of human rights, which he grounds in the created dignity and eschatological destiny of humanity as the image of God. It is by means of the concept of human rights that Moltmann's political theology is able to formulate specific political goals. The two earlier themes of revolutionary hope and solidarity with victims gain concreteness especially in this form. Eschatological hope finds its immediate application in striving for the realization of human rights – new dimensions of which can constantly come to light in the movement of history towards the fulfilment of human destiny in the kingdom of God. Solidarity with victims takes political effect in the attempt to secure their rights and dignity as full members of the human community. One could almost claim that human rights come to play the kind of role in Moltmann's political theology that Marxism plays in the liberation theology of Latin America. The concept of human rights is a way of specifying the concrete implications of political theology, and a way of doing so which makes contact with non-Christian political goals and activity, thus enabling Christians to join with others in a common struggle for liberation.

(7) Christology

In *The Way of Jesus Christ,* Moltmann returned to Christology, which had been at the centre of his early work, but was now able to develop a much more comprehensive Christology. The dialectic of cross and resurrection, interpreted in eschatological perspective and trinitarian context, is retained from the early work, as is the stress on the Old Testament/Jewish framework of theological interpretation for the history of Jesus. The latter is now developed in a more distinctively messianic, rather than simply eschatological, form: the Christian dialogue with Judaism must keep Christology messianic, looking not only to Jesus' past but also to his future, which is the messianic future of the as yet still un-redeemed world. Whereas Moltmann's early theology focused on the way the resurrection of Jesus opened up the eschatological future for the world, but did not especially stress the parousia of Jesus himself, the range of Moltmann's Christology is now extended to the coming Christ, as in the Creeds. The metaphor of Jesus Christ 'on his way', which is exploited in a variety of ways in the book, indicates, among other things, that Jesus is on his way to the messianic future. Christology therefore is necessarily *Christologia viae,* not fixed and static, but provisional and open to the future.

As well as this more explicit development of the eschatological aspect of Christology, there is also much more attention to the earthly life and ministry of Jesus than in Moltmann's previous work – more, indeed, than in most Christologies. This has at least two important consequences. In the first place, Moltmann develops a Spirit Christology, which stresses that the life and ministry of Jesus, as the messianic prophet, take place in the power of the Spirit. This emphasis belongs within Moltmann's mature view of the trinitarian history of God with the world, in which the trinitarian Persons interrelate in changing and reciprocal ways. The history of Jesus is not to be understood in a narrowly christological, but rather in a fully trinitarian way, in which Jesus lives in relation to his Father and the Spirit. The uniqueness of Jesus' trinitarian relationship to the Father and the Spirit prevents this Spirit Christology from being a 'degree Christology', as other forms of Spirit Christology have often been. Secondly, Moltmann highlights, unusually in a Christology, the distinctive ethical way of life which Jesus taught his disciples. Christology, he claims, is inextricably related not only to soteriology, but also to Christian ethics;

Christology must be done in close conjunction with 'Christopraxis'; and the 'total, holistic knowledge of Christ' entails living a life of following his way, in the community of his disciples, in fellowship with him.

Finally, holistic Christology requires holistic soteriology, in the sense of a view of salvation which encompasses body and soul, individual and community, humanity and the rest of nature, in a vision of the universal abolition of transience and death and the new creation of all things. This is not new, in Moltmann's theology, but the explicit development of the universal aspect of Christology and soteriology as involving the non-human creation is the result both of Moltmann's development of his theology of creation and of his perception of the universal peril in which all creation on this planet now stands. In the situation of nuclear threat and ecological destruction, the world is now in a literally 'end-time' situation, in which 'the great apocalyptic dying, the death of all things' looms – not, of course, as a fatalistic prophecy, but as an unprecedented peril which puts humanity and the rest of nature in a common danger. In this apocalyptically understood context, Moltmann is easily able to take up again the eschatological dialectic of the cross and the resurrection, which was central to his early theology, and to highlight the contextuality of its soteriological force. In his cross Jesus enters and suffers vicariously the end-time sufferings that threaten the whole creation. He identifies with dying nature as well as with abandoned humans. He undergoes the birth pangs of the new creation, and his resurrection is the eschatological springtime of all nature.

(8) *Pneumatology*

Moltmann's theology has become more and more strongly pneumatological. This is in part a consequence of his trinitarian doctrine, which stresses the reciprocal and changing relationships of the three Persons, and rejects the subordination of pneumatology to Christology. The principle for relating pneumatology to Christology is that they must be understood in relation to each other within an overall trinitarian framework, rather than that pneumatology should be developed exclusively from Christology. This allows Moltmann to give far more attention to the Spirit's role for its own sake than the Western theological tradition has often done. His attention to pneumatology also, however, corresponds to his growing stress on the immanence of God in creation, as his eschatological panentheism (the hope that God will indwell all things in the new creation) has been increasingly accompanied by a stress on the coinherence of God and the world already, by the presence of the Spirit both in suffering the transience and evil of the world and in anticipating the eschatological rebirth of all things through the Spirit. Thus pneumatology first came into its own in *The Church in the Power of the Spirit,* gained a more thoroughly universal dimension in relation to the whole of creation in *God in Creation,* was correlated with – without being sub-ordinated to – Christology in *The Way of Jesus Christ,* and finally receives a full treatment for its own sake in *Spirit of Life.*

Moltmann's developed pneumatology understands the Holy Spirit primarily as the divine source of *life:* 'the eternal Spirit is the divine wellspring of life – the source of life created, life preserved and life daily renewed, and finally the source of eternal life of all created being' (SL 82). This emphasis serves a number of important purposes. In the first place, it breaks out of the narrow association of the Spirit with revelation, which was characteristic of Barth's theology, and so enables Moltmann, in one of his more emphatic rejections of Barthian positions, to give *experience* – the experience of God in the whole of life and of all things in God – a place in theology, not as alternative to but in correlation with the revelatory word of God. The Spirit of life is God experienced in the profundity and vitality of life lived in God. As the Spirit is the wellspring of all life, so all experience can be a discovery of this living source in God.

Secondly, an 'holistic pneumatology' corresponds to Moltmann's holistic Christology and soteriology. As the Spirit of life, the Spirit is not related to the 'spiritual' as opposed to the bodily and material, or to the individual as opposed to the social, or to the human as opposed to the rest of creation. The Spirit is the source of the whole of life in bodiliness and community. Life in the Spirit is not a life of withdrawal from the world into God, but the 'vitality of a creative life out of God' (SL 83), which is characterized by love of life and affirmation of all life. This is a relatively new form of Moltmann's characteristic concern for a theology of positive involvement in God's world.

Thirdly, the notion of the Spirit as the divine source of all life highlights both the continuity of God's life and the life of his creation, such that the creatures are not distant from God but live out of his life, and also the continuity of creation and salvation, in that the Spirit is the source both of the transient life which ends in death and of the eternal life of the new creation. The Spirit gives life to all things, sustains all things in life, and brings all things to rebirth beyond death and beyond the reach of death. But finally, this continuity of creation and new creation is not to be understood as excluding the eschatological dualism which has always been a key to Moltmann's thought. Creation is subject to the powers of death and destruction, and the Spirit is the power of the liberating struggle of life against death, the source of life renewed out of death. The continuity of creation and new creation is created by the Spirit's act of restoring the old creation in the eschatologically transcendent new creation. The christological centre of Moltmann's theology – the dialectic in which the Spirit raises the crucified Jesus to eschatological life – still holds.

4. Debate

Some of the issues which have been raised in criticism of Moltmann's work are as follows:

(1) Critics of Moltmann's early work frequently complained of one-sided emphasis on some theological themes at the expense of others. Especially this was said of the emphasis on the future in *Theology of Hope*, which appeared to deny all present experience of God. However, in retrospect this one-sidedness can be seen to be a result of Moltmann's method, in the early works, of taking up *in turn*

a number of complementary perspectives on theology. In the context of the whole trilogy, the one-sidedness of each book is balanced by the others. Present experience of God, polemically played down in *Theology of Hope,* is fully acknowledged in later work, but given an eschatological orientation which preserves the intention of *Theology of Hope.*[4]

(2) Much criticism focused on the political implications of *Theology of Hope,* though not always with due attention to the subsequent essays in which these were fully developed. From the Liberation theologians of Latin America, themselves influenced by Moltmann, came the criticism that the eschatological transcendence of the kingdom beyond all its present anticipations sanctions the typical European theologian's detachment from concrete political movements and objectives.[5] From some more conservative theologians comes the opposite complaint that Moltmann reduces eschatology to human political achievements.[6] Both criticisms miss the careful way in which Moltmann relates the eschatological kingdom to its anticipations in history, though there is something in the Liberationists' charge that Moltmann's political theology is *relatively* lacking in concrete proposals. From a different perspective, Pannenberg[7] blames Moltmann's dialectical eschatology for the commitment to *revolutionary change* which characterizes both European political theology and Liberation theology, and it is certainly true that Moltmann's dialectical language was sometimes too simplistically applied to the political sphere.

(3) Criticism of Moltmann's doctrine of God has claimed that, in rejecting the traditional doctrines of divine aseity and impassibility, he compromises the freedom of God and falls

---

[4] See chapter 11 below.

[5] See chapter 5 below.

[6] More extreme is the extraordinary argument of R. E. Otto, *The God of Hope: The Trinitarian Vision of Jürgen Moltmann* (Lanham/London: University Press of America, 1991), that 'Moltmann's God is the idea of human community' (p. 11). The book is a remarkable example of understanding grossly distorted by polemical determination.

[7] W. Pannenberg, *Christian Spirituality and Sacramental Community* (London: Darton, Longman & Todd, 1983), chapter 3.

into the 'Hegelian' mistake of making world history the process by which God realizes himself. To some extent such criticisms provoked Moltmann, after *The Crucified God,* into clarifying his view.[8] He does not dissolve God into world history, but he does intend a real interaction between God and the world. The problem of divine freedom leads him to deny the reality of the contrast between necessity and freedom of choice in God. Because God's freedom is the freedom of his love, he cannot choose not to love and as love he is intrinsically related to the world. A different kind of criticism finds it hard to distinguish Moltmann's social trinitarianism from tritheism,[9] a charge which careful reading of his later trinitarian work fails to support. The fundamental point – that the trinitarian Persons relate to each other as personal subjects – has, in fact, much more claim to represent the mainstream Christian theological tradition than has the modern tendency to conceive God as the supreme individual.

(4) Many critics, especially in the Anglo-Saxon tradition, find Moltmann's work lacking in philosophical analysis and logical rigour. This is a question of theological style, and Moltmann's way of doing theology has other merits, such as breadth of vision, which more analytical treatments lack. But it is true that it sometimes obscures conceptual problems in his work which could otherwise come to light and be overcome more quickly. Related to this criticism is the charge that Moltmann is insufficiently aware of the necessarily analogical nature of talk about God, so that his discussion of the divine experience too often becomes unconsciously mythological.

(5) Though not often commented on, two related tendencies in some of his later work call for criticism. In the first place, elements of undisciplined speculation appear, and secondly, whereas his earlier work was carefully rooted in current biblical scholarship, his use of biblical material in

---

[8] See Bauckham, *Moltmann: Messianic Theology in the Making,* pp. 106–10.
[9] E.g. G. Hunsinger, 'The Crucified God and the Political Theology of Violence,' *Heythrop Journal* 14 (1973), p. 278.

the later work seems rather often to ignore historical–critical interpretation and to leave his hermeneutical principles dangerously unclear. One reason for both tendencies is that, whereas his earlier work at its best moved between the concreteness of the biblical history and the concrete situations of the modern world, he seems more recently to have been increasingly drawn into the concerns of the theological tradition for their own sake (or, in some cases, such as the *Filioque* issue, by ecumenical discussions).

5. Achievement and Agenda

Perhaps Moltmann's greatest achievement in the earlier works was to open up hermeneutical structures for relating biblical faith to the modern world. The strength and appropriateness of these structures lie in their biblical basis, their christological centre and their eschatological openness. They give Moltmann's theology a relevance to the modern world which is achieved not only without surrendering the central features of biblical and historic Christian faith, but much more positively by probing the theological meaning of these in relation to contemporary realities and concerns. By recovering a christological centre which is both dialectical and eschatological, Moltmann's theology acquired an openness to the world which is not in tension with the christological centre but is actually required by the christological centre, and which is not an accommodation to conservative, liberal or radical values, but has a critical edge and a consistent solidarity with the most marginalized members of society.

His later work continues to bring both the biblical history and the central themes of the Christian theological tradition into productive relationship with the contemporary context. In doing so, he has recently become the contemporary theologian who has perhaps most successfully transcended the dominant (theological and non-theological) paradigm of reality as human history, recognized in this a reflex of the modern ideology of domination, and attempted to enter theologically into the reciprocity of human history and the rest of nature as the history of God's creation. That he has been able to do so by developing and expanding the structures of his earlier thought, rather than rejecting and replacing them, demonstrates the hermeneutical fecundity of his theological vision and its ability to relate illuminatingly to fresh situations and insights.

A very notable feature of the later work is Moltmann's sustained attempt to reconceive the doctrine of God in order to do better justice than the tradition to the Christian perception of God as trinitarian love. In a period when many major theologians, questioning the axioms of metaphysical theism, have recognized the need to envisage God as receptive and suffering as well as active, and have also rediscovered the potential of thorough-going trinitarianism, Moltmann's has been one of the boldest and fullest explorations of such a doctrine of God. Its merits lie in the attempt to take utterly seriously those claims about God which lie at the heart of the Christian revelation. The attempt has its problems, but the issues are indisputably important for the credibility of the God of Christian faith today.

Moltmann himself has already stated his agenda for completing his series of systematic contributions to theology (see section 2 above), but within this scheme new developments, such as have occurred in all his major works so far, must certainly be expected. As he works towards the final projected volume on theological method, we may hope that some of the methodological problems mentioned above (section 4) will be addressed.

2

Theology of Hope Revisited*

1. Introduction

Jürgen Moltmann's first major work, *Theology of Hope*, first published in 1964, is arguably one of the truly great theological works of the last few decades, and indisputably one of the most influential. Though Moltmann's own theology has developed considerably, in many subsequent works since *Theology of Hope*, it remains one of his greatest achievements, perhaps rivalled only by his second major work, *The Crucified God*. These two books, which constitute the core of Moltmann's early theology, have a concentrated power of argument, focused on their central integrating ideas, which is lacking in the more diffuse structure and argument of some of the later works, significant though these are in their own way. The two early books also have a certain polemical extremeness, which, by contrast with the more balanced and rounded quality of the later works, gives them the sort of impact which one also finds in the passionate extremity of the young Luther or the dialectical rhetoric of the young Barth. The comparison is appropriate, not only because the influence of these two predecessors on Moltmann's work is very evident, but also because, in adopting something of their dialectical and prophetic style of theology, Moltmann had a parallel purpose: that of reorientating theological work. If, having accomplished this, Moltmann has sub-

* This chapter originated as the Ninth Hartley Victoria Commemoration Lecture, given at Hartley Victoria Methodist College in the Northern Federation for Training in Ministry, Manchester, on 13 November 1987. It was first published as: 'Moltmann's *Theology of Hope* Revisited,' *Scottish Journal of Theology* 42 (1989), pp. 199–214.

sequently become more and more like the older Barth of the
Church Dogmatics, this is understandable and brings both
advantages and disadvantages with it.

Of course, part of the greatness of a theological work, and
certainly much of its influence, must derive from its ability to
speak relevantly to a contemporary situation. The reasons
why *Theology of Hope* was able to do so in the later 1960s are,
no doubt, complex. Against the background of previous
twentieth-century theology's consistent refusal to take
seriously the future eschatological dimension of biblical
faith, Moltmann's assertion of the overriding significance of
future eschatology for Christian theology seems, from one
point of view, remarkable, but, from another point of view,
perhaps inevitable. The constitutive importance of eschatology for biblical faith was so obvious a conclusion of biblical
scholarship that systematic theology could not evade the
challenge for ever – at least not if it aimed, as Moltmann's
theology did, to be a theology of the word of God. But the
rehabilitation of future eschatology, which appeared simultaneously in the work of Wolfhart Pannenberg and other
German theologians, as well as, most influentially, in
Moltmann's *Theology of Hope,* was more than an appropriation of biblical theology. It was a *contemporary* appropriation
of biblical theology, which did something that Schweitzer,
Dodd, Bultmann and many others had thought impossible.
Whereas they had thought that the future eschatology of the
New Testament could appear only an incredible mythology
to the modern world, Pannenberg, Moltmann and others
saw in future eschatology precisely the way to make Christian
faith credible and relevant to the modern world. They did so
in somewhat different ways. Moltmann's interpretation of
eschatology proved particularly influential because of its
strongly practical thrust: it made Christian hope the
motivating force for the church's missionary engagement
with the world, especially for Christian involvement in the
processes of social and political change. By opening the
church to the eschatological future, it also opened the
church to the world, casting the church in the role of an
agent of eschatological unrest in society, whose task is to keep

the world on the move towards the coming kingdom of God.

Now in one sense Moltmann, in *Theology of Hope*, was deliberately engaging critically with the modern world. He wished to show how the modern experience of history as a process of constant and radical change, in hopeful search of a new future, should not be rejected by the church, as though Christianity stood for reactionary traditionalism, nor ignored by the church, as though Christianity represented a withdrawal from history into purely subjective authenticity. (The latter Moltmann takes to be the position of Bultmann, a highly polemical dialogue with whom runs right through *Theology of Hope*.) Rather the eschatological orientation of biblical Christian faith towards the future of the world makes it possible, indeed imperative for the church to engage with the possibilities for change in the modern world, promote them against all tendencies to stagnation, and give them eschatological direction towards the future kingdom of God. The Gospel proves relevant and credible today precisely through the eschatological faith that truth lies in the future and proves itself in changing the present in the direction of its future. So Moltmann argued.

Nevertheless, the immensely enthusiastic reception of the book in so many circles took Moltmann by surprise. Looking back one has to acknowledge that an element in the book's immediate impact was its rather transient and superficial appeal to the general optimistic mood of the 1960s. It was published right in the midst of that 'outburst of hope' (as Moltmann later called it) in which a sense of the unlimited possibilities of the future combined with an eager discarding of the past and an enthusiastic confidence that freedom and fulfilment, once desired, could easily be seized. But since the 1960s hope has become much more problematic. The culture of the 1960s itself was rapidly commercialized and consumerized, its naive hopes for real change translated into our consumer society's self-indulgent obsession with mere novelty. Utopian hope has run into the resistant and conflictual realities of a world in which the expectations of the affluent are at the expense of the poor and the hopes of the poor threaten the prosperous.

So was *Theology of Hope* simply a book of the 1960s? Is revisiting it just an exercise in nostalgia for some of us, historical theology for others? I would like to suggest that the roots of hope in *Theology of Hope* go much deeper than the shallow soil of 1960s optimism, and that an attempt to retrace those roots may help us to recover the kind of resilient, patient and creative hope that is needed in the 1990s. In order to suggest this, I want to approach *Theology of Hope* in a rather different way from the more comprehensive account of it in my previous book on Moltmann,[1] and to go straight to the heart of the book: Moltmann's treatment of the resurrection of Jesus. For what makes Christian faith eschatological, for Moltmann, and what determines the nature of the Christian eschatological hope is the raising of the crucified Jesus from death by God. *Theology of Hope* is as much a book about the resurrection of Jesus as it is a book about eschatology, since, for Moltmann, the resurrection is only properly understood in eschatological perspective, while eschatology is Christian only when it concerns the future of the risen Christ. A focus on Moltmann's treatment of the resurrection may also help us to see the relevance of *Theology of Hope* to more recent theological discussion, in which the resurrection of Jesus has been considerably more prominent than eschatological hope.[2]

2. The Meaning of the Resurrection of Jesus

'Christianity stands or falls with the reality of the raising of Jesus from the dead by God' (TH 165) – claims Moltmann, and few would disagree. But the reality which is here at stake

---

[1] *Moltmann: Messianic Theology in the Making* (Basingstoke: Marshall Pickering, 1987), chapter 2.

[2] See, for example, P. Perkins, *Resurrection: New Testament Witness and Contemporary Reflection* (London: Geoffrey Chapman, 1984); P. Carnley, *The Structure of Resurrection Belief* (Oxford: Clarendon Press, 1987); G. O'Collins, *Jesus Risen* (London: Darton, Longman & Todd, 1987). It is rather remarkable that neither Perkins nor Carnley makes more than passing reference to Moltmann.

cannot be separated from the significance which the raising of Jesus from the dead by God is understood to have. It is because theologians disagree as to the significance of Jesus' resurrection that they seem to disagree as to its reality: one person's reality is another's unreality. So we must begin by setting out rather carefully the full significance of the resurrection in Moltmann's thinking – and its significance is very considerable.

Two fundamental concepts combine to create the core of the meaning of the resurrection in *Theology of Hope*. The first is the *identity* of Jesus in the total contradiction of cross and resurrection. For Moltmann, the cross and the resurrection of Jesus represent total opposites: death and life, the absence of God and the nearness of God, godforsakenness and the glory of God. Jesus abandoned by his Father to death and Jesus raised by his Father to eschatological life in the divine glory represent an absolute contradiction, yet it is the *same* Jesus who was crucified and is now raised. An essential element in the resurrection appearances is Jesus' identifica-tion of himself as Jesus, the same Jesus who died. By raising him to life, God created continuity in this radical discontinuity. We could call this a *dialectical* Christology, in which Jesus' identity is sustained in contradiction.

The second fundamental concept is that this divine act of raising the dead Jesus to new life is an event – the definitive event – of eschatological promise. Here the meaning of Jesus' resurrection is dependent on recovering the Jewish roots of Christian theology – something very characteristic of Moltmann's theological enterprise. The God who raised Jesus from the dead was the God of Israel, whose action can be properly understood only against the background of the Old Testament history of promise. The God of Israel revealed himself to Israel by making promises which opened up the future. The very notion of resurrection was meaningful only as deriving from that background: it represented the point at which Jewish hopes for the future became thoroughly eschatological, in envisaging a future in which even death will be overcome in God's new creation. Against this background, God's act of raising Jesus from the dead was the culminating event of promise. In it God *guaranteed* his promise by, so to speak, *enacting* it in Jesus' person. The promise of God's new creation of all things remains outstanding, because only Jesus is raised, but he has been raised for the sake of the future eschatological resurrection of all the dead, the new creation of all reality, and the coming of God's kingdom of righteousness and glory. His resurrection *entails* this universal future. Without the future of the risen Christ, which is the eschatological future of all reality under his lordship, his resurrection *in the past* has no meaning.

Now by bringing these two fundamental interpretative concepts together we can see the resurrection of Jesus as an event of *dialectical* eschatological promise: the dialectical element is important because it distinguishes Moltmann's thinking at this point from Pannenberg's otherwise rather similar eschatological view of the resurrection. To Moltmann's dialectical Christology – in which the resurrection contradicts the cross – corresponds a dialectical eschatology, in which the promise contradicts present reality. The crucified Jesus in his death is identified with all the negative qualities of present reality, its subjection to sin and suffering and death, its godlessness and godforsakenness and transitoriness. But the same Jesus is raised to eschatological life. Therefore his resurrection is God's promise of new creation for the whole of the godforsaken reality which the crucified Jesus represents. The contradiction of cross and resurrection represents the contradiction between present reality and reality as it will be in the new creation. The eschatological kingdom is no mere fulfilment of the immanent possibilities of the present. Rather it represents a radically new future, the promise of life for the dead, righteousness for the unrighteous, new creation for a creation which is subject to evil and death.

At this point, the absolute contradiction of cross and resurrection and the identity of Jesus crucified and risen are both important for the nature of Moltmann's eschatology. The resurrection was not the survival of some aspect of Jesus which was not subject to death. Jesus was *wholly* dead and

wholly raised by God. The continuity was given in God's act of
new creation. Similarly God's promise is for a radically new
future, but a radically new future *for this world.* Just as it is the
same Jesus who was crucified and raised, so God's promise is
not for *another* world, but for the new creation of *this* world.
The promise of the resurrection is given to the world in
which Jesus' cross stands. And it is given to that world in all
its material and worldly reality. It is not that some aspect of
our world can survive into another, but that the whole of
creation, subject as it is to sin and suffering and death, will be
transformed in God's new creation. It is this which gives
Jesus' resurrection its universal cosmic significance, and
which gives it a present significance for the world, in so far as
the world is already transformable in the direction of its
future eschatological transformation.

From the account so far given of the meaning of Jesus'
resurrection, we should be able to see how it gives to
Moltmann's theology at the same time a christological *centre*
and a universal eschatological *horizon*. Christian theology,
Christian faith and, as we shall see, also Christian praxis take
place *between* the particular historical events of the biblical
revelation, culminating in the resurrection of Jesus, and the
universal eschatological horizon which the resurrection of
Jesus projects. They are always in movement from one to the
other, seeking the universal future of the risen Christ. The
resurrection, as a particular event full of universal significance and as a past event which opens up the future, gives
the biblical revelation its claim to universal significance for
all people and all reality. Its universality is not that of
correspondence to universal human experience, but the
eschatological universality of a promise for the coming of
God's lordship over all reality.

In order to fill out Moltmann's understanding of the
significance of the resurrection, I need to relate it to three
further topics: theodicy, knowledge of God, and the mission
of the church. It is, in the first place, highly characteristic
of Moltmann's theology to give prominence to the theodicy
question: the problem of God's righteousness in the face
of the suffering and evil of the world. Jewish–Christian

eschatology, and the very notion of resurrection, have their roots in this question. Apocalyptic eschatology gave no theoretical explanation of suffering and oppression, but it offered the hope that God's righteousness must in the end prevail. In this sense it was dialectical eschatology: it set the hope for God's righteousness against present experience of an unrighteous world and looked for God's kingdom as the negation of all the negatives of present experience. The hope of resurrection, which is the hope that God's righteousness will be finally vindicated even for the dead, sums up this eschatological theodicy. Thus Jesus' resurrection, understood in the context of the theodicy question, is the promise of God's righteousness for an unrighteous world. Its radical contradiction of the cross, its promise of a radically new future which cannot develop out of the present but can come only as divine recreation, correspond to a perception of the world as subject to sin and suffering and death and in need of radical transformation. The resurrection, says Moltmann, is 'God's great protest against death' and against all the manifold forms of evil and suffering which death takes already in the midst of life (EG 31–2; cf. TH 21).

It is worth noting here a sociological comment about the credibility of eschatology which Moltmann made at a later date (EG 33) but which coheres closely with his argument in *Theology of Hope*. Future eschatology, in the form of hope for a radically new future, an alternative to the present, lost its credibility in the bourgeois Christianity of the nineteenth and twentieth centuries, among people who were satisfied with their lot and wished only to secure the future as more of the same. The eschatological message of Jesus' resurrection attains its full significance only where it exposes the unrighteousness of the present and sustains the hope of those who hunger for change. The further question, whether it may not function as opium for the people, postponing change until the *eschaton* and encouraging people to put up with present unrighteousness, is a question I shall take up shortly. In Moltmann's view, however, the eschatological hope kindled by the resurrection of Jesus may not function as a substitute for action in the present, but rather motivates and directs action in pursuit of righteousness now.

In the light of the connexion between the resurrection and eschatological theodicy we should also be able to understand the relationship of the resurrection to the question of the knowledge of God. The Christian God has made himself known as the God who raised Jesus Christ from the dead and so as 'the God who raises the dead' (Romans 4:17) (TH 30). He is the God who promises a different future and awakens hope for it. His reality is therefore indissolubly linked with the hope that the world *will be* different from what it is now. He is not the explanation or guarantor of its present condition so much as the source of hope for its transformation. Therefore the existence of God cannot be concluded from the world as it is or from universal human experience. God is not evident in the world in its present state because the world in its present state does not correspond to God. But if the world in its present state, its subjection to evil and suffering, makes God questionable, conversely the God of resurrection, the God who raised Jesus Christ from the dead, makes the present state of the world questionable. He opens it in hope to a different future. This God can finally prove himself, his lordship over all reality, only in the new creation of all things, and provisionally only by kindling and sustaining hope which contradicts and resists the godless state of present reality.

This argument, which ties the reality of God to the hope of the new creation, is very important. The fact that the resurrection of Jesus does not correspond to the modern experience of reality is here not, as for so many modern theologians, a theological embarrassment but a crucial theological advantage. If the modern experience of reality, which is an experience of the absence of God, were accepted as the final arbiter of what is possible, then God and hope would both be dead. Faith in God is possible only as hope that the world can be different. Only the God of resurrection can successfully challenge the modern experience of the death of God.

Whether hope in the God of resurrection is more than an illusory escape from reality can be known only in the context of my final topic in this section: the mission of the church. For Moltmann, the resurrection of Jesus was an utterly unique event, without historical cause, but not at all without historical effect. On the contrary, as the event of eschatological promise, the resurrection set in motion a historical process of movement towards the coming kingdom, a process in which the promise already affects the world and moves it in the direction of its future transformation. This process is the universal mission of the church. Hope for the future of the world, given in the resurrection of Jesus, entailed and entails a call to universal mission.

At this point it is important to remember that Christian hope is not for *another world,* but for *the divine transformation of this world.* In Moltmann's view this is the crucial point which distinguishes authentic Christian hope from the kind of other-worldly eschatology which, projecting hope entirely into another world, is resigned to the inalterability of affairs in this world and therefore serves to justify the *status quo.* 'There has been,' he says,

> running through the actual history of . . . the Christian church a constant struggle between a religious faith in the beyond, which leaves this world to its own devices, and a hope for the future, which accepts responsibility for transforming this world (RRF 136).

The authentic effect of resurrection hope is to show present reality to be *not yet* what it can be and will be. It is seen as transformable in the direction of the promised future. In this way believers in the promise are liberated from accommodation to the present state of things and set critically against it. They suffer the contradiction between what is and what is promised. But this critical distance also enables them to seek and activate those present possibilities of world history which lead in the direction of the eschatological future. Thus, by arousing active hope the promise creates anticipations of the future kingdom within history. These can be no more than anticipations, but they are real anticipations of the coming kingdom, and precisely the transcendence of the kingdom beyond all its anticipations is the source of its power to affect history. Hope for the universal divine transformation of all reality thrusts believers into the worldly reality for whose future they hope, but keeps them always unreconciled to its present condition, 'a constant disturbance in human society', and 'the source of continual new impulses towards the realization of righteousness, freedom and humanity here in the light of the promised future that is to come' (TH 22). Thus, faith in the God of resurrection proves itself, in so far as a provisional indication of its validity is possible, not as an interpretation of the world as it is, but as a source of resistance to the world as it is for the sake of its transformation.

3. The Contrast with Reductionist Views of the Resurrection

Moltmann's understanding of the cosmic eschatological significance of the resurrection of Jesus contrasts strikingly with the tendency in much recent theology to *reduce* the significance of the resurrection, and I have little doubt that Moltmann's understanding is closer to the significance the resurrection had for those who first preached it and made it the foundation of Christian faith. Naturally, any modern interpretation of the resurrection must be a *modern* interpretation. The question is whether the task of modern interpretation is that of accommodating the resurrection within the constraints of the modern experience of the world, or whether, as I think Moltmann conceives it, it is to bring the resurrection into a critical and productive relationship to the modern experience of the world, opening it up to new possibilities.

It may be helpful at this point to indicate how Moltmann maintains the full significance of the resurrection in contrast to various different forms of reduction of its significance.

(1) An interpretation of the resurrection which reduces it to the apostles' interpretation of the cross or of the significance of Jesus' life deprives it of its meaning as an event of divine promise. Only as a real event which happened to Jesus, in which God raised the crucified Jesus to new

eschatological life, can the resurrection be a ground of hope for a really new future, transcending present experience.

(2) An interpretation of the resurrection as a purely past event, which tells us something about who Jesus was, is inadequate. Moltmann rightly explains that the church recalls past history, not for the sake of backward-looking traditionalism, but for the sake of the unfulfilled promise contained in the past. Especially this is true of the resurrection. It is the remembrance of the resurrection as an event of eschatological transcendence that keeps the church on the way to a kingdom which beckons us beyond every present achievement.

(3) An interpretation which reduces the resurrection to our present experience of it is likewise inadequate. Moltmann does not deny our present experience of the risen Christ and the powers of the new creation in the Holy Spirit: indeed in later work he emphasizes it. But this is an experience of the resurrection under the form of the cross: it proves itself in the encounter with sin and suffering and death. In this experience the promise has not yet attained its goal of a creation delivered from sin and suffering and death. Only as the resurrection retains a surplus value, beyond our present experience of it, can it serve to direct our present experience in hope and mission towards a future which transcends present experience.

(4) The resurrection should not be reduced, in existentialist fashion, to its significance for our subjective experience, excluding the objective world of nature and history. Rather, as promise for the new creation of all reality, it involves believers in a movement of world-transformation, in which they find themselves, not in abstraction from external reality, but in hopeful engagement with it.

(5) Finally, the alternative of transcendent hope (beyond history) and historical hope (within history) is a false one, and the resurrection need not be reduced to either. There are those for whom the resurrection concerns only hope beyond death, while others, particularly some liberation

theologians, have felt that eschatological hope is a distraction from the task of transforming the world now. Moltmann's claim is that eschatological hope for a new creation transcending historical possibility is, properly understood, not an alternative to active hope within history, but motivates, stimulates and sustains it. Precisely because hope of resurrection goes as far as hope can go – to God's triumph over death – it encompasses and includes all lesser hopes for the realization of God's righteousness within history (TH 33–4; RRF 120).

4. The Credibility of the Resurrection

The ground for belief in the resurrection of Jesus is usually discussed in terms of historical grounds for believing in the resurrection as a past event and present experience as a means of knowing the risen Christ in the Spirit. This is true, for example, of the recent, very significant discussion of the epistemology of resurrection faith by Peter Carnley in his *The Structure of Resurrection Belief* (1987). What is missing from such discussions is the element of hope: that to believe in the resurrection of Jesus is at once to accept that God raised him from the dead and to embrace the hope for a universal future corresponding to his resurrection. Since the resurrection is not understood unless it is understood as eschatological promise, it cannot be believed without eschatological hope. Carnley, whose book is notable for its careful attention to the treatment of the resurrection by most modern theologians except Moltmann, might, had he taken Moltmann more seriously, have seen the need for an epistemology of hope to complement his treatment of Easter faith as remembering and knowing.[3]

Moltmann is quite clear that the resurrection of Jesus was a real event in space and time, but refuses to follow Pannenberg in regarding it as therefore accessible to the historian *qua* historian. The problem is that the resurrection

---

[3] By contrast, O'Collins does pay attention to Moltmann (*Jesus Risen*, pp. 67–76) and therefore gives hope a place in his epistemology of resurrection faith (pp. 131–2, 134).

calls in question the very concept of history which modern historical method presupposes: that of the fundamental similarity of all experience. The problem is not simply, as it is often represented, that the resurrection of Jesus is an unparalleled event. We all know that strange and inexplicable events happen, and it is an arrogant historian who rejects reliable testimony to an event simply because he has never heard before of anyone experiencing such an event. But the most one can usually do with such events is to file them away in a catalogue of curious happenings. They do not really rupture the basic similarity of all historical experience. But it would hardly be an adequate response to the possibility that Jesus rose from the dead to put it in the same category as the possibility that someone once saw a yeti. Why not? Because the resurrection, as understood in Christian faith, is an event of *eschatological* novelty, which transcends the whole order of historical occurrence. It is altogether without any kind of analogy in the history known to us, and must be, because it is the promise of a radically new future for the world, which *will* be analogous to *it*. Thus, it can be accepted only as an event which sets in question the modern secular concept of history and itself creates an understanding of history as subject to the promise of its eschatological transformation by God, history as open to the radically new.

As such the resurrection can only be known in a combination of remembrance and hope, and therefore only in a self-involving knowledge which thrusts the believer into the active hope of the church's missionary vocation to the world. I am not myself convinced that this understanding of resurrection faith, as necessarily involving practical and hopeful elements and therefore not susceptible to historical *proof*, need renounce any form of historical basis. But it seems that Moltmann is not prepared to allow this. If we ask how resurrection hope can be distinguished from sheer wishful thinking, his consistent answer seems to be that it proves itself in practice. The promise of the resurrection can be definitively verified only eschatologically, when God redeems his promise in new creation, but it is provisionally verifiable now as it proves its power to make history. As the promise liberates people from acceptance of reality as it is and provides an initiative for change, it passes at least the Marxist test that truth must be practicable. Resurrection hope proves itself not an illusory myth of the existing world, but a critical force for change.

There must, of course, be a sense in which, if the resurrection as promise already creates anticipations of the new creation within history, then in fact it creates *analogies* to itself and is no longer an event totally without analogy. At a later date, Moltmann agreed that:

> If in the history of death there are no analogies to Jesus' resurrection, there are at least analogies in the category of the Spirit and his effects. For us today, the experiential form of the resurrection is . . . the justification of the godless in a world of unrighteousness, the experience of faith, certainty in the midst of uncertainty, the experience of love in the midst of death (FH 163).

Moreover, as Moltmann's later work has increasingly stressed the extent to which the Spirit's activity, not only in the church but throughout creation and history, creates provisional anticipations of the new creation, his stress in *Theology of Hope* on the totally non-analogous nature of the resurrection must be significantly qualified. This may in fact make resurrection faith more explicable than it is in *Theology of Hope*.[4] But nevertheless it remains the case that the resurrection far transcends these analogies and can find an adequate analogy only in the future new creation. Belief in it is therefore inseparable from hope.

5. Christianity as Radical Hope

It is not only Christians who hope. Indeed, in the 1960s, it was Moltmann's frequently expressed opinion that in the modern period hope had largely migrated from the Christian church to the secular movements of human hope.

[4] Cf. the sharp criticism by P. C. Hodgson, *Jesus – Word and Presence* (Philadelphia: Fortress Press, 1971), pp. 240–1.

He saw this as the great schism in modern Western history: 'a Christian faith in God without hope for the future of the world has called forth a secular hope for the future of the world without faith in God' (RRF 200). One aim of Moltmann's theological work was to help to heal this schism, and I think we must grant him some measure of success. But the schism raises the question whether hope, after all, really needs God. This question, which concerned Moltmann considerably in the period when he was writing *Theology of Hope* and soon afterwards, was the more acute for him because of the debt which his theology of hope owed to the work of the Jewish Marxist philosopher Ernst Bloch. Bloch's great work, *The Principle of Hope,* was not only a powerful atheistic philosophy of hope, but one which aimed to *inherit* biblical eschatology in a non-religious form, taking the biblical God of hope to be a symbol of hope, a projection of the immanent power of history to transcend itself in a hopeful movement into the future.

Bloch's catchphrase, 'transcending without transcendence',[5] neatly puts the difference between him and Moltmann. It raises the question whether hope has sufficient ground within itself and in the immanent possibilities of the world, or whether it needs a foundation of trust in a transcendent Creator of the future? Is real transcending possible without divine transcendence? Moltmann's discussion of this point in dialogue with Bloch focuses on the power of hope to overcome the power of the negative in history. For Bloch, hope negates the negative and transcends it by turning every 'not' into a 'not yet'. But Moltmann responds that such hope can surmount only such *relative* negatives as have within them the possibility of becoming a 'not yet'. It cannot transcend the absolute negative, what Moltmann, borrowing the description from Hegel, calls 'the abyss of nothingness into which all being sinks'. At the point where all possibilities of humanity or nature run out, in utterly hopeless suffering or in the face of death, it offers no negation of the negative (EH 34–5). Hence, for Moltmann, the significance of the fact that biblical eschatology arose precisely at the point where immanent possibilities of hope run out, as hope in the God who creates out of nothing and gives life to the dead. Death has no seeds of resurrection within itself, it cannot become a 'not yet', but the really transcendent God of hope can negate even its absolute negativity in giving new life to the dead. Hence precisely the point which Bloch's principle of hope cannot reach – the resurrection of the dead – is the foundation of Christian eschatology.

Death is no mere residual problem for an immanent hope which can deal with everything else. Rather, as the final contradiction of all hope, death casts its shadow over all life, saps the power of all hope, and threatens the meaning of all life lived in hope. But conversely, Christian hope, which does not confront death as the final, intractable problem, but actually *begins* from the promise of resurrection given in God's raising of the crucified Jesus, by no means concerns itself only with death and resurrection. Rather, from its ability to transcend the final enemy of human life, it derives the inspiration and the strength to confront every lesser enemy. Instead of threatening proximate, this-worldly hopes with a horizon of ultimate meaninglessness and hopelessness, it sets them within a horizon of ultimate meaning and hope and so sustains them in every contradiction and calls them to new life when they sink into despair. It also, very characteristically, ensures that none need be left behind without hope. Every movement of human progress within history has to forget some people, those who are already past helping, those to whom it cannot offer hope. But just as the crucified Jesus was identified in his dying with the most wretched of the earth, so his risen future is open to the forgotten, the despairing and dying.

Christianity at its most authentic has always been radical hope. This is why the martyrs, in their hopeful resistance to death, have so often been seen as the witnesses to Christ *par excellence*. Only in aberrant forms, and probably less often than is sometimes supposed, has resurrection faith been an opiate, a justification for leaving this world unchanged. It has indeed often sustained people in otherwise unbearable conditions which they had no means of changing and enabled them to resist the dehumanizing power of such conditions. But it can also, as the power of resistance to all the negatives of life, be the source of the creative expectation with which Christians need to confront both the false hopes and the stagnating hopes of the 1990s.

3

Divine Suffering*

This chapter will focus on Moltmann's discussion of divine passibility in relation to the cross in *The Crucified God*, with some reference to his later work, but without attempting to cover the later discussions comprehensively. The first part of the chapter will concentrate on exposition and explanation of Moltmann's argument for divine passibility. In the second part of the chapter, I shall set out a line of argument, different from but complementary to Moltmann's, which will in general support his view of divine passibility, but with some qualification.

I

(1) *Three reasons for speaking of God's suffering*

Although Moltmann does not explicitly set out these three reasons as such, they can be identified in *The Crucified God* and Moltmann's subsequent treatments of the subject as three reasons – or, perhaps it would be better to say, three elements in Moltmann's single reason for requiring Christian theology to speak of God's suffering. They are closely interconnected:

(*a*) *The passion of Christ.* Only if we can say that God himself was involved in the suffering of Christ on the cross can we do justice to the place of the cross in Christian faith:

* This chapter was originally a lecture given at the third Edinburgh Conference in Christian Dogmatics in 1989, and was first published as: 'In Defence of *The Crucified God*,' in N. M. de S. Cameron (ed.), *The Power and Weakness of God: Impassibility and Orthodoxy* (*Scottish Bulletin of Evangelical Theology* Special Study 4; Edinburgh: Rutherford House Books, 1990), pp. 93–118.

'How can Christian faith understand Christ's passion as being the revelation of God, if the deity cannot suffer?' (TKG 21). To realize the full force of this argument, we must realize that in *The Crucified God* Moltmann was developing a theology of the cross in the sense of Luther's *theologia crucis* and explicitly as a modern continuation of the radical direction of Luther's *theologia crucis.* This makes the cross, in all of its stark negativity, the basis and criterion of Christian theology, 'the test of everything which deserves to be called Christian' (CG 7). In particular, it means that God is decisively revealed in the suffering and death of Jesus on the cross. The cross must be the criterion which distinguishes the Christian understanding of God from all others. Moltmann's criticism of the early Church's understanding of the two natures of Christ, which distinguished the impassible divine nature from the passible human nature and attributed the suffering of Jesus only to the latter, is an application of this principle. The metaphysical concept of God which the Fathers took over from Greek philosophy defined the divine nature as the opposite of everything finite and made suffering and death axiomatically impossible for God. The two-natures Christology was a way of affirming the deity of the Christ who suffered and died, without redefining divine nature in the light of the cross. It understood divine nature in terms of a natural theology (cf. TKG 22) – in Luther's terms a *theologia gloriae* – which had no place for the cross, and then attempted to speak of the incarnation and the cross. The result could only be para-doxical talk of God suffering impassibly (TKG 22). In reality, Moltmann claims, the cross as the revelation of God is incompatible with the philosophical concept of the impassible God. If the cross is found to contradict understandings of God derived from elsewhere, then the attempt must be made rigorously to understand the being of God from the event of the cross. It is in this sense that *The Crucified God* claims that taking seriously the theology of the cross calls for a 'revolution in the concept of God' (CG 4, 204):

> Within the Christian message of the cross of Christ, something new and strange has entered the metaphysical world. For this faith must understand the deity of God from the event of the

suffering and death of the Son of God and thus bring about a
fundamental change in the orders of being of metaphysical
thought and the value tables of religious feeling (CG 215).

(*b*) *The nature of love.* Metaphysical theism has to
eliminate from the notion of God's love for the world any
element of reciprocity. God cannot be affected by the objects
of his love. They can neither cause him pain nor increase his
joy, which is perfect without them. Suffering, along with all
feeling, cannot belong to God's love, which has to be understood rather as purely active benevolence: God's will and
action for the good of his creation. Moltmann's approach is
quite different: God's love is his 'passion' in the double sense
of passionate concern (*Leidenschaft*) and suffering (*Leiden*).
Love is not just activity on others but involvement with others
in which one is moved and affected. Vulnerability to suffering is essential to it. The clash with the Greek concept is most
apparent when Moltmann represents the Greek concept of
God's inability to suffer as a deficiency rather than, as it was
for Greek philosophy, a perfection:

> A God who cannot suffer is poorer than any man. For a God who
> is incapable of suffering is a being who cannot be involved.
> Suffering and injustice do not affect him. . . . But the one who
> cannot suffer cannot love either. So he is also a loveless being
> (CG 222).

Two important points need to be made about this
argument from the nature of love. First, although we shall
have to return to the question of anthropomorphism and
analogy in speaking of divine and human love, it is evident
that Moltmann is not simply saying that God's love must be
like human love in every respect. Rather he claims that being
affected by the beloved and therefore vulnerable to suffering
is essential to what is best and most valuable in human love.
Pathos is not a deficiency of human love, which must be
stripped from our concept of divine love, but is rather love's
greatness, without which it is not recognizably love.

Secondly, however, it is not strictly accurate to regard this
argument as an argument from the nature of human love to
the nature of God. In that case, it would be just another kind

of natural theology, independent of the cross. Moltmann uses it in the context of a discussion of protest atheism's rebellion against metaphysical theism. It functions as no more than a negative demonstration that the apathetic god of metaphysical theism has nothing to offer the protest atheist who values his own human capacity to love and to suffer and to die (CG 222–3; cf. 253). It is not this argument, but the cross which reveals God's love to be suffering love. To say that God is love is to refer to the cross (TKG 82–3). Thus, the argument about the nature of love is valid only in strict relation to the cross. Moltmann's point is that the only concept of God's love which can do justice to the cross is that of passionate concern which suffers from, with and for those it loves.

(*c*) *The problem of human suffering.*   The theodicy question is the main context for Moltmann's discussion of the doctrine of God in chapter 6 of *The Crucified God.* The basic problem of traditional theism, with its purely active, impassible God, is the problem of theodicy: how can an all-powerful and invulnerable creator and ruler of the world be justified in the face of the enormity of human suffering? If such a God is not to function as a justification for innocent suffering, silencing all protest against it and inculcating meek submission to it as his will, then there must be rebellion against him in the name of goodness and righteousness. So metaphysical theism (to which Moltmann links the political theism which depicts God in the image of the absolute despot) has as its counterpart 'the only serious atheism' (CG 252), the atheism of protest, which Albert Camus describes as a 'metaphysical rebellion' (CG 221) against the God who sanctions suffering. So Moltmann, recognizing the justification of atheism's protest against the God of metaphysical theism on the ground of innocent suffering, seeks a way beyond both metaphysical theism and protest atheism, an understanding of God which neither suppresses nor evades the problem of suffering. He finds this in 'a theology of the cross which understands God as the suffering God in the suffering of Christ and which cries out with the godforsaken

God, "My God, why have you forsaken me?" For this theology,
God and suffering are no longer contradictions, as in theism
and atheism, but God's being is in suffering and the suffering
is in God's being itself, because God is love' (CG 227).

Two points must be made also about this topic. First, once
again, we should be cautious about regarding the problem of
suffering as an argument for the suffering of God. The widespread modern Christian feeling that the loving God cannot
be understood as remaining impassively aloof from the
suffering of the world he loves is clearly shared by Moltmann,
but he does not make this in itself an argument. In *The
Crucified God* there is no discovery of the suffering God apart
from the cross. The theodicy question, as sharpened by the
impasse between theism and protest atheism, provides the
context for fresh theological perception of the cross: 'Only
when [Christian theology] has understood what took place
between Jesus and his Father on the cross can it speak of the
significance of this God for those who suffer and protest at
the history of [suffering in] the world' (CG 227).

Secondly, it is important to recognize that the theodicy
question is for Moltmann an aspect of soteriology as well as
the primary contemporary context for the doctrine of God.
In *The Crucified God* Moltmann understands the soteriological significance of the cross more broadly than it has
usually been understood in the tradition, as including 'both
the question of human guilt and man's liberation from it,
and also the question of human suffering and man's
redemption from it' (CG 134). Moltmann by no means
underrates the former. In a later comment, having claimed
that 'the universal significance of the crucified Christ is only
really comprehended through the theodicy question', he
continues that, 'the interpretation of Christ's death on the
cross as an atoning event in the framework of the question of
human guilt is the central part of this universal significance;
but it is not the whole of it, or its fullness' (TKG 52). In
chapters 4 and 5 of *The Crucified God* he holds closely
together the double soteriological significance of the cross:
for justification and theodicy. Only in chapter 6 does the
theodicy question become the dominant one, because it is so

closely involved in the modern problematic of the doctrine of God. But it remains a soteriological issue: in other words, the point of relating God to suffering is not to explain suffering, but to redeem from suffering. Thus, although Moltmann in chapter 6 probes the theology of the cross as a question which goes beyond soteriology to the doctrine of God – the question of who God himself is in the event of the cross (and cf. FC 62–4) – the effect is not to detach the doctrine of God from soteriology but to relate the doctrine of God to soteriology. Just as Moltmann recognizes the soteriological interest in the patristic doctrine of the impassibility of God (CG 228, 267–9), so his interpretation of the cross as the event of God's suffering is strongly soteriological: all suffering becomes God's *so that he may overcome it* (CG 246). God's suffering is with those who suffer for the sake of their redemption from suffering.

Thus, the three elements we have identified as contributing to Moltmann's need to speak of God's suffering are very closely connected: the cross reveals God to be love which suffers with and for those who suffer. Because God is love he is for himself (the doctrine of God) what he is for us (soteriology) in the event of his suffering love.

The three elements are probably the three major reasons why many other Christian theologians since the mid-nineteenth century have questioned the doctrine of divine impassibility.[1] But it is noteworthy that whereas the second and third have often been given independent validity, in Moltmann's *The Crucified God* they function not as independent reasons but only in the closest connexion with the first. Paul Fiddes's recent book on divine suffering[2] identifies these three as three major reasons why recent theology has come to speak of divine suffering, and adds a fourth: 'the world-picture of today', by which he means the picture of the world as process and therefore of God as involved in the

---

[1] See the survey in R. Bauckham, '"Only the suffering God can help": divine passibility in modern theology,' *Themelios* 9/3 (1984), pp. 6–12, with bibliography.

[2] P. S. Fiddes, *The Creative Suffering of God* (Oxford: Clarendon Press, 1988), chapter 2.

process and interacting with its freedom.[3] This idea of God's suffering the freedom he grants the non-human creation does later appear in Moltmann's doctrine of creation (GC 69, 210–11).

(2) *Jesus' cry of dereliction as central to Moltmann's understanding of the suffering of God*

Moltmann takes the words of Psalm 22, 'My God, my God, why have you forsaken me?', spoken by the dying Jesus in Mark's account of the crucifixion (Mark 15:34), to be, though not as such a historical report of what Jesus said, an authentic interpretation of Jesus' dying cry which takes us closest to the theological reality of Jesus' dying and death (CG 146–7). The crucified Jesus' abandonment by God his Father is the deepest theological reality of the event of the cross and dictates the terms in which a theology of the cross must speak of God's suffering. It is worth noticing that a recent full study of the cry of dereliction, from both a biblical and a theological perspective, by the Italian theologian Gérard Rossé,[4] strongly supports the weight Moltmann gives to the cry and to a large extent, though with some qualifications, the significance Moltmann finds in it.[5]

In relation to the cry of dereliction we can take further what we have already said about soteriology and the doctrine of God. The cry has both dimensions. Its soteriological significance is Jesus' (and therefore God's) identification with the godless and the godforsaken in the depths of their abandonment. Here Moltmann makes a strong contemporary restatement of a traditional understanding of the cry.[6] But he is anxious to press beyond this to the cry's revelation of the significance the cross has for God himself. It is Jesus' cry to the Father who has abandoned him.

---

[3] Fiddes, *Creative Suffering*, pp. 37–45.

[4] G. Rossé, *The Cry of Jesus on the Cross* (tr. S. W. Arndt; New York: Paulist Press, 1987).

[5] Rossé denies that the cry expresses despair (cf. TKG 78–9) or rebellion (cf. CG 227): *Cry of Jesus*, pp. 102, 108. He also questions the way Moltmann sees a real separation between the Father and the Son on the cross: *Cry of Jesus*, pp. 136–8.

[6] For the history of interpretation, see Rossé, *Cry of Jesus*, chapter 5.

Moreover, we do not take the incarnation seriously if we distinguish at this point between the humanity of Jesus and the divine Son. In the relationship between Jesus and his Father on the cross, it is a question of 'the person of Jesus . . . in its totality as the Son' (CG 207). Thus, the cry of dereliction signifies an event of suffering between the Father and the Son, that is, in God himself: 'there God disputes with God; there God cries out to God; there God dies in God' (FC 65). This insistence on the cry of dereliction as having an inner-trinitarian significance which points to suffering in God is immensely important for understanding Moltmann's view of divine suffering. He wants to make clear that the cross is not just, as in traditional theology, an act of God external to himself for our salvation – an *opus trinitatis ad extra* – by which God in himself is unaffected. Rather, as an event in which the Son suffers abandonment by the Father, the cross is God acting in himself: 'But if God is acting in himself, then he is also suffering his own action in himself' (FC 65).

This is why Moltmann is not content with the way in which Chalcedonian Christology could speak of God's suffering and death, in terms of the doctrine of the two natures, nor even with the ways in which Rahner and Barth tried to take the traditional approach further (cf. CG 201–4; FC 62–4). However seriously these theologians had tried to attribute the suffering and death of the cross to God, it remained a matter of God's outward relationship to the world, not of his inner trinitarian relationships with himself. Moltmann takes the cry of dereliction to mean that the suffering of the cross affects God in his inner trinitarian relationships. This is why the soteriological approach to the cross is not enough. At this point, Moltmann tends to give the rather misleading impression that he is leaving soteriology behind in order to discuss an aspect of the cross (how it affects God) which is *not* of soteriological significance (cf. FC 62; CG 201). His tendency to separate, in discussion, what the cross means for God from what it means for us has some unfortunate consequences. But the separation, as we have already indicated, does not really mean that soteriology is left behind. Moltmann's point is rather that we do not understand the full soteriological significance of the cross until we have probed its significance for God himself. The depth and effectiveness of God's solidarity with the godforsaken are seen when it is realized that God suffers the godforsakenness of Jesus in himself. God's saving relationship to us takes place within and affects his trinitarian relationships to himself. The distinction between God in himself and God for us disappears (cf. FC 76).

(3) *The suffering of the cross as internal to the Trinity*

As Moltmann unpacks the meaning of the cry of dereliction, he describes a differentiated suffering of both the Father and the Son. That the Father and the Son both suffer, but in different ways, is essential to his location of the suffering of the cross in the relationship between the Father and the Son, and so within God, not just in the relationship between God and the world. It is not that only the incarnate Son suffers. Nor is it that the human Jesus suffers and God shares Jesus' experience of suffering by empathy.[7] Rather, while Jesus the Son suffers dying in abandonment by his Father, the Father suffers in grief the death of his Son. 'The grief of the Father is here as important as the death of the Son' (CG 243). In other words, Father and Son experience a mutual loss – the Son of his Father, the Father of his Son – but differently in that it is the Son who is left by the Father to die. Although Moltmann does not perhaps make this point as clear as he might, this mutual loss is the estrangement of godforsaken humanity from God taken, as it were, within the divine experience, through the Son's identification with the godforsaken, and suffered by God. But the nature of the suffering is peculiarly God's, since the mutual loss ruptures the unparalleled closeness of the Son and the Father.

Moltmann has been criticized for the way he divides the persons,[8] but to understand him we need also to appreciate the paradox he presents, according to which Father and Son are most deeply united precisely in their division. The event of the cross is the act of God's love for the world, in which

[7] So, apparently, Fiddes, *Creative Suffering*, p. 168.
[8] Rossé, *Cry of Jesus*, pp. 136–8; Fiddes, *Creative Suffering*, pp. 138–40, 202.

Father and Son are united in a 'deep community of will' (CG 243). It is in their common love that the Father surrenders the Son to death and the Son surrenders himself to death. 'On the cross Jesus and his God and Father are divided as deeply as possible through an accursed death, and yet they are most deeply one through their surrender' (FC 73). It is this paradox which makes the cross salvific. God suffers the estrangement of sinful and suffering humanity from himself and includes it within the loving fellowship of his trinitarian being. Thus the Holy Spirit, the third trinitarian person, who unites the Father and the Son in their love at the point of their most painful separation, is 'the creative love proceeding out of the Father's pain and the Son's self-surrender and coming to forsaken human beings in order to open to them a future for life' (TTC 294–5). In this way it is God's inner-trinitarian suffering which reaches the godless and the godforsaken with his love. The cross makes the human situation the situation of God, from which neither guilt nor suffering nor death can exclude anyone (GC 276–7).

(4) *The cross as a unique event of divine suffering*

Paul Fiddes rightly points out that one of the major tasks of a doctrine of divine suffering is to talk coherently of 'a God who suffers universally and yet is still present uniquely and decisively in the sufferings of Christ'.[9] He finds Moltmann attempting to do this, but failing to do so satisfactorily.[10] In Moltmann's work after *The Crucified God* it is clear that he does not intend to confine God's suffering to the event of the cross (cf. CPS 62–4; TKG 118; GC 15–16, 69, 210–11). This is less clear in *The Crucified God* itself, but even there his discussion of Jewish theology – both Abraham Heschel's interpretation of the divine *pathos* in the theology of the Old Testament prophets and the rabbinic understanding of the *Shekinah* in the sufferings of Israel – requires that the God of Israel already suffered in his relationship with Israel (CG 270–4). Yet it is clear that Moltmann does not regard the

[9] Fiddes, *Creative Suffering*, p. 3.
[10] Fiddes, *Creative Suffering*, pp. 5–12.

cross as merely the revelation to us of the suffering God constantly experiences in his relation to his creation – a position which is found in some representatives of the English tradition of thought about divine passibility.[11] The cross, it seems, is unique not only for us but also for God. Even in Moltmann's later work, where he develops a much broader account of God's trinitarian history with the world from creation to consummation, the cross retains a unique and decisive place. If Moltmann is not fully successful in stating the character of this uniqueness, I think it can be interpreted in a way which does better justice to his thought than Fiddes' discussion of it.[12]

Not using Moltmann's words, one could say that the cross is the event in which God makes all human suffering his *own*. Here God does not merely enter by empathy into the suffering of all who suffer, but by an act of solidarity in suffering makes their suffering his own. In Moltmann's own words, God 'does not merely enter into [the human] situation of [godforsakenness]; he also accepts and adopts it himself, making it part of his own eternal life' (TKG 119). The differentiated suffering of Father and Son in the event of the cross, even if approached by God's suffering with Israel (CG 274; TKG 118), is unique, and essential to the cross as God's act of solidarity with the godless and the godforsaken. God the Son suffers abandonment *himself*, actually as one of the godforsaken; God the Father suffers the death of *his own* Son as one of the godforsaken. This understanding of the uniqueness of the cross of course

[11] E.g. H. R. Rashdall, *The Idea of Atonement in Christian Theology* (London: Macmillan, 1919), pp. 450–4; F. Young in J. Hick (ed.), *The Myth of God Incarnate* (London: SCM Press, 1977), pp. 36–7.

[12] Fiddes, *Creative Suffering*, p. 9, misses the point: 'If God has always been really dwelling with people in their suffering, then he must have been having the same kind of experience which Moltmann attributes to the cross.' But this is to assume that God experiences the sufferings of Jesus only by empathy, as he does other sufferers' sufferings. This is Fiddes' own view (cf. *Creative Suffering*, pp. 168, 200) but it is not Moltmann's, for whom Jesus' sufferings are experienced by God the Son, not as someone else's sufferings, but uniquely as his own human sufferings.

requires the 'Alexandrian' type of Christology which Moltmann takes for granted (cf. TKG 118–19) – and of which Fiddes is critical from the point of view of his own more 'Antiochene' Christology.[13] But to be fully comprehensible it requires thought about the distinction, to which Moltmann gives no attention, between God's suffering *as God* and God's suffering *as human* (in the incarnation). We shall return to this point.

(5) *The God–world relationship as reciprocal*

Finally, we turn to the wider question of Moltmann's understanding of the relation between God and the world and its difference from the classical theistic understanding. The doctrine of divine impassibility was part and parcel of the view that God relates only actively to the world. Because he is complete in his own perfection in himself, he cannot be affected by the world, which would mean being changed by it. Moltmann, from *The Crucified God* onwards, develops, by contrast, a view of God's history with the world which is a history of reciprocal relationships. God's creation both causes him suffering and augments his joy. Moltmann calls this the trinitarian history of God, because, in conformity with the relationship of the Trinity to the cross which we have sketched, he sees God's relationship with the world taking place within the trinitarian relationships of Father, Son and Spirit. It is a relationship which really affects God because it is internal to his trinitarian self-relationship. God's changing relationships with his creation are at the same time changing relationships between the trinitarian persons. In experiencing the world God experiences himself differently. This idea is worked out in detail in *The Trinity and the Kingdom of God*.

However, the contrast with the classical view is not absolute, because Moltmann maintains a strong emphasis on

---

[13] Cf. Fiddes, *Creative Suffering*, p. 138. By calling Fiddes' Christology Antiochene in approach, I do not mean that he separates the two natures. I mean that his christological model is the Antiochene one of the union of God the *Logos* with a human person, such that Jesus is the most perfect instance of God's union with people. For Alexandrian Christology, on the other hand, Jesus is constituted a person only as the humanity of God.

the priority of God's voluntary love towards the world. It is only because God voluntarily opens himself in love to the world that he can be affected by it. This emerges, in the first place, in his criticism of the patristic doctrine of divine *apatheia*. Moltmann does recognize that the doctrine contained an important truth: that God is not *subjected* to suffering against his will *as creatures are* (CG 229–30). The Fathers made the mistake of recognizing only two alternatives:

> either essential incapacity for suffering, or a fateful subjection to suffering. But there is a third form of suffering: active suffering – the voluntary laying oneself open to another and allowing oneself to be intimately affected by him; that is to say, the suffering of passionate love. . . . If [God] is capable of loving something else [than himself], then he lays himself open to the suffering which love for another brings him; and yet, by virtue of his love, he remains master of the pain that love causes him to suffer. God does not suffer out of deficiency of being, like created beings. . . . But he suffers from the love which is the superabundance and overflowing of his being (TKG 23; cf. CG 230).

It should also be noted that God's suffering is not only consequent on God's loving initiative. It also contributes to the fulfilment of God's loving purpose for his creation. God's suffering is powerful. It is a moment in his creative and redemptive activity. It is through his suffering that God liberates his creation for its participation in his eschatological joy (cf. TKG 59–60).

The notion of an important degree of reciprocity between God and the world (cf. TKG 98–9) has very broad effects on Moltmann's later theology, which we cannot fully explore here. The idea of divine suffering is increasingly subsumed under the broader notion of divine self-limitation or *kenosis*, as involved in the act of creation as such and as characteristic of all of God's relationships with his creation. Suffering in the sense of pain follows as a further step from suffering in the sense of allowing: God's letting creation be itself as other than himself and giving it a degree of freedom in relation to himself (cf. TKG 108–11, 118–19; GC 86–90). But Moltmann

insists that this self-limitation in respect of God's omni-
potence is at the same time a de-limitation in respect of his
goodness (TKG 119; cf. GC 88–9). In other words, it enables
his love to evoke the free response of his creation. It becomes
clear that the issue of divine passibility is closely connected
with the issue of divine and human freedom and their relationship, itself a major preoccupation in Moltmann's later
work (e.g. TKG 52–60, 105–8, 191–222; GC 79–86).

II

Moltmann's understanding of the cross as an event of divine
suffering contains valuable insights, but needs certainly some
clarification and perhaps some qualification.

(1) *The problem of patristic Christology*

A discussion can usefully begin with the problem of patristic
Christology, which, as Moltmann correctly sees, enshrined
the contradiction which has always hampered the development of a thorough-going theology of the cross: 'since that
time most theologians have simultaneously maintained the
passion of Christ, God's Son, and the deity's essential
incapacity for suffering – even though it was at the price of
having to talk paradoxically about "the sufferings of the God
who cannot suffer". But in doing this they have simply added
together Greek philosophy's "apathy" axiom and the central
statements of the gospel. The contradiction remains – and
remains unsatisfactory' (TKG 22).

From the point of view of the problem of divine suffering,
patristic Christology had two rather different sides to it. On
the one hand, it should be recognized that in Alexandrian
Christology, as represented especially by Cyril of Alexandria,
and in Chalcedonian orthodoxy, especially as clarified by the
fifth ecumenical council, the Council of Constantinople of
553, it was very important to be able to say that God the *Logos*
was the subject of the passion and death of Jesus. Such
language was as old as Ignatius of Antioch, who spoke of
'the passion of my God', and the paradoxes it engendered
were equally traditional: Melito of Sardis (frg. 13) already
writes, 'the invisible was seen . . . , the impassible suffered,

the immortal died, the heavenly one was buried'. In the Alexandrian tradition a major concern in Christology became the need to maintain the single divine subject of the whole incarnate life, so that to be able to say that 'God was born' (and therefore Mary was 'Mother of God') and 'God suffered' were treated as the shibboleths of orthodoxy. The Antiochenes resisted such statements because they seemed to make divine nature passible, but the Alexandrians insisted on them because only in this way could the work of salvation be God's work. God the *Logos* must be the one and only subject of the whole of the incarnate life of Christ, including especially the redemptive passion and death. They allowed no human subject in Christ to whom such experiences could be attributed. That Chalcedon itself taught this Cyrilline doctrine of a single divine subject of the incarnation, to whom the suffering of Christ must be attributed, was not clear in the period immediately after Chalcedon, when its defence against the so-called Monophysites was in the hands of theologians who interpreted it in an Antiochene way, but its meaning was eventually clarified through the theopaschite controversy of the sixth century, in which the so-called Neo-Chalcedonians promoted a Cyrilline interpretation of Chalcedon, which was endorsed by the Council of Constantinople of 553. The significance of the theopaschite controversy has been undeservedly neglected by modern theologians who have tended to see Chalcedon as the conclusion of the patristic christological debate, so far as its relevance for later theology goes. Moltmann, who notes the controversy, incorrectly states that the theopaschite formula, 'One of the holy Trinity suffered in the flesh', was rejected (CG 228).[14] In fact, it was endorsed by the Council of Constantinople, which maintained that 'Jesus Christ who was crucified in the flesh is true God and the Lord of glory and one of the Holy Trinity' (the statement alludes to 1 Corinthians 2:8 as the prooftext for saying that God was crucified). Such language was nothing new, but the Council

[14] Fiddes, *Creative Suffering*, p. 115 n.11, says that 'while approved by the second Council of Constantinople in 553, it was finally rejected by the Western Church'. This is also incorrect.

established, probably quite correctly,[15] that Chalcedonian orthodoxy entailed it.

Moltmann probably underestimates this side of patristic Christology,[16] but he correctly notes that the Fathers found it well-nigh impossible to see the suffering thus attributed to God as a real experience of suffering for God (CG 227–9). According to the doctrine of the two natures, also established at Chalcedon, God in the incarnation is the subject of two natures, his own impassible divine nature and the passible human nature he assumes in incarnation. To say that God suffered meant that he was the subject of the sufferings of his human nature. He who in his own divine nature is impassible suffered in his human nature. The Fathers might have resolved the paradox by saying that only in incarnation can God suffer, but in fact the axiom of divine impassibility was so strong that they usually resolved the paradox by minimizing the reality of the suffering for God. What Cyril seems to mean by the claim that God 'suffered impassibly' is that the *Logos* was aware of the sufferings of his human nature, accepted them as his own, because the human nature is his, but did not experience them as sufferings. No doubt this did not seem as docetic then as it does to us, because of the contemporary ideal of human detachment from suffering.[17] But it is logically unsatisfactory, because there can be no such thing as suffering unless *someone* actually suffers. Since Cyril denies a human subject in Christ, the crucifixion can be described as suffering only if God experiences it as suffering. He cannot simply acknowledge the suffering as his own without experiencing it as suffering, because unless he experiences it as suffering no suffering exists for him to own. In this sense the Antiochenes were

---

[15] For the view that neo-Chalcedonianism was faithful to the intentions of Chalcedon, see P. T. R. Gray, *The Defence of Chalcedon in the East (451–553)* (Leiden: Brill, 1979).

[16] The discussion in CG 231–2 uses the term 'person' in a more Antiochene than Alexandrian–Chalcedonian way ('the whole of the divine and human person of Christ'), and so seems to miss the point that the divine person suffers and dies, though not in his divine nature.

[17] Cf. F. M. Young, 'A Reconsideration of Alexandrian Christology,' *Journal of Ecclesiastical History* 22 (1971), pp. 103–14.

correct: the only way to preserve the reality of Christ's human experience and the absolute impassibility of God was to attribute the former to the man Jesus, a human subject not identical with the *Logos*. Chalcedonian orthodoxy, with its single divine subject in Christ, must logically deny either that any suffering took place when Jesus was crucified or that God is absolutely impassible. But it would be quite coherent to claim that God can suffer *only* in incarnation, that is, only by experiencing the human experience of Jesus as his own.

(2) *God's incarnate suffering*

While it is true that the Fathers' Christology was hampered by their Platonic definition of divine nature, the problem raised by patristic Christology cannot be solved simply by rejecting their definition of divine nature, as Moltmann does. Taking incarnation seriously requires us to assert that divine nature – what it is for God to be God – includes the possibility of being human, that is, of making his own all the finite experience of a fully human life, of course without ceasing to be God. It is not possible to define divine nature in such a way as to exclude the properties of being human, as the Fathers did, and then unite the two natures, without separation or confusion, in the divine person of the *Logos*. Unless divine nature includes the possibility of being human incarnation is not possible. But, on the other hand, incarnation does not mean a general dissolution of the difference between divine and human natures. Only in the unique instance of the man Jesus is God human in the full sense that he is all that it means to be a finite human creature. At this point, isolating the issue of suffering can be misleading. Whatever we may say about suffering, we are bound, if we take incarnation seriously, to distinguish between what can be said of God *as human* (in the incarnation) and what can be said of him *as God* (outside incarnation). Even if we took the most anthropomorphic language of the Old Testament as the criterion of what can be said of God, still many statements remain which can only be made of God as the subject of the human life of Jesus: that he eats, gets tired, sleeps, is afraid, dies. In fact, Moltmann's title makes just such a statement about God: that he was crucified. Precisely in order to preserve the reality of the incarnation, we must not abolish the difference between what is possible for God in incarnation and what is otherwise possible for God. In order to say that God suffered crucifixion, we need to be able to assert, not that some kinds of human experience have analogies in the divine experience, but that incarnation, which entails all the utterly and precisely human experience of a fully human life, is really possible for God. Then it follows that God suffered crucifixion in exactly the same way as it follows that God was suckled at Mary's breast and slept in a boat on the sea of Galilee.

I do not make this point in order to deny that God can suffer outside the incarnation. That question is still open. But it is important to be clear that, whatever may be said about God's suffering outside the incarnation, his human suffering as Jesus is unique, since this is precisely human suffering. There is a danger that a doctrine of divine passibility can promote its own peculiar kind of docetism. In other words, we may think of the suffering of Jesus as the kind of suffering which we suppose to be attributable to God, unconsciously reducing its fully human character and forgetting that the point of the doctrine of the incarnation is that in Jesus' case his utterly human suffering – his fear in Gethsemane, his loneliness as friends desert him, the excruciating physical agony, and so on – is precisely as utterly human suffering attributable to God. The inattentive reader of Moltmann's account of the cross as an event between the divine persons may succumb to this kind of docetism. It is not Moltmann's intention. What he wishes to say is that the thoroughly human history of Golgotha takes place within the relationships of the Trinity. But his general discussion of divine passibility, which does not distinguish God's suffering as human from his suffering as God, could mislead. We have noted Moltmann's admission that the doctrine of divine impassibility was legitimate in so far as it 'really says that God is not subjected to suffering in the same way as transient, created beings' (TKG 23). But applied too simply to God's suffering in Jesus this could seriously mislead. In Jesus God suffered precisely the sufferings of a transient, created being. Moltmann's statement applies to God's incarnate suffering only in the sense that in the act of incarnation God voluntarily assumed all the human experience of the man Jesus.

(3) *God's non-incarnate suffering*

In the incarnation God the Son suffers human suffering. Should we, with Moltmann, go on to say that in the event of the cross the Father also suffers, though differently? Three lines of argument may take us in that direction: (*a*) If incarnation is possible for God, then God is not limited by the traditional metaphysical attributes. (*b*) In the human life of the Son of God, the Father is revealed. But what is most revelatory of God in the human life of Jesus is his loving identification with the godless and the godforsaken by which he shares and suffers their fate. The supreme revelation of the Father's love is not a human example of purely active benevolence, but the *suffering* love of the crucified Jesus. So it is to this kind of love – love which through involvement with the beloved suffers – that we should consider God's love analogous. God's incarnate love in Jesus is of this kind because the incarnation is grounded in this kind of love in God. Of course, to speak of God's suffering love – other than in the incarnation – is to use anthropomorphic analogy. All personal language about God is anthropomorphic analogy. But this no more enables us to conclude that God does not really suffer than it enables us to conclude that God does not really love. The point is that whereas the tradition of metaphysical theism held that purely active benevolence was the only kind of human love which has an analogy in God, the cross requires us to say that it is human suffering love to which God's love is analogous. Moltmann's claim that the Father suffers in grief the death of the Son on the cross is bold anthropomorphism, but consistent with much biblical language. As theology it may be criticized only if its analogical character is neglected and it is supposed to claim that we know what it was like for the Father to suffer the death of Jesus. Of course, we do not know what anything is like for God, only that some things in human experience have an analogy in divine experience. What does lay Moltmann open to the charge of speaking mythologically about the divine experience is his failure to distinguish, in his account of the cross as a trinitarian event, the human suffering of Jesus, which is human suffering, from the divine suffering of the Father, which is only analogous to human suffering. If we could speak as literally about the Father's experience as we can about the human experience of the incarnate Son, incarnation would not be necessary.

(*c*) The third line of argument is to take seriously the Old Testament revelation of God as the context for understanding the incarnation and the cross. Against the background of the Old Testament, the incarnation is in one sense something quite new, but in another sense continuous with the God of Israel's involvement with his people and their sufferings. Moltmann adumbrates this line of argument in his use of Abraham Heschel's pioneering study of the *pathos* of God in the prophets,[18] but it could be taken further with the aid of other studies in Old Testament theology,[19] such as Terence Fretheim's book on the suffering of God in the Old Testament.[20] Such studies not only show that the suffering of God is a far more pervasive theme in the Old Testament than the classic passages usually cited might indicate. They also take the Old Testament's anthropomorphic language about God seriously as revelatory of God, instead of dismissing as

---

[18] On Heschel, see Bauckham, '"Only the suffering God",' 9–10, and more fully: J. C. Merkle, 'Heschel's Theology of Divine Pathos,' in *Abraham Joshua Heschel: Exploring His Life and Thought*, (ed.) J. C. Merkle (New York: Macmillan/London: Collier Macmillan, 1985), pp. 66–83; J. C. Merkle, *The Genesis of Faith: The Depth Theology of Abraham Joshua Heschel* (New York: Macmillan/London: Collier Macmillan, 1985), pp. 130–5.

[19] E.g. E. S. Gerstenberger and W. Schrage, *Suffering*, tr. J. E. Steely (Nashville: Abingdon, 1980), pp. 98–102; E. Jacob, 'Le Dieu souffrant, un thème théologique vétérotestamentaire,' *Zeitschrift für die alttestamentliche Wissenschaft* 95 (1983), pp. 1–8.

[20] T. E. Fretheim, *The Suffering of God: An Old Testament Perspective* (Overtures to Biblical Theology 14; Philadelphia: Fortress, 1984).

mere anthropomorphism, not to be taken seriously, whatever does not accord with the traditional metaphysical concept of God.

One way of relating the Old Testament tradition of God's suffering to the cross as an event of divine suffering between the Father and the Son might be, in summary, as follows. God in the Old Testament suffers empathetically *with* his people in their sufferings. He also suffers grief *because of* his people when they reject him and are lost to him. Finally, both these kinds of suffering constitute a redemptive suffering *for* his people.[21] In Jesus God's identification with people in their sufferings reaches a new and absolute depth. He goes beyond empathy to an act of solidarity in which he suffers as one of the godless and the godforsaken, sharing their fate of abandonment. But this identification of God with those who suffer (in the person of the Son) at the same time causes him grief (in the person of the Father). In the Father's suffering of the death of Jesus God's grief at the loss of those who are estranged from him reaches a new and absolute depth. He suffers that loss as the loss of his own Son identified with the godless and the godforsaken. Thus, human estrangement from God comes between the Father and the Son, they suffer it in their common love for the world, and their mutual, but differentiated suffering overcomes the estrangement and so proves to be redemptive suffering for the world.

(4) *Anthropomorphism and apophaticism*

Finally, we return to what Moltmann calls metaphysical theism and offer a critique somewhat different from (though not contradictory to) Moltmann's. The tradition of metaphysical theism in Christian theology could be seen as having two rather different strands in it, both deriving from its origins in Platonism. The two strands may be called anthropomorphic[22] and apophatic. The first, dependent on the

---

[21] These three kinds of suffering of God in the Old Testament are distinguished and discussed by Fretheim, *Suffering of God*, chapters 7–9

[22] I use the term 'anthropomorphic' in the general sense of applying to God language which we otherwise use of human persons, not merely in the sense of attributing the physical features of human persons to God.

Platonic view that the human intellect is the element in human nature which is akin to the divine, conceives God as the supreme *Nous*. The human being is most akin to God when the mind, which is the true self, abstracted from the body and all relations with the material world, contemplates eternal, unchanging truth. God is 'without body, parts or passions', as in the Platonic view the human mind can be when it recollects its true nature. Divine *apatheia*, therefore, is not so much a definition of God as wholly other than us, but rather the ideal to which Platonic humanity itself aspires. For this view of God as the supreme Mind, to attribute knowledge and will to God is appropriate, if analogical, but to attribute emotion or bodily sensation to God is inappropriate. The latter is considered anthropomorphic, the former not. In reality, of course, this view is selective anthropomorphism. It speaks of God in terms of one facet of human personality (impassive reason), not of others, and corresponds to an anthropology which treated this facet as the highest element of human nature. Biblical anthropomorphism is also selective, but not in this way. The biblical God does not, for example, eat, sleep, fear, doubt or die, but he is, for example, grieved and roused to anger, he desires and feels compassion, he hides his face and shows strength with his arm, just as much as he knows and wills. The deep-rooted prejudice that reference to God's reason and will is more literal than reference to God in emotional and physical terms derives from Platonism, rather than the Bible. It would be better to recognize that all personal language about God is equally anthropomorphic. Such language should be justified not by a Platonic anthropology in which the human mind is the image of God, but by a biblical anthropology in which human personality as a psychosomatic whole and in community is the image of God.

The second strand in the tradition of metaphysical theism is negative theology. It does not tell us what God is like (he is the supreme intellect) but what he is not (he is not finite like us). All the traditional metaphysical attributes can be understood in this sense: God is not limited by time as we are, God is not limited by space as we are, God is not limited in knowledge or power as we are, God is not subject to change or suffering as finite creatures are. God transcends finite existence in every respect: this is all the metaphysical attributes really tell us about God. In Platonism, this kind of negative theology gave God a transcendence which removed him from all relationship with the world: the metaphysical attributes exclude their finite opposites and make it impossible for God to relate to this world. The great struggle of patristic theology was to recognize God's transcendence as the wholly other whose incomparable difference from creation does not exclude but enables his incomparably intimate relationship with his creation, in immanence and incarnation. Probably the most effective way of continuing that struggle is to understand the metaphysical attributes not as excluding but as including their opposites.[23] That God transcends time need not mean that he cannot also relate to us in time. That God transcends space need not mean that he cannot also relate to us in space. That God is not subject to change or suffering as we are need not mean that he cannot change or suffer in any way at all. That God transcends every human limitation need not prevent him also assuming every human limitation in incarnation.

To speak as adequately as we can of God we need to use both anthropomorphic and negative language, but not to confuse the two.[24] Negative theology should not inhibit the use of anthropomorphism, but stands as a permanent qualification of all anthropomorphism. God suffers, but as the one who transcends all finite suffering. We may say that there is something analogous to human suffering in the divine experience, but we may not thereby claim that we know what it is like for God to suffer. We might even say, with Cyril, that God suffers impassibly, but not, as he did, of the incarnation. The incarnation, in which God is not like us but actually one of us, anchors all our language of God in his concrete human history. But the ocean in which it floats is the boundless mystery of God's infinity.

---

[23] Cf. H. Küng's notion of the 'dialectic of the attributes': *The Incarnation of God* (tr. J. R. Stephenson; Edinburgh: T. & T. Clark, 1987), pp. 445–53.

[24] On this, cf. S. Tugwell, 'Spirituality and Negative Theology,' *New Blackfriars* 68 (1987), pp. 257–63.

4

Theodicy*

The question of the justification of God in the face of the
problem of suffering – which in the modern age can be
named Auschwitz – is one of the central threads in the
complex argument of Moltmann's *The Crucified God*. An
attempt to disentangle this thread will be worthwhile because
Moltmann's response (not solution) to the problem of
suffering has two considerable merits, which are not both to
be found in many other recent treatments of theodicy. In the
first place, he responds to the problem of suffering in the
particular shape which it has assumed in the modern period,
and secondly, he responds to it from the resources offered by
the christological centre of historic Christian faith, i.e. from
an incarnational understanding of the cross and resurrection of Jesus Christ. Like the best features of the rest of his
theology, therefore, Moltmann's treatment of theodicy is an
authentically Christian response to the characteristically
modern perception of the world.

In order to highlight this characteristic, the first part of
this chapter will sketch the shape of the problem of theodicy
in its modern form, without reference to Moltmann, but
through consideration of three writers to whom Moltmann's
discussion of the problem is indebted: Dostoyevsky, Camus
and Wiesel. This first part of the chapter will be structured as
a discussion of three crucial texts and their interpretation.
The loose ends which this discussion leaves hanging will then

* This chapter was originally a lecture given to the Manson Society in the
University of Manchester in February 1986. It was first published as: 'Theodicy
from Ivan Karamazov to Moltmann,' *Modern Theology* 4 (1987), pp. 83–97. The
Appendix has not previously been published.

be gathered up in the discussion of Moltmann in the second part of the chapter.

I

The first two texts are passages from modern literature which have attained virtually scriptural status in modern discussions of theodicy. The first is Ivan Karamazov's famous argument against theodicy in discussion with his brother Alyosha in book V chapter 4 of Dostoyevsky's *The Brothers Karamazov*.[1]

It is essentially an argument against any eschatological theodicy of the kind which justifies suffering as the price to be paid for the achievement of some eschatological purpose of God in the future, when it will be seen to have been worth the price. But it is an argument which is valid against any theodicy which explains suffering as necessary to the divine purpose, and so against the most popular types of modern theodicy: that suffering is the calculated risk God took when he created free creatures,[2] that suffering is an inevitable part of an evolutionary natural world,[3] that suffering has an educative role as part of the 'soul-making' which is the purpose of this world.[4] The difficulty with such explanations of suffering is not that they do not explain anything, but that they do not, or *should* not explain everything. The real

[1] For recent theological discussion of Ivan Karamazov's argument, see CG 220–3; HFM 58; D. Soelle, *Suffering* (London: Darton, Longman & Todd, 1975), pp. 174–7; B. Hebblethwaite, *Evil, Suffering and Religion* (London: Sheldon Press, 1976), pp. 64–7, 105–6; S. R. Sutherland, *Atheism and the Rejection of God: Contemporary Philosophy and The Brothers Karamazov* (Oxford: Blackwell, 1977); R. Harries, 'Ivan Karamazov's Argument,' *Theology* 81 (1978), pp. 104–11; K. Surin, 'Theodicy?,' *Harvard Theological Review* 76 (1983), pp. 236–40; idem, *Theology and the Problem of Evil* (Oxford: Basil Blackwell, 1986), pp. 96–105. Cf. also S. Weil, *Gravity and Grace* (tr. E. Craufurd; London: Routledge, 1963), p. 72.

[2] E.g. S. T. Davis, 'Free Will and Evil,' chapter 3 in S. T. Davis (ed.), *Encountering Evil: Live Options in Theodicy* (Edinburgh: T. & T. Clark, 1981). A Jewish post-Auschwitz version of this type of theodicy is that of Eliezer Berkovitz: see the critical account in S. T. Katz, *Post-Holocaust Dialogues* (New York/London: New York University Press, 1983), pp. 163–7, 268–86.

[3] E.g. J. Cowburn, *Shadows and the Dark* (London: SCM Press, 1979), part II (explaining only some evil in this way).

[4] E.g. J. Hick, *Evil and the God of Love* (London: Macmillan, 1966); idem, 'An Irenaean Theodicy,' chapter 2 in Davis (ed.), *Encountering Evil.*

problem of suffering for theistic belief is not that there is suffering, but that there is too much suffering. All these explanations of suffering leave unexplained an excess of suffering which is the real problem of theodicy.[5] Attempts to explain even the excess by explanations of this kind – which make it part of God's purpose – are the targets of Ivan's attack.

From this point of view it is significant that Ivan deliberately chooses as his evidence the sufferings of small children, inflicted on them by the cruelty of adults. His examples of parental cruelty, culled from the newspapers, are depressingly familiar, since they resemble those which have featured in our own news media in recent years. Ivan's final, clinching story is of an eight-year-old serf-boy who accidentally injured his landowner's favourite dog. The landowner had him hunted, like an animal, with huntsmen, whips and hounds, who tore the boy in pieces before the eyes of his mother.[6]

Ivan's initial point is that this is innocent and *senseless* suffering. It is impossible to explain it either as due to the child's own fault or as serving the child's own ultimate good, even in heaven. If God's allowing such suffering is to be justified as part of some ultimate divine purpose for the world, it can only be for someone *else*'s benefit. But this is morally unacceptable:

> Listen: if all have to suffer so as to buy eternal harmony by their suffering, what have the children to do with it . . . ? It is entirely incomprehensible why they, too, should have to suffer and why they should have to buy harmony by their sufferings. Why should they, too, be used as dung for someone's future harmony?[7]

But Ivan goes further. Not only is it incomprehensible. Even if it were to become comprehensible to him at the eschaton, he would not accept an eternal harmony bought at this price. The real force of the argument comes in this question to Alyosha:

[5] So F. Sonntag, 'Anthropodicy and the Return of God,' chapter 5 in Davis (ed.), *Encountering Evil*, p. 141.

[6] F. Dostoyevsky, *The Brothers Karamazov* (Harmondsworth: Penguin, 1982), p. 284.

[7] Dostoyevsky, *Brothers Karamazov*, p. 286.

Tell me frankly . . . imagine that it is you yourself who are erecting
the edifice of human destiny with the aim of making men happy in
the end, of giving them peace and contentment at last, but that to
do that it is absolutely necessary, and indeed quite inevitable, to
torture to death only one tiny creature, the little girl who beat her
breast with her little fist, and to found the edifice on her unavenged
tears – would you consent to be the architect on those conditions?[8]

Alyosha would not.

Thus the effect of the argument is that the facts of innocent and senseless suffering ought to make theodicy, in the
usual sense, impossible (cf. TKG 47–8). The argument sets
our sense of justice against any alleged divine purpose. Since
theodicy of this kind can only justify God by justifying the
suffering, we can only accept it by suppressing our moral
outrage at the injustice of the suffering. Therefore we *ought*
not to accept it. Though Ivan ironically, for the sake of argument, accepts the existence of the God of classical theodicy,[9]
he finds this God's world morally unacceptable. Therefore,
as Alyosha points out, he rebels,[10] and Dostoyevsky's chapter-
title (Rebellion) indicates that this is in fact why Ivan is an
atheist. In the name of justice, he *rebels* against the God who
can only be justified by calling injustice just.

Among the many modern writers who have been deeply
influenced by Ivan's argument is Albert Camus, who must
have felt its influence at least from the time when he played
the part of Ivan in a dramatic adaptation of Dostoyevsky's
novel.[11] The point at which Camus's interpretation of Ivan
becomes important for our discussion is in his great book
L'homme révolté (*The Rebel*), which had considerable influence
on Moltmann's thinking in *The Crucified God*.[12] Ivan's
argument plays a key role in Camus's book, because Ivan's
revolt against the God of traditional theodicy is interpreted

[8] Dostoyevsky, *Brothers Karamazov*, p. 287.

[9] For the sense in which Ivan 'accepts God', see Sutherland, *Atheism*, pp. 31–6.

[10] Dostoyevsky, *Brothers Karamazov*, p. 287.

[11] H. R. Lottman, *Albert Camus* (London: Weidenfeld & Nicolson, 1979), pp. 175–6.

[12] Ivan Karamazov's influence is also to be seen in Camus's *The Plague*, but I am not aware that this book influenced Moltmann. Moltmann first referred to Camus's *The Rebel*, in the context of a discussion of theodicy, in 1968 (HP 34).

as typifying the revolt of the whole modern age and the source of its revolutionary history. For Camus, the problem of the modern age, with which *The Rebel* is a philosophical wrestling, is that it began, in effect, with Ivan's principled revolt against the injustice of the world and therefore against the God who sanctions this injustice, but it ends (for Camus writing in 1951) with the unprecedented injustices of Nazism and Stalinism. His purpose in the book is to *understand* the guilt of 'a period which, within fifty years, uproots, enslaves, or kills seventy million human beings',[13] and does so in the name of political *principle:* 'slave camps under the flag of freedom, massacres justified by philanthropy or the taste for the superhuman'.[14] How did a movement – the modern rebellion against God – which began by rejecting the God who justifies innocent suffering end by *itself justifying* the infliction of innocent suffering on an unprecedented scale?

Camus sees this result foreshadowed in Ivan.[15] Ivan's revolt initially contained not only the negative element of a rejection of the world as it is, but also a positive affirmation of value, a sense of human dignity and human solidarity from which the desire for justice in the face of the world's injustice arises. But Ivan's revolt *itself undermines* this positive element, because there is another aspect to his rebellion, which is prominent in the novel but which we have not yet mentioned. Without God and immortality, without the immortal value of the human soul in the sight of God,[16] concludes Ivan in a key sentence of the book, 'everything is permitted'.[17] Camus comments: 'With this "all is permitted" the history of contemporary nihilism really begins.'[18] Ivan's own tragedy is

---

In *The Crucified God*, the relevant explicit references to Camus are on pp. 80 n. 65, 221–2, 226, 252; but the influence of *The Rebel* on Moltmann's thinking in *The Crucified God* is greater than these references might suggest. Cf. also FC 171, 193 n. 28; EH 116, 142.

[13] A. Camus, *The Rebel* (Harmondsworth: Penguin, 1971), p. 11.

[14] Camus, *Rebel*, p. 12.

[15] Camus, *Rebel*, pp. 50–6.

[16] M. Friedman, *Problematic Rebel: Melville, Dostoievsky, Kafka, Camus* (Chicago/ London: University of Chicago Press, ²1970), p. 194.

[17] Dostoyevsky, *Brothers Karamazov*, p. 77.

[18] Camus, *Rebel*, p. 52.

that he is caught between the sense of justice on account of which he rebels against the God of theodicy and the rational justification for murder which he deduces from his rebellion. And the story of the Grand Inquisitor, which Ivan tells, prophesies with chilling accuracy the political consequences to which Ivan's nihilism will lead. For Camus, the Grand Inquisitor represents the totalitarian logic which inflicts suffering and murder for the sake, ostensibly, of an abstract ideal of universal happiness in the future.[19]

As Camus sees it, what has happened, in the history of the modern age which Ivan's revolt so remarkably encapsulates, is that theodicy has been replaced by anthropodicy. In the ancien régime, the God of theodicy served to sanction the injustices of society, justifying suffering by means of his eschatological purpose. This God had to be rejected in the modern revolt against the injustices of his world. But the rebel who wishes to replace that world by a new just world must himself replace God. Humanity – or at least the political élite, who know there is no God – must take control of human destiny in order to replace the unjust world of the dead God with its own new world of human justice. But in order to subject history to this purpose, the revolutionary élite justifies any means. Innocent suffering may be inflicted for the sake of *future* justice, and so the tyranny of the revolutionary régime silences revolt just as effectively as God did in the tyranny of the old divine right monarchies. For an eschatological theodicy which justified suffering the modern age has substituted an eschatological anthropodicy which also justifies suffering.

Thus, Camus's interpretation of Ivan throws important light on the problem of theodicy in our age. It gives it the practical, political thrust which the problem of suffering in the age of Auschwitz, Hiroshima and Stalinism must have. It also makes clear that Ivan's atheism is not in itself a solution to the problem of theodicy, because it simply gives rise to another form of the problem: that of anthropodicy. What is

[19] Camus, *Rebel*, pp. 55–6. For this interpretation of the much discussed story of the Grand Inquisitor, cf. Friedman, *Problematic Rebel*, pp. 199–206.

needed is a basis for Ivan's protest against innocent and senseless suffering, a basis for rejecting any justification of such suffering, whether as theodicy or as anthropodicy. How can Ivan's protest be maintained and not lapse into the cynical terror of the Grand Inquisitor?

Our second text is by the Jewish holocaust survivor and novelist Elie Wiesel, in his book *La Nuit* (*Night*), which is an autobiographical memoir of his experience of Auschwitz. In this case the text is not a classic argument, but a classic story, which has been subject to a variety of midrashic interpretations in Jewish and Christian theologians attempting 'theology after Auschwitz'.[20] The story takes place in Buna, the camp attached to Auschwitz. A young Jewish boy was hanged, along with two adults, by the SS in front of the thousands of inmates of the camp, who were then obliged to file past the three hanged bodies, looking them full in the face. The two adults were dead, but the child, being so light, was still alive.

> For more than half an hour he stayed there, struggling between life and death, dying in slow agony under our eyes. And we had to look him full in the face. He was still alive when I passed in front of him. His tongue was still red, his eyes were not yet glazed.
>
> Behind me, I heard [a] man asking:
> 'Where is God now?'
> And I heard a voice within me answer him:
> 'Where is He? Here He is – He is hanging here on this gallows. . . .'
> That night the soup tasted of corpses.[21]

Though this is undoubtedly a key passage in Wiesel's book, it is, as John Roth points out, a highly enigmatic key, whose

---

[20] For Christian theological interpretation of the story, see CG 273–4, 278; Soelle, *Suffering*, pp. 145–50; K. Surin, 'The Impassibility of God and the Problem of Evil,' *Scottish Journal of Theology* 35 (1982), pp. 111–12; idem, 'Theodicy?,' pp. 240–3; idem, *Theology*, pp. 116–18; J.-B. Metz, 'Facing the Jews: Christian Theology after Auschwitz,' in F. S. Fiorenza and D. Tracy (ed.), *The Holocaust as Interruption* (Edinburgh: T. & T. Clark, 1984) = *Concilium* 175 (5/ 1984), pp. 29–30.

[21] E. Wiesel, *Night* (New York: Hill & Wang, 1960), p. 71.

power as an image no doubt lies in its openness to interpretation.[22] But in considering, initially, its meaning within the book, we must resist the Christian reader's temptation to find in it some kind of echo of the *crucified* God,[23] even though at a subsequent stage a deliberate reinterpretation in this sense, such as Moltmann attempts, may be justified. To me at least it is clear that within the book the story marks the final, crucial step in Wiesel's loss of faith in God. God hangs on the gallows because the possibility of faith in him is dying with every moment the dying child suffers and the God of Israel fails to deliver him. God is dead because the holocaust makes theodicy impossible.[24]

What has gone unnoticed in the discussion of Wiesel's work is the clear influence of Ivan Karamazov as interpreted by Camus, who was writing *The Rebel* when Wiesel knew him in Paris after the War.[25] On the one hand, Wiesel recognizes, with Camus, the root of the Nazi terror in Ivan's nihilism. Arriving in Auschwitz and seeing for the first time a lorry-load of dead babies being consigned to the incinerator, Wiesel tells his father he cannot

[22] J. K. Roth, *A Consuming Fire: Encounters with Elie Wiesel and the Holocaust* (Atlanta: John Knox Press, 1979), p. 63; idem, 'Telling a Tale That Cannot Be Told: Reflections on the Authorship of Elie Wiesel,' in A. H. Rosenfeld and I. Greenberg (ed.), *Confronting the Holocaust: The Impact of Elie Wiesel* (Bloomington/London: Indiana University Press, 1978), p. 61.

[23] Cf. E. L. Fackenheim's warning against this: 'Midrashic Existence after the Holocaust: Reflections Occasioned by the Work of Elie Wiesel,' in Rosenfeld and Greenberg (ed.), *Confronting*, p. 111.

[24] For *Night* as an 'anti-Exodus' in which the covenant people lose the God of the covenant, see L. S. Cunningham, 'Elie Wiesel's Anti-Exodus,' in H. J. Cargas (ed.), *Responses to Elie Wiesel* (New York: Persea Books, 1978), pp. 23–8. Against Roth, *Fire*, pp. 63–4, *Night* does not seem to me to suggest that faith in some God survives Wiesel's loss of faith in the God of the covenant, the God of providential justice. On the problem of the death of God in Wiesel's works, see also B. L. Sherwin, 'Elie Wiesel and Jewish Theology,' in Cargas (ed.), *Responses*, pp. 143–5.

[25] See R. C. Lamont, 'Elie Wiesel: In Search of a Tongue,' in Rosenfeld and Greenberg ed., *Confronting*, pp. 88–9. On pp. 89–96, Lamont discusses Camus's influence on Wiesel, but without reference to *The Rebel*. J. Knopp, 'Wiesel and the Absurd,' in Cargas (ed.), *Responses*, pp. 92–101, compares Wiesel's work with Camus's, but again without reference to *The Rebel*.

believe that they could burn people in our age, that humanity would never tolerate it . . .

'Humanity? [replies his father] Humanity is not concerned with us. Today anything is allowed. Anything is possible, even these crematories. . . .'[26]

Wiesel's father here echoes Ivan's catchphrase.

On the other hand, Wiesel himself repeats Ivan's rebellion against God, as protest against God's permission of Auschwitz wells up and gradually extinguishes his faith in a God of providential justice.[27] At the Jewish New Year, when thousands of Jews in the camp gather to worship, he finds he cannot join in the benediction:

Why, but why should I bless Him? In every fiber I rebelled. Because He had had thousands of His children burned in His pits? Because He kept six crematories working night and day, on Sundays and feast days? Because in His great might He had created Auschwitz, Birkenau, Buna, and so many factories of death?[28]

In accusing God Wiesel finds himself without God, as though the death of the boy on the gallows had killed him.

But there is also another aspect to God in the book. If the death of God is the recurrent theme of the first part of the book, the theme which overtakes it in the second part is that of the struggle against the dehumanizing effect of extreme suffering. Wiesel portrays powerfully the way in which, when sheer survival becomes the only concern, all human feelings for others threaten to disappear before the mere animal instinct for self-preservation. This is again, in a very different way, the danger of relapse into nihilism, this time for the victims of suffering. The issue is dramatized in Wiesel's struggle to continue to care about and to help his father, who becomes an impediment to Wiesel's own survival. At one

---

[26] Wiesel, *Night*, p. 42.
[27] Cf. Wiesel, *Night*, pp. 43–4, 53, 73–5. B. L. Sherwin, 'Wiesel's Midrash: The Writings of Elie Wiesel and Their Relationship to Jewish Tradition,' in Rosenfeld and Greenberg (ed.), *Confronting*, pp. 117–32, points out Wiesel's indebtedness to the Jewish theological tradition of believing protest against God, but it seems to me that in *Night* the influence of Ivan Karamazov predominates.
[28] Wiesel, *Night*, p. 73.

desperate point he meets an old man, Rabbi Eliahou, who has become separated from his son and is searching for him. Wiesel knows that the son has deliberately abandoned the father in order to increase his own chances of survival.

> And, in spite of myself, a prayer rose in my heart, to that God in whom I no longer believed.
> My God, Lord of the Universe, give me strength never to do what Rabbi Eliahou's son has done.[29]

The prayer is answered, though only just.

What Wiesel here recognizes – because, unlike Camus, he knew religion from the inside – is that the idea of God stands in a *dialectical* relationship to the problem of suffering. God is not only the authority over history to whom the rebel directs his accusation; he also represents and so sustains the human values which alone keep human beings human in the face of unacceptable suffering. If God dies under the sentence passed at his trial in Auschwitz, he also lives in the affirmation of human dignity and human solidarity which prevents the rebel's lapse from protest into nihilism.

Our third text is a genuinely scriptural one, from Mark's account of the crucifixion:

> At the ninth hour Jesus cried with a loud voice, . . . 'My God, my God, why hast thou forsaken me?'. . . And Jesus uttered a loud cry, and breathed his last (Mark 15:34, 37).

The death of an innocent sufferer lies at the heart of the Christian faith – an innocent sufferer identified, in incarnational terms, with God himself. Consequently, Alyosha, for example, does not recognize the God against whom Ivan directs his protest as the Christian God, since he is not the crucified God.[30] But does the cross really help? Much depends on how it is interpreted.

Camus offers two interpretations[31] which constitute to some extent a challenge to which Moltmann responds in *The Crucified God.* One is Camus's own atheistic view of a purely

[29] Wiesel, *Night*, p. 95.

[30] Dostoyevsky, *Brothers Karamazov*, p. 288.

[31] On Camus's interpretation of the cross, see J. Onimus, *Albert Camus and Christianity* (Dublin: Gill & Macmillan, 1970), pp. 48–50.

human Jesus, whose dying cry of dereliction is the complaint of an innocent man against the injustice done to him. In this sense, the crucified Jesus represents a *rebellion* against God at the very beginning of Christianity.[32] But in Camus's view *Christianity's* interpretation of the cross – as the suffering of God himself – made it something quite different. If God himself suffered the evils of the human condition to the limit, as the cry of dereliction shows, then they can no longer be the ground for revolt against him: the cross quells the spirit of revolt. Indeed, by making suffering the route to heaven, the crucified Christ encourages acceptance of suffering in imitation of himself.[33] Thus, Camus's complaint against Christianity is that by putting the crucified God at the centre of its faith it sanctifies and sanctions suffering.[34] So neither of Camus's interpretations of the cross, not even the one he represents as the Christian interpretation, meets Ivan's argument: indeed, both reinforce it. If the cross is divested of deity, Jesus is just one more victim, protesting his innocence against divine injustice.[35] If the cross is invested with deity, it becomes the most effective, but also the most objectionable theodicy, justifying suffering and silencing protest. In neither case is there a possibility of justifying God without justifying suffering.

From this discussion of the three texts which we have taken to illustrate the modern shape of the problem of suffering may be drawn, for the moment, two requirements, one negative and one positive, which an adequate theological response to the problem of suffering must meet.

(1) Innocent and involuntary suffering must not be justified. It must be justified neither by theodicy, which explains it as necessary to God's purpose, nor by

---

[32] Camus, *Rebel*, pp. 27 n., 56–7.

[33] Camus, *L'homme révolté* (Paris: Gallimard, 1951), pp. 50–1 (this passage is not in the English translation); idem, *Rebel*, p. 81.

[34] Cf. P. Thody, *Albert Camus: A study of his work* (London: Hamish Hamilton, 1957), pp. 22, 55. This complaint of Camus is shared by Wiesel: see Roth, *Fire*, p. 89; M. Berenbaum, 'The Additional Covenant,' in Rosenfeld and Greenberg (ed.), *Confronting*, p. 177.

[35] Camus, *L'homme révolté*, p. 53 (this passage is not in the English translation); cf. Camus, *The Fall* (Harmondsworth: Penguin, 1963), pp. 83–4.

anthropodicy, which explains it as necessary to some higher human purpose. Such justifications suppress the sense of moral outrage against evil, silence protest against it, and therefore at the very least reduce the motive for relieving and overcoming suffering. At worst they justify infliction of innocent suffering by totalitarian régimes both theocratic and atheistic.

(2) An adequate theological response to the problem of suffering must contain an initiative for overcoming suffering. If it is not to justify suffering, it must, on the contrary, help to maintain the protest against suffering and convert it into an initiative for overcoming suffering. These two requirements are presupposed in Moltmann's approach to theodicy.

II

Moltmann's early theology has the merit of making the cross and resurrection of Christ its determining centre. A particular interpretation of the cross and resurrection *together* – Moltmann's dialectic of cross and resurrection[36] – lies at the heart of Moltmann's theology, and a simplified, schematic description of the first two phases of his work, represented by the two books *Theology of Hope* and *The Crucified God*, would be that in the first he focuses on the resurrection, interpreted by the concepts of divine promise and hope, whereas in the second he focuses on the cross, interpreted by the concepts of divine suffering and love. In both phases, the dialectical interpretation of cross and resurrection *together* underlies the focus first on the resurrection in particular and then on the cross. The two phases are therefore complementary. In Moltmann's response to the theodicy problem a foundation is laid in the first phase, in

---

[36] For a straightforward account of this dialectic in Moltmann's theology, see J. A. Irish, 'Moltmann's Theology of Contradiction,' *Theology Today* 32 (1975–6), pp. 21–31; and for a much fuller study, see M. D. Meeks, *Origins of the Theology of Hope* (Philadelphia: Fortress Press, 1974). Also, for fuller treatment of the aspects of Moltmann's theology summarized in this chapter, see my *Moltmann: Messianic Theology in the Making* (Basingstoke: Marshall Pickering, 1987), chapters 2–3.

which the response is made from the perspective of Jesus' resurrection and in terms of the concepts of promise and hope. But Moltmann engages more deeply with the problem in the second phase, in which the response is made from the perspective of Jesus' cross and in terms of the concepts of divine suffering and love.

The dialectic of cross and resurrection means that the cross and the resurrection of Jesus represent complete opposites: death and life, the absence of God and the presence of God, godforsakenness and the glory of God. Yet the crucified and risen Jesus is the same Jesus in this total contradiction. God, who creates out of nothing and raises the dead, raised the crucified Jesus to new life, thereby creating continuity through this radical discontinuity: the same Jesus, crucified and risen (cf. TH 197–201, 210–11). In *Theology of Hope* the interpretation of this divine act of raising the crucified Jesus from death is controlled by the concept of promise. The resurrection of the crucified Jesus is the definitive event of divine promise for the eschatological future of the world. The crucified Jesus in his death was identified with the present reality of the world in all its negativity: its subjection to sin, suffering and death, or what Moltmann calls its godlessness, godforsakenness and transitoriness. Not that the world in its present reality is simply evil (cf. RRF 12–14), but it is subject to evil and ends in nothingness. In this sense the cross represents the plight and the fate of the world. But the same Jesus was raised, and therefore his resurrection is God's promise of new creation for the whole of the reality which the crucified Jesus represents. The contradiction of cross and resurrection corresponds to the contradiction between what reality is now and what God promises to make it: it constitutes God's promise of life for the dead, righteousness for the unrighteous, freedom for those in bondage, God's presence for those abandoned by God (TH 201, 211).

Thus, the dialectic of cross and resurrection creates a dialectical concept of divine promise. The God of promise redeems the world by contradicting it and transcending the contradiction, i.e. he confronts the world in its godlessness and godforsakenness with the promise of righteousness and divine presence, and he transcends the contradiction by recreating the world to accord with the promise. This dialectic of promise in turn gives rise to a dialectical under-standing of Christian life and mission in the form of the dialectic of hope (TH 18–19, 195–7, 225–7). The promise sets believers in contradiction to the state of the world in which they live. By promising a quite different reality it gives them a critical distance from reality as it is, and they begin to suffer the contradiction between the two, as the promise exposes the lack of righteousness and freedom in the world around them (TH 118–19, 222). But the contradiction between experience and hope then leads to attempts to transcend the contradiction, as Christians seek possibilities of bringing reality into closer correspondence to the promise. Hope for the future divine transformation of reality becomes the motive for Christian involvement in the present transformation of life – individual, social, economic, political – in accordance with and in anticipation of the promised eschatological transformation by God (TH 22, 34–5, 288–90; RRF 137–8).

As a response to the problem of suffering, therefore, Moltmann is proposing an eschatological theodicy, *not* in the sense that suffering will prove justified as contributing to the final fulfilment of God's purpose, but in the sense that God will finally *overcome* all suffering (see HP 49–50; HFM 58; TJ 56–7; CG 165, 278).[37] The divine promise gives no explanation of suffering, but hope for liberation from suffering, and thereby also an initiative for Christian praxis in overcoming suffering now. By identifying the divine purpose not with what reality is but with what it will be – and, under the impact of the promise, can to some extent begin to be – Moltmann in effect aligns the divine purpose *with* Ivan's protest against the unacceptable face of present reality. Christian 'hope finds in Christ not only a consolation in suffering, but also the protest of the divine promise *against* suffering' (TH 21). Moreover, hope in

---

[37] In this rejection of any justification of suffering, Moltmann is also influenced by the Frankfurt school, especially by Walter Benjamin.

God's promise gives strength to the protest and converts it into action. In a remark which he must later have thought superficial, Moltmann even called his political theology, which converts hope into political praxis, 'the practical answering of the theodicy problem' (FH 47–8).[38] This illustrates how even in this first phase of his response to the theodicy problem Moltmann is concerned to meet our two requirements for an adequate response. But we are left wondering how a God who responds to the unjustified suffering of the world *only* with promises can ever justify himself, even when he fulfils the promises.

However, the elements of promise and hope lay a foundation which is presupposed in Moltmann's deeper and fuller response to the theodicy problem in *The Crucified God* and without which the latter cannot be fully appreciated. In *The Crucified God* Moltmann's thinking moves back from the resurrection of Jesus as the event of divine promise to the cross of Jesus as the event of divine love. In this movement, Moltmann is asking the question: how does the divine promise, established in Jesus' resurrection, reach those to whom it is addressed, the godless and the godforsaken, i.e. sinners who suffer their own turning away from God and innocent sufferers who are the victims of pointless suffering?[39] How does the promise of liberation from suffering in God's presence, given in the resurrection, reach those who in their meaningless suffering feel abandoned by God? Moltmann's answer is that it reaches them through Jesus' *identification* with them, in their condition, on the cross. His resurrection represents salvation *for them* only because he dies for them, identified with them in their condition (CG 24, 185–6, 192; DGG 178). This identification involves above all a sharing of their suffering

---

[38] On Moltmann's political theology from this point of view, see D. L. Migliore, 'Biblical Eschatology and Political Hermeneutics,' *Theology Today* 26 (1969–70), pp. 116–32.

[39] For Moltmann, the soteriological significance of the cross embraces 'both the question of human guilt and man's liberation from it, and also the question of human suffering and man's redemption from it' (CG 134). In this chapter we are concerned only with the latter theme.

in God's absence. The central concept of *The Crucified God* is love which suffers in solidarity with those who suffer: identifying love or solidarity in suffering. This is love which meets the suffering of the godforsaken – the meaningless suffering of those who suffer innocently and involuntarily – with another kind of suffering: voluntary fellow-suffering. It is love which willingly, out of love, comes alongside those it loves and identifies with them in their suffering. Moltmann is careful to stress that identification, in this sense, does not mean assimilation (CG 25–6, 28). Jesus on the cross is not simply one of the godless and the godforsaken, another sinner or another innocent sufferer. As such he would do them no good. Rather he is one who *voluntarily* identifies with them, takes their side and shares their fate (CG 50–1). Jesus' suffering and dying on the cross are God's act of loving solidarity with all who suffer apparently abandoned by God.

Of course, the cross is *God's* act of loving solidarity with sufferers only because Jesus is the divine Son of God incarnate.[40] Fully to understand Moltmann's view of the cross we have to put the dialectic of cross and resurrection together with the incarnational Christology and trinitarian doctrine of God with which Moltmann is working in *The Crucified God*. The cross and resurrection represent the opposition between a reality which does not correspond to God, the world subject to sin, suffering and death, and a reality which does correspond to God, a new creation indwelt by God's presence and reflecting his glory. But incarnational Christology means that this dialectic is internal to God's own experience. He suffers it in the person of the crucified and risen Son of God. He not only, in the resurrection, contradicts the reality which does not correspond to him; he also, on the cross, identifies with that reality. He is present in his own contradiction – the godlessness and godforsakenness of the cross – because in his love he embraces the reality which does not yet correspond to him. And therefore he suffers. The crucified God does not keep his

---

[40] Moltmann's progress from the largely functional and representative Christology of *Theology of Hope* to the explicitly incarnational Christology of *The Crucified God* occurred in close connexion with the theodicy issue.

impassible distance from those who suffer.[41] His love is not simply active benevolence which acts on humanity. It is dialectical love which in embracing its own contradiction must suffer (CG 248–9). A most important point in this argument for our purpose is that in identifying with the godforsaken the crucified God does not sanction their suffering as part of his purpose, because the dialectic of cross and resurrection remains. God's purpose is liberation from suffering, promised in the resurrection, where God is present in a reality corresponding to him. On the cross he embraces the godforsaken reality which precisely does not correspond to him. Thus the element of protest against the unacceptable features of present reality, which characterizes promise and hope in *Theology of Hope*, is not suppressed in *The Crucified God* but included in the concept of identifying love which dominates this book.

Moltmann's view of the cross as divine solidarity with the godless and the godforsaken involves neither allowing God's presence in the cross to reduce its utter negativity nor allowing the utter negativity of the cross to reduce God's presence in it. Hence his insistence on the language of contradiction: God is present in his own contradiction (CG 27).[42] Moltmann's response to the theodicy problem requires what he calls restoring 'the profane horror and godlessness of the cross' (CG 33), which comes fully to light only in the cry of dereliction: 'My God, my God, why hast thou forsaken me?' Like Camus, Moltmann puts this cry at the heart of his interpretation of the cross. The deepest dimension of the cross is not seen in Jesus' rejection by the Jewish leaders or in his condemnation by the Roman authorities, though both of these have a place in Moltmann's interpretation of the cross.

[41] On Moltmann's understanding of divine suffering, see R. Bauckham, 'Jürgen Moltmann,' in P. Toon and J. D. Spiceland (ed.), *One God in Trinity* (London: Bagster, 1980), pp. 121–3; idem, '"Only the suffering God can help": divine passibility in modern theology,' *Themelios* 9/3 (1984), pp. 6–12 (placing Moltmann's view in the context of modern discussion of the topic); idem, *Moltmann*, chapter 4.

[42] On the meaning of this language in *The Crucified God*, see R. Bauckham, 'Moltmann's Eschatology of the Cross,' *Scottish Journal of Theology* 30 (1977), pp. 304–8; idem, *Moltmann*, chapter 3.

The deepest dimension of the cross is seen only in Jesus' abandonment by his God and Father, when God leaves him to die (CG 4, 145–3; TKG 78). Hence it is understandable only in a trinitarian context as an event between Jesus the incarnate Son and his Father, an event of divine suffering in which Jesus suffers dying in abandonment by his Father and the Father suffers in grief the death of his Son. As such it is the act of divine solidarity with the godforsaken world, in which the Son willingly surrenders himself in love for the world and the Father willingly surrenders his Son in love for the world. The great abyss of the world's godforsakenness is thus taken within the trinitarian love between the Father and the Son (CG 190–3, 241–9; CPS 93–6; TKG 75–83).[43]

In order to show how Moltmann's argument meshes with our earlier discussion of Dostoyevsky, Camus and Wiesel, we shall take up our three texts again in reverse order. In the first place, Moltmann's crucified Christ is neither of the crucified Christs offered by Camus.[44] He is neither just another innocent man protesting against divine injustice nor the suffering God who sets an example of meek submission to suffering. Rather he is 'the protesting God' (CG 226). Moltmann divests the cross neither of deity nor of protest against suffering. The incarnate God identifies with the suffering of those he loves and, as those who suffer in loving solidarity with innocent sufferers must, he takes up and expresses their protest against their pointless suffering. In the cry of dereliction the crucified Christ protests on behalf of all innocent sufferers. And the example he sets is not of fatalistic acceptance of suffering, but of voluntary, loving identification with the desolate and the abandoned. Thus protest, moral outrage against suffering, is not quelled but sustained by the cross, and becomes an essential element in that loving solidarity which the crucified Christ both

---

[43] On Moltmann's interpretation of the cross, see Bauckham, 'Jürgen Moltmann,' pp. 117–24; idem, *Moltmann*, chapters 3–4; J. J. O'Donnell, *Trinity and Temporality: The Christian Doctrine of God in the Light of Process Theology and the Theology of Hope* (Oxford: Oxford University Press, 1983), pp. 116–20.

[44] For Moltmann's explicit interaction with Camus's view of the crucified Christ, see CG 226.

practises and encourages in his followers (see CG 48–53, 227, 252–4; CPS 97–8, 273–4; OC 42–3).

Secondly, what of Wiesel's narrative? The cross, for Moltmann, is God's demonstrative *act* of solidarity by which he identifies with all human suffering. Thus he can re-interpret Wiesel's story of the boy on the gallows: 'in a real, transferred sense . . . God himself hung on the gallows, as E. Wiesel was able to say' (CG 278). This reinterpretation is justified in the light of the cross, which would be enough to end faith in God were it not seen as God's presence precisely in abandonment by God.[45] Hence, in Auschwitz as on the cross, God is present in his own contradiction. He is present not simply in silence, but in the protests of the rebels, like Wiesel, who in the name of divine righteousness protest against his silence, and present too in the human love and solidarity which give point to their protest (HP 33–5, 43, 51; CG 252–6). But none of this can absolve him of respon-sibility for allowing the holocaust. So what, finally, of Ivan Karamazov's argument?

Moltmann's response does not solve the problem of suffer-ing in the sense of explaining suffering.[46] Nor should it do so, because any such explanation is subject to Ivan's criticism: that it justifies suffering (TKG 52). What is needed is a response to the theodicy problem which, instead of Ivan's impotent protest which lapses into nihilism, sustains Ivan's protest and converts it into liberating praxis.[47] How does the crucified God do so?

Consider, first, the victims of suffering, since any response to the problem of suffering must attempt to adopt their per-spective.[48] The person who suffers the excess of meaningless suffering feels abandoned by God and cries out in protest against the God who has incomprehensibly left him to suffer. But in the crucified God he finds God actually taking his side against himself (CG 252). God is no longer just the heavenly

---

[45] Cf. the important quotation from Iwand on CG 36.
[46] This is G. M. Jantzen's criticism of Moltmann: 'Christian Hope and Jesus' Despair,' *King's Theological Review* 5 (1982), p. 5.
[47] Cf. CG 223: 'what keeps Ivan Karamazov's protest alive?'
[48] Cf. Surin, 'Theodicy?,' p. 232; idem, *Theology*, p. 52.

authority whom he accuses, but also the one who shares his suffering in love and protests with him against his suffering in love. This in itself begins his liberation from suffering. It removes what Moltmann calls 'the suffering in suffering': the lack of love, the abandonment in suffering (CG 46; CPS 94). In the experience of God's love the sufferer recovers his sense of human worth and the hope which maintain his protest against suffering and enable him to resist its de-humanizing power (CG 47–52).

Consider, secondly, the person like Ivan who protests on behalf of the suffering. The protest against God is valid and can only be answered when God fulfils his promises and finally overcomes all evil and suffering. But the crucified God stands in a dialectical relation to the problem of suffering. He is not only in some sense responsible for the world which arouses our moral outrage (T 565; CG 252),[49] he also endorses that protest against himself. This dialectic of divine responsibility and protest must remain an open dialectic to be resolved only at the eschaton when suffering is overcome (HP 43–4; UZ 137–8; CG 178; T 565; TKG 49). Meantime, God's solidarity with the suffering provides a *ground* for that longing for divine righteousness from which the protest arises, keeps it from lapsing into nihilism, and empowers it with hope and love (CG 278). Ivan's protest is impotent, because, as he confesses, he 'never could understand how one can love one's neighbour'.[50] Therefore it leads from theodicy to anthropodicy and the totalitarian terror of the Grand Inquisitor. The protest of the crucified God is the protest of love which always takes the side of the victims of injustice (CG 52–3; FC 57; CPS 97–8), and therefore it leads believers in the crucified God into liberating praxis on their behalf. By keeping the theodicy question alive and open, the crucified God leads into concrete struggles for justice and liberation from suffering (HP 51). And by meeting the problem of suffering with voluntary *fellow* suffering, the crucified God promotes that loving solidarity with victims

[49] If he were not this, his solidarity with the suffering would be no ground for hope for his overcoming of suffering at the eschaton.
[50] Dostoyevsky, *Brothers Karamazov*, p. 276.

which refuses every justification of suffering. This is *his* only justification short of the new creation.

Appendix to Chapter Four: Elie Wiesel's *Twilight*

After this chapter was first written, Wiesel published a novel[51] which contains his most mature reflections on the themes of theodicy which he first tackled in *Night*. The French title *Le Crépuscule, au loin*,[52] was reduced in English translation to the simple *Twilight*, which corresponds, surely deliberately, to *Night*. *Twilight*, however, is in fictional rather than auto-biographical form. It is narrated by a Polish Jew, Raphael Lipkin, who, alone of his family, escaped arrest by the Nazis. In Paris after the war he was befriended by Pedro, a hero of the Briha, the clandestine Jewish organization which helped survivors of the Holocaust. Pedro enabled Raphael to go on living when his experiences had extinguished all desire to live. But Pedro disappeared on an unsuccessful mission to rescue Raphael's brother from a Russian gaol. Raphael settled in America, married, had a daughter, was divorced. His haunted life as a survivor[53] is finally shattered by an anonymous telephone caller who casts serious doubts on Pedro's integrity. On the caller's advice, he spends a period in a sanatorium for the mentally ill, which specializes in schizophrenics who think they are characters from biblical history. Raphael goes there in search of the truth about Pedro, feeling his own basis for living to be at stake in the threat to Pedro's reputation (cf. pp. 36, 71, 117–18).[54] He feels he is himself going mad. The book intertwines Raphael's interviews with the patients, many of whose extraordinary delusions serve to voice the theological issues surrounding the holocaust and to take Raphael back into its horrors, and Raphael's own recollections of his youth before

---

[51] *Le Crépuscule, au loin* was first published in 1987 (Paris: Grasset & Fasquelle).

[52] The French title ('Twilight, in the distance') refers more precisely to the end of the book. See E. Wiesel, *Twilight* (London: Penguin, 1991), p. 206: 'Twilight no longer seems distant.'

[53] On the issue of what it means to be a survivor, which recurs throughout the book, see, e.g., pp. 123, 132, 174, 185, 197.

[54] Page references in the text are to the Penguin edition of *Twilight* (see n. 2).

and during the war. In the end the question of Pedro gives way to the question of God. Raphael's final dialogue is with the schizophrenic who thinks he is God.

There can be no doubt that this recent book consciously resumes and rethinks the issues of Wiesel's first book. Prefaced to it is a quotation from *Night*:

> Never shall I forget that night, the first night in the camp, which turned my life into long night, seven times cursed and seven times sealed. Never can I forget those flames that consumed my faith for ever. Never shall I forget that nocturnal silence which deprived me, for all eternity, of the desire to live (*Twilight*, p. 9).

But in *Twilight* Raphael does not experience darkness in this unambiguous finality. Rather he enters the twilight world in which darkness struggles with light but has not won. 'Day and night are in mortal combat,' says the mad patient 'God' to Raphael as they gaze at the darkening evening sky: 'Since creation they have been at a stalemate. Why do they fight? They alone understand their struggle' (p. 207). Twilight is the sphere of struggle between good and evil. It is also 'the domain of madness' (p. 202) which the mad people at the clinic inhabit, and which Raphael, as he becomes mad or thinks he becomes mad, finally also enters (pp. 202, 206, 217). While *Night* told the story of Wiesel's loss of faith, *Twilight* broaches the possibility of a new kind of faith, which inhabits the twilight world where evil does its worst in the conflict with the good, and which, in its open-eyed, suffering awareness of the dark,[55] has to be a kind of madness.

Twilight contains significant echoes of *Night*. When the young Raphael first hears from his brother what Germans are doing to Jews, he asks his father:

> 'How can this be true? How can man be so cruel?' 'Remember,' replied his father, 'once evil is unleashed, anything is possible' (p. 211).

Three times, in relation to the holocaust, Raphael asks the 'terrible question': '*And what about God in all this?*' (pp. 210,

---

[55] Cf. p. 14: 'Remember: a madman is someone whose eyes are always open.'

212, 214).[56] Referring to a man who had survived the death camps, Raphael asks Pedro:

> '*and what about God in all this?* One of the two men is a believer; he put on his *tefillin* this morning, I saw him with my own eyes. Tell me, Pedro, where was God while this pious Jew endured twenty-five lashes of the German's whip? Do you want to know what I really think? That very morning, God should have revealed Himself to him and said, "Wait a minute, you still say your prayers? You still believe in my kindness, my justice? My poor man, you are mad . . ."' (p. 212).

Praying to a God who is kind and just is not impossible, as Wiesel found it in *Night* – but it is madness. When Raphael persists in pressing Pedro to say whether he agrees 'that in these times one must be mad to believe in God,' Pedro at last answers:

> 'I can think of another explanation: What if it is God who is mad?' Raphael was shaken. He wanted to take a deep breath. He wanted to scream. But no sound left his throat.

Of the echoes of *Night* in *Twilight* , the most interesting is the one which offers a variant of the famous scene of the child on the gallows. When the Germans first occupy the Polish town in which Raphael and his family live, the residents are required to assemble in the main square, where the German commander makes an example of a Jew alleged to have assaulted a German soldier. The Jew is brought forward to be hanged. Raphael thinks he recognizes the man. He is an old madman who had befriended Raphael, who used to make weekly visits to the asylum to see him. When Raphael was close to death from typhus, the old man had visited his bedside and revealed to him that he had asked and had been allowed by the Celestial Tribunal to die in place of all those threatened with death by the epidemic.

---

[56] Cf. the earlier questions: '*And Rachel* [Raphael's daughter] *in all this?*' (p. 102), '*And Pedro in all this?*' (p. 204). The series of questions mark the progress of his concerns back from his recent preoccupation with his failed marriage, to the basis for living he acquired with Pedro's help after the war, and finally, through the shaking of this foundation, back to the most fundamental question which he had asked as a boy in and after the war and to which he now, at the end of the book, returns: '*And God in all this?*'

Now he thinks it is the old man he sees on the scaffold. But then the old man is by his side, speaking to him.

> 'If you are here, who was that on the scaffold?'
> The old man did not answer.
> Raphael whispered, 'I had to be sure it wasn't you.'
> 'You're not sure? That's good. I like it that way. Then again, even if it had been me, I would still stay close to you and your family. You see, whenever one of our people dies, I die for him and with him. Oh, I know: it's difficult to understand. Never mind. It's not necessary to understand everything in life, especially at your age' (pp. 34–5).

Since the old man turns out in some sense to represent God (cf. p. 217), Wiesel is clearly here alluding to the ambiguity of the famous episode in *Night* – the question of the sense in which God hangs on the gallows. He is now taking up the interpretation some have put on that scene: that God suffers with his people in their sufferings. But he is not neglecting the primary meaning the scene had had for him: that God died for his faith. On Raphael's first encounter with the old madman, the madman said: 'I'll be here even when I'm no longer here' (p. 12). The 'mad old man who died more than once' (p. 28) is present even when he is absent.

The old man seems to be God, not *simpliciter* – since he prays to God (p. 34) – but as the *Shekinah* presence of God with his people in exile and suffering (cf. p. 13). (Moltmann in CG 273–4 actually cites the episode of the boy on the gallows from *Night* as an expression of this rabbinic and kabbalistic *Shekinah* theology. Cf. also TKG 27–30; JM 49–52.) This *Shekinah* theology is expounded within the book by the patient who thinks he is Abraham (pp. 95–6), and it is what Raphael remembers having learned from the old madman:

> Long ago, in Rovidok, the old madman with veiled eyes persuaded him that it was possible for one man to die in another man's place, and that divine redemption depends upon human redemption (p. 100; cf. also pp. 13, 175, 213).

The last clause alludes to the kabbalistic idea that God himself is in need of redemption which will come only with

Israel's redemption, when the exile and suffering of the
Shekinah will come to an end and God be reunited with
himself.[57]

But this is pre-Holocaust theology, which the book seems to
indicate cannot remain unchanged by the Holocaust. If the
old madman could die in place of the potential victims of the
typhus epidemic, saving them from death, why can he not die
in place of the victims of the Holocaust, saving them from
death? The question is not explicitly asked in the book but it is
implicit. It probably explains the most puzzling passage in this
enigmatic book. At the end of the book Raphael is in conversation with the patient who thinks he is God – not the
Shekinah but the Creator. Of course, the patient is not God.
The device enables Wiesel to distance what is said from any
notion of divine revelation, since, as Pedro says: 'while the
question [the theodicy question] never changes, the answer is
ever-changing' (p. 197). But nevertheless what the patient
'God' says represents insight Raphael believes he has gained.
While not the answer, it is an answer, a post-Holocaust answer.
It must be taken seriously. That this 'God' is mad is wholly
appropriate, for as Pedro suggested, the God in whom it is
possible to believe after the Holocaust must be mad.

The conversation highlights God's suffering for his creation, and Raphael's own suffering. 'God' says:

> 'There is suffering and there is suffering. Who is more odious
> than the man who laments a lost object in the presence of one
> who has lost a friend; or the man who complains of a trifle in the
> presence of one who is condemned to die? I am not suggesting
> you should not cry when you hurt. But if you cry only for your-
> self, your cry, in spite of its echo, will remain hollow. Without
> others, you would never know love. Without life, death would be
> meaningless. I repeat: What matters is not to cry for yourself.
> Cry for others. And for me too.' . . .
>
> 'You are right,' Raphael tells his neighbour. 'There are
> different degrees of suffering. Yours is surely deeper, more
> lasting. But why must it negate mine?'

---

[57] A statement of this doctrine by a modern but pre-Holocaust Jewish
theologian whose work Wiesel certainly knows is F. Rosenzweig, *The Star of
Redemption* (Notre Dame: Notre Dame Press, 1985), pp. 409–10.

'It doesn't,' says the man. 'No one can suffer in place of
another. No one can live or die in place of another.'
'Not even you?'
'Not even I' (pp. 213–14).

The point seems to be that *substitutionary* suffering is
impossible. Certainly God suffers because of humanity and
with humanity (p. 214), but he cannot suffer instead of
humanity, sparing them the suffering.

Though substitutionary suffering is impossible, tears for
others in their suffering, the Creator's tears for others (cf.
p. 209), and even our tears for the Creator (cf. pp. 213–14)
are redemptive. In Paris after the war, Raphael encountered
the old madman for the last time before his visit to the
sanatorium. He is a rabbi who leads prayers for the Jewish
children, but the children – children of the Holocaust
generation – do not wish to pray:

> The rabbi, wrapped in his ritual shawl, closed his prayer book
> and said, 'Children, you are right. Perhaps we need a different
> kind of prayer.'
> And he began to weep soundlessly, until he was choked with
> sobs . . .
> 'Thank you rabbi, your tears have freed us,' said one of the
> older boys. 'Now we can pray' (pp. 122–3).

Tears, we should perhaps infer, unite sufferers with God,
unite the Creator with his *Shekinah* , and so bring about the
redemption.

The pervasive metaphor of madness also, of course, serves
the needs of a post-Holocaust theology. The mad God is the
God who has seen (cf. pp. 209–10) the irrational horror of
the Holocaust and himself suffers it. To believe in God in
spite of the Holocaust and to understand the possibility of
redemption in spite of the Holocaust one must enter the
twilight zone of madness, eyes wide open to evil. The 'path to
enlightenment', Pedro had told Raphael, 'leads through the
ravaged landscape of madness' (p. 75). But enlightenment is
not likely to be rational understanding. Right through the
book runs an emphasis on the impossibility of understanding
the ultimate matters of good and evil, of giving a rational

answer to the theodicy question. On his very first encounter with the old madman, Raphael reflects:

> The old man was mad, and madmen put little store in being understood. Madmen can say anything, do or undo anything, without ever having to explain. Madmen are free, totally free (p. 12).

Pedro, 'a madman in his own way',

> was forever telling Raphael that one must not seek to understand, that one must understand without seeking, that it is sometimes necessary to seek in order not to understand (p. 100).

And about the theodicy question, Pedro (who believed in humanity more obviously than in God) said:

> 'Like the question, the answer needs freedom. But while the question never changes, the answer is ever-changing: What is important for man is to know that there is an answer. What is important for man is to feel not only the existence of an answer, but the presence of one who knows the answer. When I seek that presence I am seeking God.'
>   'Are you telling me you believe in God?' I asked you.
>   Ignoring my question, you went on:
>   'As I move closer to man, I move closer to God . . .' (pp. 197–8).

Raphael's enlightenment can take the form only of a vision, not an explanation. He is promised it and set on the path to it in his youth, when the old madman would teach him Jewish mystical theology, though he never understood. The old man spoke of the heavenly palace

> where the Creator of the world awaits the *Shekhina* to restore his creation to the origins of innocence. And the eagle's nest where a lone, melancholy Messiah prays for time to accelerate its rhythm . . .
>   'The place I want to show you is farther still,' said the old man. 'Promise to follow me always' (p. 13).

The place is farther than the traditional images of redemption because it lies beyond the Holocaust. On another occasion in his youth, when the old man visits his sickbed and reveals that he is going to die in Raphael's place, he receives another intimation of future enlightenment:

> 'But if you die, it means I'll never see you again!'
> 'It does mean something, but not that,' said the old man. 'I'll be dead, but you'll go on seeing me.'
> 'Then nothing will change?'
> 'Something will. My eyes.'

Raphael looks at the mysterious eyes which have always been described as veiled. The promise is that, beyond the death of God's *Shekinah* in the Holocaust, Raphael will still see him, but differently.

Following his old friend, the madman, into his own domain, the twilight of madness, Raphael receives finally his enlightenment:

> From far away, a star appears. Uncommonly brilliant, it captures the essence of twilight.
>
> The patient sitting beside Raphael raises his head to look at the sky. Raphael too looks and looks, but his eyes retrieve only twilight and it has a face, a face he has never forgotten. That of the old man from Rovidok. Only his eyes, infinitely kind and wise, are veiled no more (p. 217).

The vision surely alludes to the Jewish theologian Franz Rosenzweig's *The Star of Redemption,* in particular to the passage where he speaks of recognizing the star of redemption in the divine countenance as it shines on the redeemed world.[58] The difference from Rosenzweig is that Raphael sees it in the twilight.

---

[58] Rosenzweig, *The Star of Redemption,* p. 418.

5

Political Theology*

Jürgen Moltmann's political theology has the considerable merit that it is thoroughly and deeply theological. The political concerns which he has maintained throughout his long career and his considerable theological output have never led him away from theology but always take him back to strictly theological questions. As he remarks in an essay on political theology,

> As long as a Christian does not know what true Christian faith is, he or she cannot relate in a reflective way to political questions. . . . This, of course, is overlooked today when out of an inner uncertainty in faith one plunges into political engagement in order to find a more certain standpoint (HD 62).

In other words, for Moltmann Christian political engagement is no substitute for Christian faith, but one of the forms which faith must take in action; and political theology is no substitute for dogmatic theology, but theology's critical reflection on its own political functions.

Moltmann's political theology cannot therefore be easily detached from the dogmatic theology in which it is rooted. If this chapter seems more theological than political, this will reflect both the merit of Moltmann's political theology – its thoroughly theological character – and also what is arguably its weakness – its relative lack of political concreteness.

1. Revolutionary hope

Moltmann's *Theology of Hope,* first published in 1964 and

---

* This chapter originated as the C. B. Powell Lecture for 1987, delivered at the University of South Africa, Pretoria, in May 1987. It has not been previously published.

undoubtedly one of the most influential theological works of the post-war period, pointed quite clearly in the direction of a political theology, but itself scarcely provided one. It was in the years immediately after *Theology of Hope* that Moltmann, following the lead of his Tübingen colleague J. B. Metz,[1] developed his thought into an explicitly political theology, in the sense in which that term came into use in Germany at that time, i.e. in the sense of a politically critical theology aiming at radical change in the political and social *status quo*. However, this first phase of Moltmann's political theology was so much a logical consequence of the thought-structures of *Theology of Hope* that it cannot be understood except in the closest possible connexion with them.

The heart of Moltmann's *Theology of Hope* and hence of the political theology which developed from it, is not simply eschatology but eschatological *Christology*. It is an interpretation of the resurrection of the crucified Jesus as the dialectical event of eschatological promise. It brings together two fundamental notions: a dialectical understanding of the cross and resurrection, and a dialectical understanding of revelation as promise.

(1) The dialectic of cross and resurrection means that, in Moltmann's view, the cross and resurrection of Jesus represent total opposites: death and life, the absence of God and the presence of God, godforsakenness and God's glory. Yet Jesus, the crucified and risen one, remained the same person in this total contradiction. By raising the crucified Jesus to new life, God created continuity in this radical discontinuity.

(2) The meaning of this divine act can be understood when it is seen as the culmination of the Old Testament history of *promise,* in which God revealed himself by making promises which opened up the future. Moltmann sees the Christ-event not so much as fulfilling the Old Testament history of promise, but rather as confirming and

---

[1] For Moltmann's relationship to Metz at this stage, see his own account in UZ 13; HTG 177. On Metz's early political theology, see R. D. Johns, *Man in the World: The Theology of Johannes Baptist Metz* (American Academy of Religion Dissertation Series 16; Missoula, Montana: Scholars Press, 1976).

guaranteeing and universalizing God's promise for the future. It is the definitive event of divine promise. This can be so because the crucified Jesus in his death is identified with all the negative qualities of present reality, its subjection to sin and suffering and death, its godlessness and god-forsakenness and transitoriness. It is not that the world in its present reality is simply evil, but it is subject to evil and ends in nothingness. The cross represents, and indeed reveals with full clarity for the first time, the plight and the fate of this world. But the same Jesus who was crucified was also raised and sustained in his own person the total contradiction of cross and resurrection. His resurrection is therefore God's promise of new creation for the whole of the godforsaken reality which the crucified Jesus represents. It is therefore an event of *dialectical* promise: it opens up a qualitatively *new* future, which negates all the negatives of present experience. It opens up a future which is not simply drawn out of the immanent possibilities of present reality, but radically contradicts present reality. It promises life for the dead, righteousness for the unrighteous, freedom for those in bondage. It offers hope where the immanent prospects of the world offer no hope. But because of Jesus' *identity* in the total contradiction of cross and resurrection, God's promise is not for another world, but for the new creation of this world in all its material and worldly reality. The promise of Jesus' resurrection is given to the world in which Jesus' cross stands.

Thus, the event of the resurrection of the crucified Christ, as an event of dialectical promise, serves in *Theology of Hope* to open theology and the church simultaneously towards the world and towards the future. The promise is for the eschatological transformation of the whole of reality. Hence Christian hope, which puts its trust in this promise, necessarily thrusts believers into the worldly reality for whose future they hope. They become involved in the church's universal mission to the world, which stems from the resurrection of Jesus and is orientated towards the future which that event projects. The task of mission is, in the first place, to awaken hope by the proclamation of the

Gospel-promise, but also to seek the *present* transformation of life in accordance with and in anticipation of the promised eschatological transformation. Not only are individual lives and the community of the church transformed in anticipation of the future new creation, but because the promise is for the transformation of all of this worldly reality, Christians must seek to realize in society at large those possibilities for change which correspond to their hope for the future. In this way the ultimate future projected by the resurrection of Jesus is brought to bear on the immediate temporal future of the world, and the church in its mission to the world is understood as an agent of eschatological unrest, charged with keeping society on the move towards the coming kingdom of God.

This is in outline the main thrust of Moltmann's thinking in *Theology of Hope*. Its significance for our present subject is that it provides a kind of hermeneutical structure for relating Christian faith to the sphere of political practice. Briefly, it is an understanding of Christian hope which requires a revolutionary political praxis. How this is so, and the problems involved in it, the following series of comments attempt to explain:

(1) The political importance of Moltmann's *dialectical* Christology and eschatology derives from the full recognition it gives to the negative, unredeemed character of objective present reality and therefore to the *difference*, even contradiction, between what reality is presently like and what in the hoped-for divine transformation of reality it can become. Since the resolution of the dialectic is reserved for the future, the concept prevents any *illusory* resolution of it by a mere religious *interpretation* of the *status quo*, which glorifies the *status quo* and veils its real evils and sufferings with a spurious religious aura. Thus, the first political effect of Christian hope is to expose the real evils of the *status quo*, to liberate the Christian from accommodation to it, and to set him or her critically against it.

(2) If theology of hope distinguishes itself sharply from religion as ideological glorification of the *status quo*, it also

distinguishes itself just as sharply from another way in which religion can support the *status quo*: by providing *compensation* for its evils. Here Moltmann finds truth in Marxist criticism of religion. Marx recognized that religion, in its hope for another world, expresses and protests against the real misery of this, but charged that by means of its *otherworldly* eschatology it provides a merely illusory compensation for human misery and thereby helps to perpetuate the conditions which cause it, instead of changing them. Marxism aimed to inherit the religious protest against human misery and direct it into the transformation of material conditions in this world. Moltmann's claim is that Christian eschatology, properly understood with reference not to another world but to the eschatological new creation of this world, must have precisely this effect. Christian hope is not the 'apocalyptic lethargy' which leaves this world to its fate and waits for another. Rather, by revealing the world to be 'not yet' what it will be, but as open to transformation in the direction of the promise, Christian hope *motivates* people to seek and to activate those present possibilities of the world which correspond to its promised future. Thus, the second political effect of Christian hope is the positive attempt to change the world in anticipation of its eschatological transformation.

(3) As a result, Moltmann stresses that theology of hope is inseparable from liberating praxis. Already in *Theology of Hope* itself Moltmann adapts Marx's famous eleventh thesis on Feuerbach: 'The philosophers have only interpreted the world in various ways; the point, however, is to change it' (quoted in TT 93). Moltmann writes: 'The theologian is not concerned merely to supply a different *interpretation* of the world, of history and of human nature, but to *transform* them in expectation of a divine transformation' (TH 84). After Marx there is no evading the insight that theory must be practicable: 'unless it contains initiative for the transformation of the world, it becomes a myth of the existing world' (RRF 138). Hence the axiom of political theology: that the criterion of theology must now be

praxis,[2] and, since the concrete possibilities of changing the world are, in the broadest sense, political, that means political praxis.

(4) Whereas Moltmann finds in Christian hope an initiative for political change, he does not *reduce* the Christian hope to something which can be realized by human activity within history. The key concept here is *anticipation*. It is not that human activity in the present builds the future kingdom, but that the future kingdom by arousing hope and obedience in the present creates anticipations of itself within history. These are real anticipations of the kingdom, forms of God's presence (cf. HD 111; CG 337) within the contradictions of a still unredeemed world, but they are precisely anticipations of a kingdom which itself remains *eschatological*, transcendent beyond all its historical approximations. This is the key point at which Latin American Liberation theology, which developed not without some influence from Moltmann's *Theology of Hope*, was at times anxious to distinguish itself from Moltmann, who is accused of detracting from the struggle for liberation by relativizing its significance in this way.[3] It is probably significant at this point that in its origins Liberation theology took the Exodus as the key to a theological understanding of liberation, whereas Moltmann gives his political theology a christological grounding in the resurrection. The Exodus has only a subordinate place as part of the Old Testament history of promise which is taken up into the culminating event of promise in the resurrection of Jesus. The promise of the resurrection is properly eschatological, including the hopes of political and economic liberation which the Exodus awakens, but extending to that new creation of the world in which all evil and suffering and

[2] For Moltmann's later view of the truth and limitations of this principle, see TT 92–4.

[3] E.g. J. Míguez Bonino, *Revolutionary Theology Comes of Age* (London: SPCK, 1975), pp. 139–42. For the debate, including other differences and Moltmann's own criticisms of Latin American Liberation theology, see T. Witvliet, *The Way of the Black Messiah* (tr. J. Bowden; London: SCM Press, 1987), pp. 51–8; G. J. Dorrien, *Reconstructing the Common Good* (Maryknoll, New York: Orbis, 1990), pp. 87–9, 98–9.

transitoriness and death will be overcome and God's glory will indwell his perfected creation.

In Moltmann's thinking this properly eschatological goal of creation does not detract from attempts to realize relative approximations to it in the present, but inspires them. Its relativizing effect has a positive importance in keeping the future open. Since the final future cannot be captured in any of its relative anticipations, these remain flexible and surpassible. New possibilities of anticipating the kingdom are constantly coming to light in the historical experiences of humanity. The transcendence of the kingdom exposes the deficiencies of every revolutionary achievement and makes frank recognition of them possible, against the tendency of revolutionary regimes to hide such deficiencies behind a glorification of the new *status quo*. Only as the eschatological source of historically inexhaustible possibilities can the future retain the 'magic' of transcendence (FC I; cf. DTH 217).

(5) The real problem of Moltmann's political theology in the 1960s was how the eschatological hope could be concretely mediated in specific political goals and strategies. On a superficial reading *Theology of Hope* could be held simply to reconcile theology to the character of the modern era as a period of continuous change. Its fascination with the ever new possibilities of the open future could, at worst, seem to endorse the optimism of Western societies in its most dubious forms: trust in technological progress and endless economic growth, and an affluent society's fashionable quest for novelty for its own sake. In reality this was far from Moltmann's purpose. The promise of the Christian Gospel does not simply endorse change, whatever its direction, but confronts the modern consciousness of historical openness with its own initiative for change in the direction of the kingdom of God. The sphere of contemporary hopes and fears for the future is the place where it addresses people, but not the content of what it says.[4]

[4] Cf. J.-P. Thévenaz, 'Vérité d'espérance ou vérité de connaissance? Les enjeux théoriques et politiques de la théologie de Jürgen Moltmann,' *Etudes théologiques et religieuses* 49 (1974), p. 242.

That the content must differ significantly from the affluent optimism of the 1960s can be seen in the dialectical character of hope and its connexion with the concern for theodicy that runs through Moltmann's theology from the beginning. Christian hope is for the manifestation of God's righteousness in a world at present characterized by suffering and injustice. It does not develop out of the prospects of a hopeful present, but brings hope into an otherwise hopeless present, hope for justice and freedom and peace where injustice, oppression and conflict presently reign. Moltmann's theology, even at this stage, can therefore have nothing really in common with an ideological optimism based on suppressing and forgetting the negativities of the *status quo*. Rather it must bring them to light for the sake of transforming them. Moltmann's political theology of hope is about bringing hope to bear on precisely the suffering and the injustices of society, but for that reason it led, by its own logic, to a new stage of Moltmann's theology. This was a political theology of the cross in which Moltmann focused on the other side of his dialectical Christology: the cross of the risen Christ, the cross by which Christ mediates the hope of resurrection to the world in its godlessness and godforsakenness.

(6) In the light of what has been said so far, it may not be surprising that the nearest Moltmann's work in the 1960s came to specifying its practical political implications was in his quite frequent talk of revolution. (The term need not, of course, imply *violent* revolution,[5] but refers to radical, structural change in society [cf. RRF 131: revolution is 'transformation in the foundations of a system'].) At least this makes clear that his sympathies in the 1960s were not with the optimism of the establishment, but with the wave of social and political protest and the pursuit of radical alternatives to the *status quo*: with the civil rights movement in the United States, with the anti-colonial struggles of the Third World,

---

[5] Moltmann in his earlier work strongly defended the legitimacy of violence in the liberation of the oppressed (e.g. EH 10), but was also sensitive to the problems which the use of violence raise for 'the humane revolution' (RRF 143–5).

with the student protest movements in the universities of Europe and North America. His participation in the Christian–Marxist dialogue of course belongs also in this context.

What gave the concept of revolution theological legitimacy for Moltmann was the dialectical character of hope: that hope *contradicts* the present as the resurrection contradicts the cross. In other words, dialectical hope calls for *radical* change. Unfortunately, this theological legitimation for talk of revolution tends to take the place of political, social and economic analysis. It lacks the material concreteness of Marxist analysis which so appealed to the Liberation theologians of Latin America. It is significant that, by contrast with them, what appealed to Moltmann in Marxism was its vision of a new society of freedom, which he found especially in the humanistic Marxism of western Europe (cf., e.g. RRF 64–5, 70), rather than scientific Marxism's analysis of the economic conditions of revolution and its strategy for proletarian revolution. Consequently, Moltmann's talk of revolution was in danger of romanticism; it had inadequate roots in concrete political conditions and possibilities; and as the radical hopes of the 1960s dissipated, Moltmann himself came to see its inadequacy as a prescription for Christian political involvement in the context of Western societies. While withdrawing none of his support for revolutionary liberation struggles in the Third World, Moltmann came to see the reformist path of democratic socialism as more appropriate in the European context.[6] This was a tacit admission that while dialectical hope may give motivation, ultimate goals and critical distance from the *status quo*, it cannot prescribe immediate political objectives and strategies, which require also concrete analysis and decision in specific contexts.

While Moltmann's political theology has achieved concreteness of this kind only sporadically, some very important developments in his theology after the 1960s have at least

[6] But see the interesting comments on messianism and democratic socialism in Bloch in HD 174. For Moltmann's commitment to democratic socialism, see especially Dorrien, *Reconstructing the Common Good,* chapter 4.

helped to show how it can be achieved. Here we can deal
with only two of these later developments in the period up to
1980: Moltmann's theology of the cross and his thinking
about human rights. Important developments beyond 1980[7]
are beyond the scope of this chapter.

2. Loving solidarity

Moltmann's dialectical Christology, with its emphasis on the
contradiction of the cross and the resurrection, contained
the potential for a radical theology of the cross. Indeed,
some of this potential was already being suggested in
Moltmann's political theology of the late 1960s, from which
the cross is by no means absent. But only with *The Crucified
God*, published in 1972, was the potential fully realized.

In *The Crucified God,* the dialectic of Jesus' identity in the
contradiction of cross and resurrection is still operative, but
whereas *Theology of Hope* focused on the resurrection of the
crucified Christ as the event of divine promise, *The Crucified
God* moves back to the cross of the risen Christ as the event of
divine love. To put this another way: in *Theology of Hope,*
Moltmann's thought moved forward from the cross to the
resurrection and the future of the world. It moved from the
unredeemed state of the world, with which Jesus on the cross
was identified, forward to its eschatological salvation. But in
The Crucified God Moltmann turns back from the promise and
the resurrection to the cross and the world with which the
crucified Jesus is identified. How does the promise,
represented by Jesus' resurrection, *reach* those to whom it is
addressed – the godless and the godforsaken, as Moltmann
repeatedly calls them in *The Crucified God*? It reaches them
through Jesus' *identification* with them, in their condition, in

---

[7] These include the political implications of the doctrine of the Trinity, for
which see, in part, chapter 8 below; the implications of his developed doctrine
of creation (including the relationship of pneumatology and Christology to
creation) for ecological concerns, for which see, in part, chapters 9 and 10
below; and Moltmann's treatment of the nuclear threat in relation to eschatology and the subject of violence and peace, for which see, in part, chapter 10
below.

the absolute negativity of the cross. His resurrection is salvation for *them* only because he first dies for them, identified with them in their condition – in an identification which involves above all a sharing of their suffering, a loving solidarity with those who suffer in God's absence. So the salvific theme of *Theology of Hope* – which is God's *promise* in the *resurrection* of the crucified Christ – is complemented by the salvific theme of *The Crucified God* – which is God's identifying and suffering love in the cross of the risen Christ. The cross is *God's* solidarity with the godless and the godforsaken, because Moltmann is now working with an explicitly incarnational Christology and trinitarian theology, so that the cross is an event of *divine suffering*, in which God overcomes the abandonment of the godless and the godforsaken by sharing their godforsaken fate in loving solidarity.

Just as the dialectical Christology of *Theology of Hope* produces a dialectical concept of promise – a promise which contradicts present reality – so in *The Crucified God* it produces a dialectical concept of divine love, i.e. a love in which God identifies with godless and suffering reality so that his salvation might reach it. He not only gives the world, in all its injustice and suffering, the promise of righteousness and freedom in a new creation. He also enters the suffering, brutal reality of this world, embraces the contradiction, suffers it in his love and overcomes it. From the God of the future who moves history forward by his promise, the focus shifts to the incarnate God who makes godless and godforsaken humanity the sphere of his presence in solidarity, and moves history forward by the power of his suffering love.

Just as the promise given in the resurrection of Christ motivates a Christian praxis of revolutionary hope, so the mediation of this promise by God's loving solidarity with the world in the cross of Christ results in a corresponding Christian praxis. The praxis of hope is complemented and deepened by a praxis of loving identification or solidarity with the world, solidarity especially with those who suffer most acutely the evils and injustices of this world, solidarity with the poor, the oppressed, the marginalized, the hopeless, the sick and the dying. The political consequences follow especially from the observation that, in concrete historical terms, Jesus died a victim of political power, as a consequence of his identification with those who were powerless and excluded by the society of his time.

Again a series of comments will make clear the way in which Moltmann's theology of the cross entails a political praxis of solidarity with victims, which does not replace but deepens the praxis of hope:

(1) The mediation of the promise by the cross means that hope becomes concretely earthed in the experience of the victims of society. The evils of the *status quo* become apparent not just by general contrast with what is promised by God, but by his self-identification on the cross with the oppressed and neglected. Christian hope for political change is in the first place *their* hope. It is they who desire a different future, and it is for their sake that possibilities of radical change must be opened up. Thus, talk of revolution, where still appropriate, is to some extent protected from romanticism: it must result from real solidarity with the victims and be rooted in their actual interests. At the same time, there is no longer any possibility of confusing the theology of hope with the ideological optimism of the affluent. In the latter case the future is planned as a mere extension of the present, in the interests of those who benefit from the present distribution of power in society. But *God's* future is anticipated on the cross, in his suffering solidarity with those who are excluded and forgotten by affluent optimism: it offers hope precisely to those to whom the *status quo* in society offers no hope. Thus Moltmann's development of the negative side of his dialectical Christology gives greater realism to his political theology:

> The divine future confronts us not in dreams of the future but in the face of the crucified Christ. . . . [Therefore] the anticipation of Christian hope is living and effective only in representing those who have no future (FC 53–4).

(2) This has an important bearing on the critical freedom of Christian hope over against all political systems and

ideologies. It becomes clear that Moltmann's insistence on this, for which the Liberation theologians have been inclined to criticize him, has nothing to do with the academic detachment of the European intellectual, who claims some kind of autonomous standpoint from which to assess all theological proposals. Rather the eschatological future which transcends every political system is allied to the cause of the victims of every such system, and so the critical distance it gives the Christian from every system and ideology is for their sake, on their behalf. The Christian's solidarity with any political movement must be a critical solidarity, *because* it can only be a consequence of, not a replacement for that solidarity with the victims to which the cross of Jesus commits his disciples.

(3) From this we can already begin to see how the cross of Christ comes to have the role of Christianity's internal principle of criticism, which unmasks ideology both within and outwith the church. At this stage of his thought Moltmann had become, through the influence of the critical theory of the Frankfurt school, more acutely aware of the extent to which all theory serves interests in society, so that even a supposedly non-political theology or a church which holds aloof from politics in fact cannot help fulfilling a political role. By failing to criticize the *status quo* it, in fact, supports it and hence the interests of the ruling class. But theology can be critical – in the sense of exposing such ideological illusions – to the extent that it is faithful to its own internal criterion: the cross of Christ. No theology which has faced up to the 'profane horror' (as Moltmann calls it) of the cross can continue to ignore the victims of society.

It is at this point that Moltmann develops the theology of the cross as a critique of political or civil religion, which he identifies as forms of idolatry (EH VIII; PR; CCR; CG 195–6, 325–9).[8] There is one form of political idolatry which gives religious sanction to political power and so absolutizes the claims of political power. But the Christ who was crucified in powerlessness and shame at the hands of the political

[8] See further R. Bauckham, *Moltmann: Messianic Theology in the Making* (Basingstoke: Marshall Pickering, 1987), pp. 73–5.

authorities deprives political power of its divinity. Those who acknowledge this politically executed Christ as their highest authority, as the point where divinity is revealed in this world, can no longer submit to political power as though to God (CCR 35). Moltmann even draws the conclusion that this requires the radical democratization of political life. The cross destroys any justification of political authority 'from above' and requires political authority to be legitimated only 'from below'.

A second form of political idolatry occurs when religion functions to integrate society and give exclusive sanction to the social values and structures of that society. A society or nation is here using religion as a form of self-confirmation, absolutizing itself, and therefore – the corollary – excluding or oppressing the 'others', those who do not conform or do not belong, those who are different. But a religion which serves in this way to integrate a society to the exclusion of others is not the religion of the cross, where God identified precisely with those who were different from himself, the godless and the godforsaken. The cross requires solidarity with those others who are the victims of society's compulsive need for self-confirmation (e.g. EH 116–17; CG 325).

(4) If the cross can function in this way as a critique of the political roles of theology and religion, it also remains a critical factor even in relation to those left-wing movements with which Moltmann had most sympathy (e.g. CG 17). The cross commits the Christian to solidarity especially with the most hopeless of humanity, not simply with the exploited proletariat but with those most wretched of the earth out of whom no revolution can be made (M 19), with those whom revolutionary realism must leave behind, even with the dying for whom the revolution will come too late. Not only with an oppressed group struggling for its liberation, but also with the forgotten victims of that group's struggle for liberation Christian solidarity is required, as well as with those who are oppressed or suffering in quite different ways. The victims are never just one group or class.[9]

[9] On the liberation not only of victims but also of oppressors, see HTG 44–56.

Not unconnected with this point is Moltmann's refusal to reduce liberation to one dimension of life – which constitutes perhaps his most important practical divergence from a Marxist approach. He identifies five dimensions of life in each of which liberation is required: the economic dimension in which liberation is needed from the vicious circle of poverty and exploitation; the political dimension in which liberation is needed from the vicious circle of domination and oppression; the cultural dimension in which liberation is needed from the vicious circle of racial and cultural alienation; the ecological dimension of the relation of society to nature, in which liberation is needed from the vicious circle of industrial pollution; and the dimension of the meaning of life, in which liberation is needed from the vicious circle of meaninglessness and apathy (CG 332–7; HD 110; cf. CPS 79; IV.4; RRF 38–41). Even these five are not really exhaustive: it is not clear, for example, where Moltmann's particular personal concern for the liberation of the handicapped (cf. PPL XVII) – by no means a non-political matter – belongs. But the point is that life is multi-dimensional and the dimensions cannot be reduced to one – say the economic one – which determines the others. Rather the dimensions mutually interact. Consequently, liberation must be multi-dimensional and must be pursued in all dimensions simultaneously. Otherwise one form of liberation may be achieved only at the cost of reducing freedom in other dimensions. This leads fairly directly to the final section of this chapter.

3. Human rights[10]

From the early 1970s onwards, human rights have come to occupy a prominent place in Moltmann's political theology, partly as a result of his involvement in the World Council of Churches' discussions of human rights but also as a coherent development within his own thought. The concept of human rights fulfils a number of important roles in his theology:

[10] This section is based especially on HD I–II.

(1) Moltmann grounds a Christian understanding of human rights in the doctrine of humanity's creation in the image of God, and thereby draws political consequences from the doctrine of creation, for the first time. But it is important to see exactly how he does this. Moltmann's earlier work had carefully avoided grounding the political order in creation in the traditional way. The traditional Protestant notion of creation ordinances was too backward-looking and conservative in tendency, as though the political task is to preserve what was already given in the created order of things (HP 112–18; HD 108). The additional problem that this notion seemed to set up a created order of things distinct from and outside the redemptive order of Christ's lordship had been overcome in Bonhoeffer's reinterpretation of the ordinances as the mandates of the single lordship of Christ encompassing all human reality. But the impression of an *ahistorical* stable order remained, and Moltmann broke with Bonhoeffer at this point in the same way in which he diverged in general from the thinking of Bonhoeffer, i.e. by introducing eschatology. Instead of conceiving politics as the attempt to restrain the unstable flux of historical change by reference to a timeless order of creation, Moltmann's theology of hope attempted to take up historical change into a movement of world-transformation towards the kingdom of God. Instead of a fixed order of society already given in creation, there is an eschatological goal towards which society must be kept open and on the move. And God's historical activity towards this goal, in mobilizing promise and suffering love, is no mere restoration of the beginning of creation, but a taking up of creation into a genuinely new creation, a kingdom of glory in which nature is perfected and surpassed.

This does not mean, even in Moltmann's early work, that new creation *replaces* creation – or, in political terms, that we must always be in search of a totally new order of things in which nothing of value in the present is conserved. It does mean that Moltmann required a doctrine of creation as *open* to the genuinely new – in political terms, that the kingdom can be anticipated not merely in preservation and backward-looking restoration, but also in innovation, in aiming for a state of human affairs for which we have no existing model but which we can only project in creative hope. Such a doctrine of creation Moltmann formulates in his understanding of the divine image in humanity. He takes the divine likeness to be not simply the given constitution of human nature, but a destiny to be realized. The image of God is the Creator's claim on his creatures which he realizes as the liberator and fulfiller of their history.[11] In his liberating and redeeming work through Christ and the Spirit God sets humanity on the way to the realization of their true future in likeness to himself. Thus the identity and dignity of human beings, as created by God, are open to fulfilment and realization in the course of history. This concept of a *created destiny* for all human beings is of great importance. It grounds the dignity of all human beings in their creation by God, preceding every form of society and government, so that there can be no doubt of the common humanity of all people and the God-given human dignity of every individual person. But it makes the fulfilment of that dignity for every human person a task to which all humanity is called. The recognition and securing of *human rights* is the way in which that task is undertaken in history.

Thus, the fundamental given is the divine image, the created dignity of every human being. Human rights – and the duties of securing the rights of others – are the specific implications of human dignity which come to light and must be undertaken on the way to the fulfilment of creation in the kingdom. The necessary openness of every political society to change in the direction of the kingdom can therefore be concretized as the need to extend its recognition and implementation of human rights. This leads to the second important function of the topic of human rights in Moltmann's thought:

(2) The concept of human rights is the way in which Moltmann's theology acquired the ability to formulate

---

[11] Moltmann develops his understanding of the divine image in humanity further in GC IX.

specific political goals.[12] The two themes of revolutionary hope and loving solidarity, which we have discussed already, gain concreteness especially in this form. Eschatological hope finds its immediate application in striving for the realization of human rights, and solidarity with the victims takes effect in the attempt to secure their rights and dignity as full members of the human community.

It could almost be said that human rights came to play the kind of role in Moltmann's political theology that Marxism played in the liberation theology of Latin America. The concept of human rights is a way of specifying the implications of political theology in a form which makes contact with non-Christian political goals and activity, and makes it possible for Christians to join with others in a common struggle for liberation:

> Church guidelines on political and social matters gain their universal significance only through reference to human rights. Through its relationship to human rights the church becomes the church for the world (HD 7).

(3) Finally, however, a Christian theology of human rights which grounds them in the created dignity of human beings as image of God can make a specific contribution to the general discussion of, and struggle for, human rights. Moltmann refers to the way in which different kinds of human rights are one-sidedly emphasized by different societies at the expense of others: for Western societies, individual civil liberties and democratic participation; for the communist societies of the Eastern block (as they then were), social and economic rights; for the nations of the Third World, the right to economic, political and cultural self-determination. Priorities in the pursuit of human rights are certainly necessary in specific, different situations, but one-sided progress which *fixes* such priorities and inhibits the pursuit of others leads to distortions of human dignity which always need to be corrected by the pursuit of neglected rights. The recognition of this Moltmann derives from the theological concept

---

[12] For a discussion of a specific example of human rights, see HD III ('The Right to Meaningful Work').

of humanity's created dignity as the divine image. Human rights are all aspects of this single created destiny which encompasses the whole of human life in all its aspects and relationships. Human rights are therefore *indivisible*. There is no ultimate priority of some rights over others, only the strategic priorities of pursuing in each situation those rights which are being denied or neglected. By such constant corrections of the balance humanity is kept on the move towards the eschatological fulfilment of human dignity in all aspects of life. This refusal to reduce human rights to individual *or* social; economic, political *or* social, corresponds to Moltmann's concept of multi-dimensional liberation: liberation takes place in the various interrelated dimensions of life through the securing of a variety of human rights.[13]

4. Conclusion

The achievement of Moltmann's political theology in the period up to 1980, which we have considered, was to provide hermeneutical structures by which to relate biblical Christian faith to political attitudes, goals and issues. The direction towards a new future anticipated in hope, the praxis of loving solidarity with victims, the implementation of humanity's created dignity and destiny in human rights: these provide the guidelines, the lines of interest and concern which can guide the concrete analysis of particular societies and specification of immediate goals and strategies. If Moltmann tends to share a common theological preference for abstraction over concreteness, at least this can be said for him: that his political theology demands that it *be* concretized by anyone who takes it seriously.

---

[13] Later Moltmann adumbrates the idea of rights for non-human creatures also: WJC 307–9; CJF 69–71 (cf. already HD 27).

6

Ecclesiology*

1. Towards a messianic ecclesiology

The *Church in the Power of the Spirit* seems to have attracted less interest and has certainly provoked far less theological discussion than Moltmann's other major works. This can hardly be because its proposals are less controversial, but it may be because, though rooted in theological argument, they are controversial in their practical thrust towards reforming the life and structure of the church. As such they cross 'the growing gulf between systematic and practical theology' (HC 128) and fall outside the central interests of academic theology, which tends to keep its distance from the church, especially from the church as actual 'grassroots' communities of Christians, which for Moltmann are the real subject of ecclesiology. This latter emphasis on the church 'from below' and the need for renewal and reform of the church to proceed 'from below' (CPS 275, 317; HC 21, 55) also distances Moltmann's ecclesiology from the general run of ecclesiological discussions in the mainstream Western denominations and in the ecumenical movement,[1] though not from ecclesiology inspired by Liberation theology and the Latin American base communities.[2]

* This chapter is a revised version of R. Bauckham, *Moltmann: Messianic Theology in the Making* (Basingstoke: Marshall Pickering, 1987), chapter 5.

[1] Note Moltmann's own comments on the reception of the book and of his ideas about the church as voluntary community in HTG 175–6. In effect, he is saying that German church leaders were not interested. For Britain, note the almost complete absence of reference to Moltmann in the significant collection of essays on ecclesiology, *On Being the Church: Essays on the Christian Community*, ed. C. E. Gunton and D. W. Hardy (Edinburgh: T. & T. Clark, 1989), although several of the essays relate to major concerns of Moltmann's ecclesiology.

[2] See, e.g., L. Boff, *Ecclesiogenesis: The base communities reinvent the church* (tr. R. R. Barr; London: Collins, 1986).

For his part, Moltmann is clear that the professional theologian should feel himself or herself in the first instance to be a member of the Christian community, which does not mean being identified with an ecclesiastical hierarchy but being identified with the local congregation of Christ's people, which, just as much as the university and the seminary, is where theology should be done (HC 41, 128–9; OC 9). This is not because theology is a matter of narrowly inner-ecclesiastical reflection, but because theology is in the service of the church's mission to the world. Theology's own critical openness to the world would remain purely abstract if it were not devoted to the church's mission and to the actual congregations of Christians as the bearers of that mission in the world.

Consequently, ecclesiology has always been integral to Moltmann's theological project and in fact as early as 1966 he was giving lectures on ecclesiology which were the forerunner of *The Church in the Power of the Spirit* (CPS xiv). His earlier works already have important ecclesiological implications which lay the foundations for *The Church in the Power of the Spirit*. In *Theology of Hope*, the eschatological promise given in the resurrection of the crucified Christ creates an *essentially missionary* church of *dialectical hope*. The church exists in mission to the world in the service of the universal future of the kingdom of God, and in its hope for the world it suffers the contradiction between the promise and the reality of the present. It is characteristically the 'exodus church', always on the move towards the new future opened up by the promise and charged with keeping the world in historical movement towards the promised future. Thus, the dialectical eschatology of *Theology of Hope* serves to open the church to history, to the world and to the future, giving the church both a dynamic existence in future-orientated mission and a critical openness to the world which is not yet but is to become the kingdom of God. In the political theology which developed out of *Theology of Hope* Moltmann then laid more emphasis on the liberating political praxis which is therefore incumbent on Christians. In recognizing that 'a missionary church cannot be apolitical' (CPS 15), Moltmann broke decisively with the German Protestant church's post-war commitment to political neutrality, just as in chapter V of *Theology of Hope* he set his face against contemporary German tendencies to integrate church and society (cf. CR 109; TGT 189). *Vis-à-vis* the civil religion which sanctions the present structures of bourgeois society, eschatological hope creates an exodus church committed to liberating and even revolutionary praxis in society.

In *Theology and Joy* the church of missionary hope becomes also the church which celebrates the *festival of freedom*, complementing its missionary ethic with the anticipated joy of the new creation. Then, with Moltmann's resolute turn to the cross in *The Crucified God*, the church's dialectical hope for the world is deepened by the addition of *dialectical love*. The church which finds its identity in identification with the crucified Christ can be involved in the world only by identification with those with whom Christ on the cross identified. The principle of its life cannot be the love of like for like, but openness to those who are different, the vulnerability of love which identifies with others, and solidarity especially with the victims of society, the most wretched and the most hopeless. The church's critical openness to the world in hope gains new dimensions when combined with the openness of suffering love.

Finally, it was Moltmann's development of the concept of the trinitarian history of God as an overarching theological context for the doctrine of the church which enabled him to integrate these earlier ecclesiological insights into a comprehensive ecclesiology in *The Church in the Power of the Spirit*. We shall see how this happens in the rest of the chapter, but first we should also notice that Moltmann's growing experience of the world-wide church, through his extensive travels and his involvement in the World Council of Churches, also contributed to the making of his ecclesiology. If *Theology of Hope* was Moltmann's most Reformed book and *The Crucified God* his most Lutheran, *The Church in the Power of the Spirit* was, in its own way, his most ecumenical book so far. This is to be seen not so much in his attention to non-Protestant theology, though this has steadily increased throughout his career[3] and in *The Church in the Power of the Spirit* there are the beginnings of the interest in Orthodox theology (CPS 36-7; cf. 256) which became stronger thereafter. The point is rather that Moltmann's ecclesiology in *The Church in the Power of the Spirit* is inspired by the actual churches he experienced in his travels outside Europe: by the commitment to political liberation in various churches of the Third World (CR 111; CPS xv), the charismatic worship of the Pentecostal and independent churches of Africa (CPS xv, 112; OC 65–6), the 'voluntary religion' of the Protestant free church tradition in the United States (TGT 190–1), the 'base communities' of Latin America (CPS 329–30), and the fellowship of persecuted Christians in many parts of the world (OC 89; EC 427). If *The Church in the Power of the Spirit* naturally speaks most often of conditions in the Protestant churches of West Germany (as it then was) and directs its reforming proposals to that situation, it is nevertheless ecumenically open in its inspiration. Moltmann believes that ecumenical solidarity with the churches of the Third World, in their sufferings and in their commitment to liberation, cannot leave the German churches unchanged (CR 111–12; CPS 343–4; OC 88–90; PPL 165–6; EC 427–8).

2. The structure and method of *The Church in the Power of the Spirit*

Moltmann describes his ecclesiology alternatively as 'relational ecclesiology' (CPS 20) or as 'messianic ecclesiology' (CPS sub-title). The meanings of the two terms are closely connected and together point to the dominant theme which holds all the facets of Moltmann's ecclesiology together and determines their character. 'Messianic ecclesiology' is shorthand for 'a christologically founded and eschatologically directed doctrine of the church' (CPS 13), or, more precisely, for an ecclesiology rooted in Moltmann's eschatological

[3] For Moltmann's view of confessional traditions in theology, see TKG xiv–xv; and, with special reference to the Protestant–Roman Catholic distinction, his 'Nachwort' in P. F. Momose, *Kreuzestheologie: Ein Auseinandersetzung mit Jürgen Moltmann* (Freiburg: Herder, 1978), pp. 174–6.

Christology. The church is the church of Jesus Christ, subject
to his lordship alone, and so 'ecclesiology can only be
developed from Christology' (CPS 66). 'Every statement
about the church will be a statement about Christ. Every
statement about Christ will be a statement about the church'
(CPS 6). But statements about Christ always also point
beyond the church to the universal future of Christ, the messianic kingdom. The Christ (Messiah) who is the foundation
of the church is 'the eschatological person' (CPS 73) whose
past history has yet to be fulfilled in his future. So his church
must be a 'messianic fellowship' (Moltmann's favourite description of the church in *The Church in the Power of the Spirit*)
orientated in mission towards the coming kingdom of God.
It participates in Christ's own mission on the way to his
future, and lives 'between remembrance of his history and
hope of his kingdom' (CPS 75). This makes the church a
provisional reality, where eschatology and history are mediated in the category of *anticipation* (CPS 191–4). 'The church
. . . is not yet the kingdom of God, but it is its anticipation in
history. . . . Christianity is not yet the new mankind but it is its
.vanguard' (CPS 196). In an anticipatory and fragmentary –
and, naturally, imperfect (CPS 167) – form, the church
represents the future of the whole of reality and so mediates
this eschatological future to the world (CPS 194–5). Therefore the church does not exist for itself but in the service of
the kingdom of God in the world (CPS 68, 164). For the
church to be the messianic fellowship means to participate
in Christ's mission in this sense.

It should be clear how much Moltmann's ecclesiology in
The Church in the Power of the Spirit is determined by the eschatological Christology of his earlier work. However, his more
recent development of this into the concept of the trinitarian
history of God with the world enables him to set the church's
eschatological mission not only in christological but also in
pneumatological perspective, so that 'messianic ecclesiology' is
at the same time and is intended by Moltmann to include
'charismatic ecclesiology' (CPS 36–7). It is this pneumatological dimension which permits a stronger emphasis on
the church's life and mission as anticipation of the kingdom

than was possible in *Theology of Hope*. Pneumatology for Moltmann is the doctrine of the eschatological fulfilment of the history of Christ. The way from the history of Christ to his future is also the history of the Spirit in his work of unification and glorification through which the eschatological future enters history. It is, therefore, the Holy Spirit who mediates eschatology and history and the church is this mediation only as it exists in the presence and power of the Holy Spirit (CPS 35, 197–8). 'Messianic ecclesiology' is a function of messianic pneumatology as well as of eschatological Christology.

Moltmann's pneumatology in *The Church in the Power of the Spirit* is christological in the sense that the mission of the Spirit follows from that of the Son (CPS 54) and the history of the Spirit fulfils the eschatological purpose and direction of the history of Christ (CPS 34). But because both Christology and pneumatology are eschatologically understood, this does not make the latter mere 'application' of 'the finished work of Christ', as Protestant dogmatics up to Barth has tended to suggest.[4] Rather than subordinating pneumatology to Christology or *vice versa*,[5] Moltmann relates the mission of the Son and the mission of the Spirit, in their common direction towards the eschatological kingdom, within the broader concept of 'the trinitarian history of God's dealings with the world' (CPS 37). The christological, pneumatological and eschatological perspectives in ecclesiology likewise all come together, as complementary rather than competing perspectives, when the church understands itself in this broadest context of the trinitarian history of God. It is this context – of the missions of the Son and the Spirit from the Father on their way to the unification of all things in the triune God and the glorification of God in all things (CPS II.4) – which constitutes the church the messianic fellowship, which is equally 'the church of Jesus Christ' (CPS III), 'the church of the kingdom of God' (CPS IV) and 'the church in the presence and power of the Holy Spirit' (CPS V and VI).

[4] For Moltmann's latest objection to this tradition, see SL 81–2.
[5] The refusal to subordinate pneumatology to Christology is a significant principle of Moltmann's work from *The Church in the Power of the Spirit* up to *The Spirit of Life*.

The same conclusion can be reached by considering the term 'relational ecclesiology'. Like everything else that exists in a living history – including the trinitarian God – the church exists in *relationships* with others. Consequently, it cannot understand itself as an entity simply in itself:

> The church cannot understand itself alone. It can only truly comprehend its mission and its meaning, its roles and its functions in relation to others (CPS 19).

Ecclesiology, therefore, cannot be a doctrine in itself, but must be developed in relation to Christology, pneumatology and eschatology. It must understand its particular subject, the church, in relation to the total context in which the church comes into being and lives. This is 'the trinitarian history of God's dealings with the world': the universal history within which alone the significance of the church's particular existence can come to light (CPS 50). In this context, too, the church is able to understand itself *in its particularity* and to avoid falsely absolutizing itself:

> In the movements of the trinitarian history of God's dealings with the world the church finds and discovers itself, in all the relationships which comprehend its life. It finds itself on the path traced by this history of God's dealings with the world, and it discovers itself as one element in the movements of the divine sending, gathering together and experience. It is not the church that has a mission of salvation to fulfil to the world; it is the mission of the Son and the Spirit through the Father that includes the church, creating a church as it goes on its way. . . . If the church understands itself, with all its tasks and powers, in the Spirit and against the horizon of the Spirit's history, then it also understands its particularity as one element in the power of the Spirit and has no need to maintain its special power and its special charges with absolute and self-destructive claims. It then has no need to look sideways in suspicion or jealousy at the saving efficacies of the Spirit outside the church; instead it can recognize them thankfully as signs that the Spirit is greater than the church and that God's purpose of salvation reaches beyond the church (CPS 64 5).

The church is *related* to the whole, through its participation in the universal mission of Christ and the Spirit on the way to the universal future of all reality in the messianic kingdom, but it *is not* the whole and will never itself become the whole (CPS 348–51). Consequently, ecclesiology can and must recognize the *relativity* of its subject and its own standpoint, without subsiding into mere *relativism* (cf. CG 11; CPS 155–7). As a particular related to the unique eschatological person, Jesus Christ, and his universal future, the church fulfils its eschatological mission in open and critical relation to other particulars, its partners in history on the way to the kingdom of God (Israel, the world religions, the secular order). Because it is itself 'on the move' (CPS 1), as one element in the movement of God's trinitarian history, it can engage in real relationships with these partners, living relationships in which both participants are open to change, and direct these relationships in hope towards the common future of the kingdom of God (cf. CPS 133–5). In other words, although the church (as 'the church of Jesus Christ', the eschatological person) does have a *special* relationship to the universal (the kingdom of God), it has this special relationship *only in relation to other particulars*. It fulfils its messianic vocation not by absolutizing itself but in open relationships of dialogue and co-operation.

This principle of relationality is a development of Moltmann's basic understanding, since *Theology of Hope*, of the church's openness to the world and to the future. Appropriately taken up in the English title (*The Open Church*) of his popular version of the themes of *The Church in the Power of the Spirit*, the concept of the church's openness runs through *The Church in the Power of the Spirit* as the corollary of its relationality. Because of the church's relative place in the wider context of the trinitarian history of God, it is 'open for God, open for men and open for the future of both God and men. The church atrophies when it surrenders any one of these opennesses and closes itself up against God, men or the future' (CPS 2).[6] The principle should also be linked

[6] For Moltmann's use of the notion that life exists in open relationship to other life, while to close oneself within oneself is to atrophy, see also (among his earlier writings) CPS 194; OC 35; CG 11; EH 13. This notion becomes even more prominent in his later work.

with the open relationality of the triune God, who is 'from eternity an open Trinity' (CPS 55) and in his trinitarian history opens himself in vulnerable love to the world. The church participates in and testifies to this history of God when it opens itself in vulnerable love to dialogue and relationship with others (CPS 160–1).

'Relational ecclesiology', Moltmann claims, 'leads to an understanding of the living nature of the church' (CPS 20), i.e. the church is understood as a *movement* within the living, moving relationships of the trinitarian history of God with the world, created by the missions of the Son and the Spirit (CPS 64). Moltmann therefore tries to avoid a definition of what the church is, which could abstract it from this movement, and instead insists that the church finds itself – through a participatory knowledge from within the divine movement in which it is caught up (CPS 52) – *where* it participates in the mission of Christ and the Spirit (CPS 65, 122). In other words, its characteristics, which make it the true church, are not its own, but those of the presence and activity of Christ and the Spirit (CPS 338): 'the whole being of the church is marked by participation in the history of God's dealings with the world' (CPS 65). *The Church in the Power of the Spirit* attempts to work out this principle consistently by understanding every aspect of the church's life and activity as a function of the mission of Christ and the Spirit, a participation in God's trinitarian history with the world. In doing so, it also performs a critical function with a view to the reform of the church (CPS 2). By enabling the church to recover its bearings within the trinitarian history of God – its christological origin, its pneumatological commission and its eschatological goal – ecclesiology should not only serve 'the theological justification of the church's actions; it also serves the criticism of those actions' (CPS 5). In part this criticism consists in liberating the church from its adaptations to and justifications of the *status quo* in society, in order for it to regain the freedom of its messianic vocation (CPS 225), and in this respect the criticism of the church in *The Church in the Power of the Spirit* follows on from the critical role of eschatology in *Theology of Hope* and the iconoclasm of the cross in *The Crucified God*.[7] 'The trinitarian history of God' includes both these critical perspectives and others. As we shall see, it is from the church's messianic vocation within the mission of Christ and the Spirit that Moltmann argues the book's broadest reforming intention: 'to point away from the pastoral church, that looks after the people, to the people's own communal church among the people' (CPS xvi).

'Every doctrine of the church starts from experiences in the church and with the church in the world' (CPS 18): because knowledge of the church in the trinitarian history of God with the world is necessarily participatory and engaged knowledge (CPS 52). Consequently, Moltmann begins with those dimensions of ecclesiology which have come to be seen as necessary as a result of the church's experiences this century: that the church is necessarily Christ's church, the missionary church, the ecumenical church and the political church (chapter I). These four dimensions form a sort of *inclusio* with the four marks of the church which are the subject of the last chapter of the book (VII): all four dimensions can easily be seen to characterize the discussion of the four marks.

However, Moltmann's project of 'relational ecclesiology' really begins in chapter II, whose first three sections lead up to the key section 4. This provides the only fully comprehensive context for the understanding of ecclesiology in its sketch of the trinitarian history of God, and so supplies the framework of understanding within which the rest of the book seeks to show how 'the whole being of the church is marked by participation in the history of God's dealings with the world' (CPS 65). The basic plan of the next four chapters is then relatively straightforward.

Chapter III deals with the church's participation in the messianic history of Christ. In section 1 Moltmann follows his favoured method[8] of reviewing various ways of understanding the relationship between Christ and the church before arriving at the most satisfactory: 'Christ as

---

[7] On these see R. Bauckham, *Moltmann: Messianic Theology in the Making* (Basingstoke: Marshall Pickering, 1987), pp. 40–1, 72–6; and chapter 5 above.
[8] Also used in TH I; CG II.

the eschatological person.' This preserves the kind of temporal structure which is basic to Moltmann's thought: that the church's remembrance of the past history of Christ does not tie the church to the past in a backward-looking relationship, as though it were a mere extension or repetition of a past event, but points it to the future, thus orientating its mission to something beyond itself: the coming kingdom of Christ (CPS 75). Moltmann then uses the structure of the traditional Protestant dogmatic scheme of the three offices of Christ as prophet, priest and king, correlating them with the ministry, death and resurrection of Christ and explaining the church's participation in each. From Jesus' messianic mission of proclamation of the Gospel and liberating action follows the church's universal mission of liberation (III.2); from Jesus' passion follows 'the church under the cross' which participates in his passion through suffering and solidarity with the godforsaken (III.3); and from Jesus' exaltation as the Lord of the coming kingdom, who changes the meaning of lordship into loving service and self-sacrifice, follows the church as the fellowship of freedom and equality in the Spirit (III.4). If the first of these three aspects of the church corresponds to the exodus church of *Theology of Hope* (though here derived from the ministry rather than the resurrection of Jesus) and if the second corresponds to the church of *The Crucified God*, identified with the crucified Jesus in his solidarity with the godforsaken, the third aspect is the one which is relatively new and most distinctive of *The Church in the Power of the Spirit*. Its christological aspect here will be complemented by its pneumatological aspect in chapter VI.

To the traditional three offices of Christ Moltmann adds two more. One is Christ in his transfiguration, which brings out the 'aesthetic' rather than the ethical significance of his resurrection. The worship and life of the church participate in the risen life of Christ as a festival of freedom (III.5). Here the ecclesiological aspect of *Theology and Joy* finds its place in Moltmann's comprehensive ecclesiology. Secondly, Moltmann restores to pride of place the neglected christological 'title' of friend. The concept of the friendship of Jesus, in which friendship signifies fellowship in freedom, makes the church's fellowship with God in Christ the source of its own fellowship as open friendship (III.6). In discussing all five of these forms of the church's participation in the mission of Christ, Moltmann is careful to represent the church's activity as having an outward and forward direction. In each case the church follows the direction of Christ's own mission, serving not itself but the world and its future.

In the final section of this chapter (III.7) Moltmann completes the christological aspect of the church's participation in the trinitarian history of God by considering, not the activities but the *presence* of Christ, on the principle that 'the true church is to be found where Christ is present' (CPS 122). Here a neat scheme gives the church its place in relation to the crucified, risen and coming Christ. According to his promises Christ is present now in two forms by identification, both of which anticipate his future presence in person at the parousia. As the exalted Christ he identifies with the church in its apostolic mission of proclamation, and in this way is present in the Gospel, sacraments and fellowship of the church, which anticipate his kingdom in the world. These are, therefore, signs of his presence and so of where the true church is to be found. But also, as the crucified Christ, he identifies with the poor,[9] who anticipate the kingdom, not in active mission but in suffering expectation. The true church is therefore to be found in fellowship with the poor. The church exists in the presence of Christ only when it links the two forms of Christ's presence by missionary presence among the poor: 'the church with its mission would be present where Christ awaits it, amid the downtrodden, the sick and the captives' (CPS 129).[10]

[9] Moltmann uses the term 'poor' in a very broad sense. Poverty is a 'multi-dimensional' concept, which 'extends from economic, social and physical poverty to psychological, moral and religious poverty' (CPS 79).

[10] Moltmann finds Christ's promise to be present in the poor in Matthew 25:31–46 (so also CCR 43–5; PR 156; HTG 47, 122; WJC 149; SL 129, 245). However, exegetical opinion is divided on the identity of 'the least of Christ's brethren' in this passage, and, as M. Tripole, 'A Church for the Poor and the World: At Issue with Moltmann's Ecclesiology,' *Theological Studies* 42 (1981), pp. 646–50, points out, they are more plausibly understood, in their Matthean

Chapter III has therefore orientated the church in the trinitarian history of God by reference to its christological origin which points to its christological future at the parousia. Chapter IV reverses the direction and orientates the church by reference to its eschatological goal as this already affects the present. The final section (IV.5) is a systematic account of how Moltmann understands the eschatological kingdom to be already present in anticipation and therefore of the church's role as mediator of the eschatological future into the present, a role which is then more fully developed pneumatologically in chapter V. But the rest of chapter IV concerns the church's relationships with those partners in history 'who are not the church and will never become the church' (CPS 134): Israel, the world religions, and the economic, political and cultural processes of the world. In this discussion the relationship to Israel, as 'Christianity's original, enduring and final partner in history' (CPS 135), has methodological priority, because it is in recalling its Israelite origins and in open relationship to contemporary Israel that the church is kept aware of the still unredeemed state of the world and therefore of its direction towards the coming kingdom.[11] Thus giving priority to the relationship with Israel ensures that the church gives messianic direction to the rest of its relationships (cf. CPS 150).

The church's place within the trinitarian history of God is given its pneumatological dimension in chapters V and VI. Since it is the Spirit who, between the history of Jesus and the

---

context, as Christian missionaries. (For a recent study which surveys the spectrum of interpretations of the passage – though oddly without mentioning Moltmann – and reaches a conclusion which, while not supporting Moltmann's idea of Christ's presence in the poor, is in a general way compatible with Moltmann's ecclesiology, see J. R. Donohue, 'The "Parable" of the Sheep and the Goats: A Challenge to Christian Ethics,' *Theological Studies* 47 [1985], pp. 3–31.) But if the specific idea of Christ's promise to be present in the poor cannot be derived from Matthew 25, Moltmann's more general notion of the church's necessary solidarity with the poor is christologically based on Jesus' fellowship with the poor in his ministry (CPS 78–80) and his identification with the godforsaken on the cross.

[11] For Moltmann's view of the significance of Israel for Christian theology's own health and integrity, see also TGT 203–4; HD XII; WJC 28–37; TT 45–6.

coming of the kingdom, is the divine presence and activity mediating the eschatological future to the world now, the pneumatological dimension to ecclesiology makes possible the fullest description of the life of the church:

> It is the doctrine of the Holy Spirit in particular that depicts the processes and experiences in which and through which the church becomes comprehensible to itself as the messianic fellowship in the world and for the world (CPS 198).

These 'processes and experiences' are the 'means' or 'mediations of salvation' (preaching, baptism, the Lord's supper, worship and lifestyle) and the ministries or charismata, dealt with in chapter V and chapter VI respectively.[12] Interpreted in the context of the mission of the Spirit, these characterize the church as the messianic fellowship open to the world and its future, existing for the world and its future, and so they are *the way in which* the church lives out its messianic vocation between the remembrance of Christ (chapter III) and the hope of the kingdom in relation to its partners in history (chapter IV). It is in these chapters V and VI in particular that the argument leads to criticism of the contemporary Protestant church in Germany and proposals for reform of its life, worship and ministry. These proposals focus on the renewal of congregational life 'from below' to produce communities which are the subjects of their own history and can therefore assume the vocation of the messianic fellowship in the world. The proposed reforms of baptism, the Lord's supper, worship, ministry and structure all lead away from civil religion, clericalism and the pastoral church 'for the people', towards the local church as a free fellowship of committed disciples, responsible for its own life and mission, a real community which is at the same time open to the world, 'the people's own communal church among the people' (CPS xvi). Only this kind of church corresponds to the mission of the Spirit within which the church exists. The Spirit creates fellowship in freedom and equality, and, just as importantly, fellowship which is orientated outwards and

---

[12] For a later treatment of the charismata, which deliberately complements, rather than repeats CPS VI, see SL IX.

forwards, to the world and its eschatological future. By keeping in the forefront of the discussion the nature of the Spirit's activity as eschatological anticipation for the sake of the future of the whole of creation, Moltmann throughout these two chapters keeps the renewal of the church's communal life and worship in unbroken connexion with its messianic mission. In the presence and power of the Holy Spirit, the church is the 'messianic fellowship' with equal stress on both words.

The final chapter (VII) is a masterly exposition of the four traditional, credal marks of the church ('one, holy, catholic and apostolic') interpreted in terms of messianic and relational ecclesiology, i.e. in terms of the church's participation in the trinitarian history of God's dealings with the world. The marks are all understood christologically, as characteristics of Christ's activity before they are characteristics of the church's participation in his mission; eschatologically, as 'messianic predicates' which point to the coming kingdom for which the church exists; and as the church's task in the world, with an outward as well as an inward direction. Finally, in order to make the marks more precisely characteristic of the church's mission in relation to the contemporary world situation ('our divided, fought over, unjust, inhuman world'), each is given an additional qualification: unity in freedom, holiness in poverty, apostolicity in suffering, catholicity in partisanship for the oppressed (CPS 341–2).

In the rest of this chapter we shall discuss some of the main themes which recur throughout *The Church in the Power of the Spirit* and Moltmann's minor ecclesiological writings.

3. Suffering and joy

Moltmann's attempt to understand the church within the trinitarian history of God explains the *dialectic of suffering and joy* in the church's experience, which colours much of his account of the church's life and especially his view of the centrality of worship in the church's life and mission. In the concept of the trinitarian history of God (according to which the divine Trinity is involved with the world in a history of reciprocal relationship whose determining centre is the cross and resurrection of Jesus Christ), Moltmann's fundamental dialectic of the cross and the resurrection leads to a dialectic of pain and joy in the divine experience with history. One side of God's history is the suffering he experiences as he opens himself in vulnerable love to the world: his suffering in the passion of Christ continues in the 'sighings of the Spirit' until he finally turns his and the world's suffering into joy at the end. But, on the other hand, in the movement of unification and glorification which leads from the resurrection of Christ to the new creation, God anticipates his eschatological joy. Since he is glorified in the liberation of his creation, he experiences joy in the Spirit's work of glorifying the Father and the Son by liberating humanity (CPS 63–4). In this movement, of course, suffering is for the sake of joy: God suffers in love for his creation in order to liberate it: 'God's pain in the world is the way to God's happiness with the world' (OC 93).

As the church participates in God's history with the world it shares this dialectic of the divine experience. As it lives in the presence of the Spirit it suffers with God's suffering with the world and experiences his anticipated joy (CPS 65). This makes the dialectic of suffering and joy in the church's life not merely the church's experience but the church's experience *of God*, and accounts for Moltmann's growing sympathy for mysticism in the period after *The Church in the Power of the Spirit* (cf. EG 55–80; TA).[13] However, in this sympathy Moltmann will not allow the contemplative mysticism of the cross (cf. CG 45–53; CPS 93) to be a substitute for what we might call the active mysticism of discipleship (EG 71–6), and the latter is the focus in *The Church in the Power of the Spirit*. 'The church shares in Christ's sufferings only when it takes part in Christ's mission. Its Christian suffering is apostolic suffering' (OC 91). Conversely, 'the church is apostolic when it takes up its cross' (CPS 361). It is as it takes part in the *mission* of Christ and the Spirit that it participates in the passion of Christ and the sighings of the Spirit. Its sufferings are therefore, like God's, messianic sufferings *with and for the world*.

The church 'is fundamentally born out of the cross of Christ' (CPS 97, cf. 86; OC 85), because it is the fellowship of

---

[13] See, in detail, chapter 11 below.

those who have been liberated by Christ's self-giving. As such, it must be *both* the 'church under the cross', which, remembering the crucified Christ, is led into solidarity with the godforsaken with whom he identified (CPS 97–8), *and* the church which celebrates the festival of freedom, glorifying God in the joy of the new exodus to eschatological freedom (cf. CPS 76–8). Consequently, it participates in Christ's mission not only in the obedience of discipleship but also in *doxology*. These two aspects influence and reinforce each other (CPS 190). On the one hand, without the 'aesthetic categories' of freedom and joy, which are the church's participation in the glorified life of the risen Christ, 'the imitation of Christ and the new obedience would become a joyless legalistic task' (CPS 109). On the other hand, doxology which did not lead into discipleship of the crucified Christ would be an irresponsible escape from the world. It is saved from this by its character precisely as *anticipation* of the new creation in the midst of this still godless and godforsaken world. As such it creates resistance to the godlessness of the world and solidarity with the godforsaken of the world (cf. CPS 97–8; OC 88). Joy in liberation won through Christ's suffering leads into suffering for the liberation of others. As always in Moltmann's early thought, the dialectical identity of the crucified and risen Christ is operative. Fellowship with the risen Christ in his eschatological glory is possible only in fellowship with the crucified Christ in his suffering, but conversely the crucified Christ mediates the joy of the new creation to those who must still suffer with him in the unredeemed world (cf. CPS 59, 273–4). So, while the church must suffer until the end of all suffering, 'there are encouraging signs of joy and even more joyful songs of liberation to be heard within and under the passion of God and the world' (OC 93–4). Even if suffering predominates, it is joy which in the cross and resurrection of Christ has gained the eschatological ascendancy which transforms the character of suffering even now.

A central role in the church's dialectical experience of suffering and joy is played by worship, because it is this which sets the Christian community, with all the pains and joys of its everyday life, within the trinitarian history of God, and enables it to understand itself as the messianic fellowship in the presence of the Spirit and to live out this vocation in the rest of its life (CPS 261–2). Worship is – or should be! – the festival of freedom, in which the new freedom of those liberated by Christ is celebrated in spontaneity and exuberant ecstasy (CPS 111–12), and the eschatological glorification of God in all things is anticipated in joyful thanksgiving (CPS 256). 'Before the liberation experienced in faith is translated into new obedience, it is celebrated in festal ecstasy' (CPS 112). This ensures that the new obedience stems from the experience of liberation in Christ. Moltmann's emphasis on worship as festival is intended to protect Christianity from the excessive moralization and rationalization which see no point in such 'play' except for the sake of work (cf. OC 64–5; LF 74, 83). 'Worship has priority over ethics' (CPS 271), because only so can Christian life be a matter of liberated love rather than compulsive legalism (cf. also TKG 6–7; TT 93–4).

There is the danger that festivals can function as mere safety-valves which, by compensating for the unfree conditions of everyday life, leave them unchanged and even reinforce them. Christian worship can all too easily fulfil this function in rationalized industrial society (CPS 111–12, 265–7). But, celebrated in the Spirit as eschatological anticipation, the Christian feast of freedom can have a quite different significance. As a *real* anticipation of the future it *demonstrates* the alternatives offered by the creative Spirit to the lack of freedom in everyday life and so encourages the search for ways of mediating this liberation into the individual lives of Christians and the public life of society (CPS 111–12, 261–2, 274). Because of its character as anticipation of the new creation, the feast will always contain an excess of freedom which cannot be translated into liberation in the rest of life yet, but this provides the transcendent eschatological stimulus which leads beyond every provisional realization of freedom:

> it points enduringly to the resurrection as the great alternative to this world of death, stimulating the limited alternatives to

death's dominion, keeping us alive and making us take our bearings from the victory of life (CPS 113, cf. 274; LF 84).

The feast not only leads into the suffering of resistance and solidarity. As celebration of the resurrection of the cruci-fied Christ, suffering is never far from it. In the presence of the crucified Christ, it can make room for the free expression of pain and grief and protest (CPS 112, 273–4; OC 79–80; cf. LF 79). In its experience of fellowship it will give expression to its solidarity with persecuted Christians (cf. OC 89–90). Moltmann has increasingly come to see real ecumenical unity as realized 'under the cross' in shared suffering (CPS 97; OC VI; EC).

4. The mature and responsible congregation

Moltmann sees himself as 'a "free-church" person in the midst of a *Volkskirche*' (CR 110). In other words, the kind of church to which he is committed in principle is the voluntary fellowship of committed disciples, a church *of* the people, while the German Protestant church to which he belongs is a pastoral church *for* the people, 'a public institution to administer the religion of society' (TGT 189). The latter still belongs to the heritage of the Constantinian adoption of Christianity as the state religion. No longer a state church, it is still civil religion, since it sees itself as the people's church for all the people and must therefore maintain a neutral stance towards all social and political divisions in society. In fact, this supposedly non-political stance is in the interests of the groups that control the *status quo* in society (CR 111). Restricting itself to the narrowly religious needs of the people, it is a clerical institution looking after the people – like the social services – and administering their religious affairs – like a government bureaucracy. Consequently, it is a church without any critical effect on society. It is a church of non-committal religion, 'an institutionalized absence of commitment' (PPL 159), since membership of the church is involuntary and the clerical institution takes care of the people's religious needs for them. 'This is the explanation of the curious situation in Germany, where 95 per cent of the people "belong" to a church, only 10–15 per cent participate actively' (CR 109). Finally, it is a 'church without community' (TGT 191). Where everyone 'belongs' but has no responsibility for the life of the church, real fellowship is impossible. (For this account of the *Volkskirche* in Moltmann's view, see CPS 224, 318–19, 326–8, 334; CR 109–10; TGT 189–92; OC 96, 98–9, 120–3; PPL 100, 158–60; HTG 175–6.)

In his criticism of this kind of church, in which Christianity has lost its character as messianic fellowship, Moltmann is not only identifying, broadly, with the 'free church' (or Congregationalist) tradition in Anglo-Saxon ecclesiology, which stems from the left wing of the Reformation (OC 117),[14] though he has some criticisms of this tradition (PPL 160–1, 162).[15] He is also impressed by the evidence that it is through the development of 'the mature and responsible congregation' that the contemporary church in many parts of the world is finding its identity as messianic fellowship and fulfilling its messianic vocation, in persecution, in experienced fellowship, in missionary service to the world, in social and political criticism and involvement (cf. CPS 329–30; CR 111).[16] Even in Europe the growth of 'grassroots communities' is a sign of the weakness of the pastoral church and a sign of hope: these 'are changing the church from the inside out and making it into the congregation' (OC 117; cf. CPS 328; PPL 104; CR 109–10). This, for Moltmann, is the great hope for the church, whose renewal must come 'from below' (HC 21).

The 'mature and responsible congregation' (HC 41; OC 117) towards which renewal must be directed is characterized by the committed discipleship of all members, in the service of the kingdom, by fellowship in freedom and

[14] Moltmann is here more accurate than in his surprising claim that 'the system of voluntary religion originated in the American republic' (TGT 190) – which, incidentally, inverts the historical relationship between ecclesiology and political democracy in a way one would not expect of Moltmann.

[15] For Moltmann's dialogue with the Anabaptist tradition, see also HD VII; WJC 118.

[16] The Confessing Church in Germany under the Nazis also has a special importance for Moltmann, since it discovered the church's own free identity and critical distance from civil society: TGT 198–201; CPS 334; CR 111.

equality, by mutual acceptance and care, and by openness to the world, especially in solidarity with the poor and the oppressed. This vision of the church is rooted theologically in its relationship to the trinitarian history of God. The hierarchical, authoritarian and clerically managed church depends, according to Moltmann, on a monarchical image of God as power and rule: fundamentally a 'monotheistic' (i.e. in Moltmann's usage, unitarian) doctrine of God. Clerical rule in the church is then legitimated by a descending authority structure in which 'the people' are subjects to be ruled and administered. But this thinking is non-trinitarian. It neglects Jesus' transformation of the notion of rule into liberating service, his open friendship and identification with 'the people', and his cross, which smashes all idols of religious power. Equally it neglects the Holy Spirit, who is not a divine or clerical instrument, but the one who liberates for free fellowship, calls and empowers all Christians for messianic service, and unites, not by subjection to a single ruler, but in loving community. As he unites the persons of the Trinity in their loving fellowship, so in his eschatological mission of liberation and unification he unites the Trinity with humanity in free fellowship. God in his trinitarian history is not a justification for clerical rule, but is the vulnerable and liberating love which makes possible open fellowship in freedom and responsibility (see CPS 225, 293–4, 305–6; HC 40; OC 115; cf. TKG 200–2; FHS 293–4).[17] In this trinitarian context ecclesiology cannot be reduced to 'hierarchology', preoccupied with the authority of the ministry, but must begin with the fact that every believer is a responsible member of the messianic fellowship (CPS 289; cf. SL 236).

Every believer is called to *committed discipleship* in the service of the kingdom in the world and thereby participates actively in the messianic vocation of the church. Against the non-committal Christianity of the pastoral church, Moltmann stresses that justification leads to liberated life (CPS

---

[17] In SL 239–41, the subordination of women in the church is blamed both on monotheistic/monarchical thinking and on 'a Christocentric concept of the church', and the remedy is 'a pneumatological concept of the church'.

36) and that faith is inseparable from discipleship of Christ (PPL 86). As disciples called to responsible participation in Christ's mission (HC 132), the Christian community becomes 'the conscious agent of its own history with God in the Holy Spirit' (HC 41; cf. OC 108–12; PPL 163–4). To this concern for a fellowship of committed disciples belongs Moltmann's interest in the description of a 'messianic lifestyle' which will witness to the coming kingdom which it reflects (CPS 275–88; OC III),[18] and also his criticism of current baptismal theory and practice (CPS 226–42; OC 124–5; HC 46–51). Moltmann sees the practice of infant baptism as the cornerstone of civil religion, since it perpetuates *involuntary* membership of the church:

> There is no possibility of creating a voluntary, independent, and mature community out of the institutional churches to which people belong simply on the basis of being baptized as children (HC 47).

But, in line with his messianic ecclesiology, Moltmann substitutes for infant baptism not 'believer's baptism', in which the believer confesses his faith (although, of course, this is presupposed), so much as 'baptism into Christian calling' (*Berufungstaufe*), i.e. baptism 'as incorporation into the Christian calling to *discipleship and service*' (HC 50–1). Baptism is each Christian's call to a task in the messianic vocation of the whole church. Obviously, the restoration of such a significance to baptism depends on and must go along with the renewal of mature and responsible congregational life (CPS 242).

As a fellowship of committed disciples, the church is also a *free* society of *equals*. Its common calling to share in Christ's messianic mission as prophet, priest and king *precedes* the particular assignments which the Spirit gives to particular members, and so the latter can never set certain 'office-bearers' who share in the offices of Christ over their fellows who do not (CPS 300–1). The Spirit in fact assigns his gifts to all members of the community, who are all 'office-bearers' in this sense. Differences are of function, not rank.

[18] Cf. now also the major account of 'The Messianic Way of Life' in WJC III.7.

Consequently, not hierarchy but 'freedom, diversity and brotherliness' characterize the community, whose principle Moltmann formulates as: 'to each his own; all for each other; testifying together to the world the saving life of Christ' (CPS 298; cf. SL 193–4).[19]

Finally, the messianic fellowship is an *open* fellowship of *friends*. Moltmann's preference for the term 'friendship' to characterize both the fellowship of Christians with God in Christ and the fellowship among Christians in the church – the latter deriving from the former – is based on the nature of friendship as a *free* relationship which combines affection with respect and loyalty (CPS 115, 316; cf. SL 255–6). It is not, like social and familial relationships, a necessary relationship but a freely chosen one, a 'simple liking-to-be-with-others' (OC 53) in total acceptance. It

> arises out of freedom, consists in mutual freedom, and preserves this freedom. . . . We are not by nature free, but become so only when someone likes us. Friends open up to one another free space for free life (OC 52).

However, friendship as characteristic of the church needs to be to some extent redefined by the friendship of Jesus which is its source. Jesus' friendship was not the closed circle of fellowship of like with like, nor was it the privatized friendship of modern society. It was open and public friendship for the unrighteous and the despised (CPS 119–21; SL 258). 'Through Jesus, friendship has become an open term of proffer. It is forthcoming solidarity' (OC 61).[20] We

[19] Moltmann's account of the charismatic structure of the church is indebted to Käsemann, usually his principal guide in Pauline exegesis, and to Küng's rather similar account: H. Küng, *The Church* (Search Press, London, 1968), section C.II. In RP 66–7, Moltmann defends his dependence on Paul rather than Luke for his theology of the charismata.

[20] It could be said that by extending the concept of friendship in this way, Moltmann is diluting the real quality of friendship, which is dependent on its being 'preferential' and 'reciprocal' (according to G. C. Meilaender, *Friendship: A Study in Theological Ethics* [Notre Dame/London: University of Notre Dame Press, 1981], chapters 1 and 2). This would not mean that friendship has to be love of like for like, but only that it is by its nature restricted and cannot be a principle of general social relationships. What Moltmann is really doing, however, is finding in certain aspects of 'preferential friendship' a

recognize here the dialectical love of God for his other which already in *The Crucified God* made identification with those who are different the social principle of Christianity (CG 28; cf. FC 79). Moltmann has now made this the principle for the renewal of the church as congregation, in the form of friendship and of the closely related principle of the acceptance of those who are different (OC II; PPL XII).

Not only God's dialectical love but also its soteriological consequence, justification by faith, lies at the theological basis of this principle of open fellowship with those who are different. Only because we have been accepted by God, in his dialectical love for us, is it possible for us to imitate his dialectical love in the acceptance of others. Only through justification by faith are we freed from the compulsion to confirm ourselves by associating only with those who are like ourselves. Accepting only those like ourselves and disparaging or fearing others is the social form of self-justification. Liberated from self-justification by God's accepting love, the church can practice 'the social form of justification by faith', which is 'recognition of the other in his otherness, the recognition of the person who is different as a person' (CPS 189). The church is then a society in which all kinds of people accept each other 'in a new kind of living together' (OC 33) and in which the *pathos* of God's dialectical love is lived out as mutual involvement in each other's joy and pain. Such a fellowship is necessarily open to others in an unqualified way. The themes of friendship and acceptance are ecclesiological themes to which Moltmann seems especially to warm in treating both their theological depth and their practical outworkings in the life of the church (CPS 114–21, 182–9, 314–16; OC II, IV; PPL XII, XIII; TA 276–8; SL 255–9).

As a society of open friendship the church is set in the history of the Spirit, as the Spirit of God's dialectical love

---

model for relating to people in a 'friendly' way: these aspects can be extended more widely than 'preferential friendship' without necessarily (though this is not explicit in Moltmann's argument) invalidating the special quality of 'preferential friendship' which must remain restricted.

flowing from the event of the cross and anticipating the kingdom:

> Open and total friendship that goes out to meet the other is the spirit of the kingdom in which God comes to man and man to man. . . . Open friendship prepares the ground for a friendlier world (CPS 121).

The fundamental openness of the church in friendship for the unlike is the essential openness of its messianic mission. Hence Moltmann is careful to protect his vision of the church from the sectarian tendencies of those free churches and fellowship groups which lack openness to others (CPS 224–5, 242, 321, 325; PPL 160–1). The 'open identity' of the friendship of Jesus makes possible a community which does not lose but finds its identity in being turned outwards to the world in evangelism, practical acts of liberation and solidarity with the poor. But its openness to the world is quite different from that of the pastoral church. Since it is not the religion of society, its own life can break free of conformity with society and offer a radical alternative: the free fellowship created by the Spirit in anticipation of the kingdom (CPS 316). This life of freedom in mutual acceptance can be the source for influencing society in the same direction: revitalizing democratic freedom and participation, promoting reconciliation in the face of racism, sexism, prejudice against the disabled, and other types of inability to accept those who are different, overcoming the apathy of modern society by spreading the passion for life which is open to suffering (cf. HC 41; CPS 292). The whole of Moltmann's section on 'Christianity in the processes of the world's life' (CPS IV.4) uses the principles of the church's own life as those by which it seeks to promote liberation in the various spheres of secular life. Furthermore, the messianic fellowship is freed from the need for the neutral stance which ties civil religion to the prevailing interests in society (TGT 111): it is free to identify with the victims of society (CPS 225). Its open friendship especially takes the form of Jesus' solidarity with the poor: not simply charitable activity for them, but fellowship with them (HC 25). Unlike the pastoral church which is for everyone in an undifferentiated way, 'the Christian community is present for everyone only when it is first present for the poor, the sick, the sinners' (HC 46; cf. CPS 334–5). It can be seen how closely Moltmann's ecclesiology of the voluntary fellowship is linked to his concern for a socially critical church which identifies with the most marginalized in society.[21]

Moltmann's concept of the church as a society of open friendship strongly influences his proposals on the meaning and practice of the Lord's supper (CPS V.4; HC 52–6; cf. already CG 44). It confers the fellowship which derives from Christ's self-giving on the cross and so 'creates solidarity among people who are in themselves different' (CPS 252). But this fellowship round the 'Lord's table must be in principle *open* to the whole world, since it is based on Jesus' table-fellowship not only with his disciples but also with the poor and the unrighteous, since it derives from the crucified Christ's open identification with all ·the godless and the godforsaken, and since it points in anticipation to the eschatological banquet of the nations. The supper represents and actualizes the open fellowship of the church's messianic mission as it is created by the universal tendency of the mission of Christ and the Spirit. Thus, 'it is the Lord's supper above all that ought to show in its eschatological openness the openness to the world of the Christian mission' (CPS 247). This means that the only condition which can be set for participation in the supper is 'that we be clear that in this meal we have to do with the Jesus who is crucified for us and that in this meal the kingdom of God stands open to us' (HC 55).

[21] For a further (somewhat corrective) dimension of Moltmann's understanding of the relationship of the church to society, see SL 231, where he speaks of 'a whole number of mutual influences: the church gets new ideas from outside, people outside derive influences from the church. To describe the relationship in a one-sided way as "prototype and example" or "model", puts an undue strain on the Christian church, makes it incapable of learning, and sets up clerical claims to domination in society. . . . The special thing about the community of Christians is not so much its character as a social model (*exemplum*) as the redeeming experiences of the fellowship of Christ found there, and the liberating experiences of the Holy Spirit. . .'

Perhaps the most cogent criticism[22] of Moltmann's concept of the church as free fellowship is that in simply opposing power and authority, on the one hand, and love and freedom, on the other, Moltmann too easily equates the former with domination. He neglects the inevitability of some kind of power and authority in human society and therefore misses the opportunity to explore the way in which power and authority can be based on consent, exercised in love, and directed to fostering, rather than suppressing, freedom and responsibility. However, his brief discussion of leadership in the congregation (CPS 309–10) and the more general discussion of the relationship between the community and the particular assignments of its members (CPS 302–6) have potential in this direction and show that he is not wholly unaware of the issues.

5. The church for the world

It has always been a basic principle of Moltmann's theology that the church exists as a provisional reality to serve the coming universal kingdom of God in the world, or, to put it another way, that the church exists in mission. This principle is fundamental to the way Moltmann develops various aspects of the church–world relationship in *The Church in the Power of the Spirit*.[23] One formal way in which he refines its meaning is in the categories of anticipation and representation. The church is the anticipation of the kingdom of God under the conditions of history, the vanguard of the new humanity (CPS 196). But anticipation involves representation. The church is *pars pro toto:* a preliminary and fragmentary *part* of the coming *whole* (the universal kingdom), and so *representative* of the whole *for the sake of* the rest of the world whose future the whole is. Consequently, the church can only prove itself as an anticipation of the coming kingdom 'through intervention and self-giving for the future

[22] S. Sykes, *The Identity of Christianity: Theologians and the Essence of Christianity from Schleiermacher to Barth* (London: SPCK, 1984), p. 297 n. 61.

[23] For criticism, see Tripole, 'A Church', pp. 656–8: I am taking up some of his points in what follows.

of others' (CPS 194–5). This is why, in Moltmann's treatment of the way the Spirit anticipates the kingdom in the life of the church (CPS V and VI), the mediations and ministries of the Spirit are always directed outwards and forwards.

> As the mediations and powers of the Holy Spirit, they lead the church beyond itself, out into the suffering of the world and into the divine future (CPS 198).

The kingdom is anticipated in the church only *as mission*, which is to say: only as the messianic fellowship of service for the kingdom of God in the world.

This clarifies the sense in which, for Moltmann, the church is a *provisional* reality, which at the end will have fulfilled its role and be superseded by the kingdom. In so far as the church anticipates the kingdom, it is continuous with the kingdom, although its necessarily imperfect anticipation of the kingdom under the conditions of history will be transcended in the perfection of the kingdom. But in so far as the church anticipates the kingdom *in mission* it is provisional. Hence in Moltmann's discussion of the four marks of the church (CPS VII), three are 'designations of the kingdom' which are applied to the church as mediating the life of the kingdom in history, but the fourth mark, apostolicity, is not a characteristic of the kingdom in its eschatological fullness at all. It designates the church in history precisely as a *missionary* anticipation of the kingdom:

> We can therefore say that the historical church *will* be the one, holy, catholic church through the apostolic witness of Christ, and in carrying out that witness; whereas the church glorified in the kingdom of God is the one, holy, catholic church, through the fulfilment of its apostolate. Historically the church has its being in carrying out the apostolate. In eternity the church has its being in fulfilment of the apostolate, that is, in the seeing face to face (CPS 358).

This passage also makes clear that the church does not disappear at the end, but, its mission accomplished, finds its fulfilment in the kingdom. In its historical form, however, the church's whole existence is characterized by the mission-ary mark of apostolicity, and this means that the other three marks take a missionary *form* in being directed outwards and forwards. The church is not, for example, '"one" for itself; it is one for the peace of divided mankind in the coming kingdom of God' (CPS 345).

None of this argument, however, seems to necessitate the kind of distinction Moltmann makes when he says that 'the real point [of the church's mission within the mission of Christ and the Spirit] is not to spread the church but to spread the kingdom' (CPS 11), or that the aim of the Gospel which the church proclaims 'is not to spread the Christian religion or to implant the church; it is to liberate the people for the exodus in the name of the coming kingdom' (CPS 84). Similarly, in criticizing the ecclesiology of the Heidelberg Catechism, he objects that 'the whole human race only seems to be material for the election and gathering of the community of the saved, as if mankind were there for the church and not the church for mankind' (CPS 69). Yet, if the church is the anticipation of the kingdom of God within history, it would seem natural to suppose that the way the church serves the coming kingdom is by calling and gathering people into its own fellowship. The church would then exist not for itself but for the world – in the sense that it exists not for the sake of those who are already its members but for the sake of extending its fellowship to others. This would not make the church's mission self-serving, since it incorporates people not for its own sake but for theirs, and, as a fellowship continually turned outwards to the incorporation of others, for the sake of others too. In rejecting this way of thinking Moltmann is far from denying that the proclamation of the Gospel, which he consistently regards as the primary, though not the only, way in which the church serves the kingdom, does create the church. By liberating people from sin and calling them to discipleship it gathers the people of the eschatological exodus, the messianic fellowship (CPS 83–4). But the church is not the goal. It is to Christ and his coming kingdom that people are converted, and it is on their way to the kingdom that they form the messianic fellowship. But is this materially different from saying that the aim of mission is the church as a fellowship continually open to the inclusion of others? It is different, in Moltmann's thinking, because, although the church has a centrally important role in preparing the way for the universal kingdom, it is not by the inclusion of the whole world in the church that the universal kingdom will come. There are movements towards the kingdom in world history independently of the church, and the church itself mediates the kingdom in history in other ways besides making disciples.

To take the latter aspect first, it is here that Moltmann's concept of multi-dimensional liberation comes into play (cf. CG 329–35; FC 109–14). The Gospel of Christ anticipates the kingdom by proclaiming and effecting liberation in all the interrelated spheres of life.

> Just as the coming kingdom is universal, so the gospel brings the liberation of men to universal expression. It seeks to liberate the soul and the body, individuals and social conditions, human systems and the systems of nature from the closedness of reserve, from self-righteousness, and from godless and inhuman pressures (CPS 223).

This means that the messianic fellowship spreads the liberation of the kingdom not only in every aspect of its own life and that of its members, but also through its members' influence in every aspect of society. The Gospel has its effect not only as people consciously respond to it in faith and discipleship, but also as it spreads freedom in the various dimensions of the life of secular society. In a hidden way and in anticipation of his presence at the end, God is present wherever people experience economic, political, cultural, ecological or personal liberation (HD 110–11). The dimensions are mutually interrelated and not reducible to one dimension which gives rise to the others, and so political liberation, for example, is not unilaterally dependent on the liberation experienced in Christian conversion. Thus, the church's influence for liberation may extend beyond its membership.

However, this need not invalidate the desire that all should join the messianic fellowship as Christian disciples: such a goal could remain desirable in addition to the church's liberating activity of other kinds. At this point, therefore, we should consider a second relevant aspect of Moltmann's thought: the idea that the mission of the Son and of the Spirit towards the kingdom includes but is not confined to the church. The church is *one element* in the history of the Spirit's liberating activity, and there are 'saving efficacies outside the church' (CPS 64–5). One might still ask whether it might not be desirable for the church to include these in its own mission. Although Moltmann rejects Rahner's notion of anonymous Christianity, there is clearly a sense in which salvation outside the church, which Moltmann believes to be the saving work of *Jesus Christ* (CPS 153), is 'anonymous' in not acknowledging Jesus Christ. Why should it not be desirable that this anonymous work of the Spirit come to explicit confession of Jesus Christ?

So, finally, we come to the uncrossable barrier which Moltmann attempts to erect in the way of any notion that the church could ever become the universal kingdom: the church has 'partners in history who are not the church and will never become the church' (CPS 134). These are Israel, which the church cannot 'succeed' (CPS 148) or 'supplant' (CPS 351); the world religions, which will 'not be ecclesiasticized . . . nor will they be Christianized' (CPS 163); and the institutions and processes of secular life 'which can neither be ecclesiasticized nor Christianized' (CPS 163). Here Moltmann is especially concerned to guard against triumphalism (cf. HD 198): 'those enthusiastic dreams of realizing the universality of God's kingdom through a universal Christian state or by supplanting Israel' (CPS 351). Why are these only dreams? The case of Israel, the primary partner, is special but also, in a way, paradigmatic. For Moltmann, Israel and the church have distinct divine callings in history, by which they complement each other and which they can only fulfil by not being each other (CPS 147–9; cf. HD 208–13). Each witnesses to the kingdom of God in its distinctive way which makes it a necessary 'thorn in the side' of the other (CPS 148). The point applies in a somewhat different way to the other partners. Because the church is only an imperfect, fragmentary anticipation of the kingdom (CPS 167), it can only serve the truth of the whole by openness to partners who can open up potentialities for the kingdom not available to the church in isolation (cf. CPS 163). It is Moltmann's profound belief in relationality and dialogue which is operative here. The church can only fulfil its special role, as the messianic fellowship which confesses Jesus Christ, in relationship to other movements in history which have different potentialities for the kingdom. As a contemporary ecclesiological strategy this is convincing enough. But one is still bound to ask why theoretical and final limits must be placed on explicit response to the Gospel through confession of faith in Christ? Of the world religions, for example, Moltmann hopes that in dialogue with Christianity 'they will be given a messianic direction towards the kingdom. For this, people of other religions, and the other religions themselves, bring a wealth of potentialities and powers with them; and Christianity must not suppress these but must fill them with hope' (CPS 163). But in gaining this messianic direction, why should they not also, without forfeiting their distinctive potentialities for the kingdom, come to believe in Jesus as the Messiah of the kingdom? But then, as liberating movements of the Spirit, orientated to the kingdom and confessing Jesus Christ as Lord, they will, by Moltmann's definition, be his church. It may well be that Moltmann's ecclesiological concerns can be maintained without setting any limits on the church's mission to call people to faith in Jesus Christ.

7

The Holy Spirit in the Trinity

1. From eschatological Christology to trinitarian pneumatology

The Holy Spirit has played an increasingly important role in Moltmann's theology. In *Theology of Hope* the Spirit is rarely mentioned, but nevertheless does play an essential role which is developed in more detail in the later books. From the beginning Moltmann's theology characteristically moves between its strongly christological centre in the events of the history of Jesus, his cross and resurrection in particular, and its universal horizon in the eschatological future of all reality. This movement is possible, indeed necessary, because the event of the resurrection of the crucified Jesus is understood as an event – the definitive event – of eschatological promise. In raising the crucified Jesus from the dead, God enacted his promise for the new creation of all things, which is a promise not of another world, but of the transformation of this world in the temporal future. Christian theology therefore has a particular starting-point in the events of the biblical history, but by the actual character of these events as eschatological promise theology is opened both to the world and to its future, or, better, to the world for the sake of its future.

Between the promise given in the resurrection of Jesus and its fulfilment in the eschatological future, the principal mediating concept in *Theology of Hope* is the mission of the church. Through the mission of the church the promise already affects the world in anticipation of the new creation and begins to transform the world already in the direction of its promised eschatological transformation. But in this connexion Moltmann also refers a number of times to the

Spirit (TH 161–2, 211–12, 216), which, he says, 'arises from the event of the resurrection of Christ and is an earnest and pledge of his future, of the future of universal resurrection and of life' (TH 211). Clearly Moltmann, whose early theology has a strongly Pauline focus in its New Testament sources and inspiration, here understands the Spirit very much in Pauline terms as the eschatological Spirit, the life of the new creation already present in the experience of the church now but present under the conditions of the un-redeemed world.

> Thus, the Spirit is the power to suffer in participation in the mission and the love of Jesus Christ, and is in this suffering the passion for what is possible, for what is coming and promised in the future of life, of freedom and of resurrection (TH 212).

What is of the greatest importance here for the under-standing of Moltmann's later development of pneumatology is that the Spirit is located historically between the resurrection of Jesus and the universal future of Christ. The Spirit, says Moltmann, 'arises from a historic event and discloses eschatological possibilities and dangers' (TH 212). It mediates between the particular history of Jesus and the universal future of the world. Moltmann's later development of pneumatology preserves this christological origin and eschatological direction.

In *Theology of Hope* it is by no means clear that the Spirit is a trinitarian Person, and Moltmann's early theology can at best be called only implicitly trinitarian. In the 1970s, however, Moltmann developed a distinctive form of trinitarian theology, which is the context for all further development of his pneumatology. So it is to Moltmann's doctrine of the Trinity that we must now turn.[1]

Moltmann's doctrine of the Trinity arises from giving a trinitarian interpretation to the basic structure of his early theology, i.e. a christological centre in the history of Jesus and a universal eschatological horizon. It therefore takes the form

---

[1] For a more detailed treatment of the material in the rest of this section, see R. Bauckham, *Moltmann: Messianic Theology in the Making* (Basingstoke: Marshall Pickering, 1987), chapter 4.

of what Moltmann later called God's trinitarian history: the history of God's involvement in the world in the history of Jesus and the Spirit by which he brings the world to its escha- tological goal. But the need for such a trinitarian inter- pretation became clear for Moltmann only as his attention moved back from the resurrection of Jesus to the cross of Jesus. If Moltmann understands the resurrection as the event of God's eschatological promise to the world, he understands the cross as the event of God's suffering love for the world. The resurrection is promise for the world only because the Jesus whom God raised from the dead was the crucified Jesus who in his cross was identified with the world in all its godless- ness and godforsakenness, its sin and its suffering. Jesus on the cross suffered the godforsakenness of the world so that the world should no longer be godforsaken. Jesus, the incarnate Son of God, suffered abandonment by his Father who left him to die. But the Father also suffers, though in a different way. He suffers in grief the death of his Son. Whereas the Son, identified with the godforsaken, suffers godforsakenness, the Father in compassion suffers his Son's participation in the fate of the godless.

This event of divine suffering is the way in which God over- comes the contradiction between himself and the godfor- saken, godless world. In his love he suffers the contradiction, is present with the godless and the godforsaken, and thereby reaches them with his love. But his trinitarian differentiation is essential to the event. In order for his love to reach and reconcile the godforsaken, the Son must identify with them and experience their alienation from God. In other words, godforsakenness must be taken within the divine experience; it must separate the Son from his Father; it must, in Moltmann's sharpest formulation, set 'God against God'. Yet at the point of their deepest separation, the Father and the Son are still united in their love, united in their love for each other and in their love for the world, which has led the Father to abandon his Son to death and the Son to surrender himself to death. In other words, on the cross the love between the Father and the Son spans the gulf of sin and suffering, bridges the chasm of the divine absence from history, and takes the whole of godless, godforsaken reality into its embrace. On the cross the relationship between the Father and the Son opens to include the whole world within it.

So far the cross appears only a binitarian, not a trinitarian event. The Spirit, in conformity with the theological structure we have already noticed, is the third element which gives the event its eschatological openness and direction. When Moltmann says that the event of the cross includes the whole of suffering and sinful reality within the love of God, he means that it does so representatively, through the Son's identification with the godforsaken and the godless. The actual reconciliation of all things in God is a process which stems from the cross and moves towards eschatological completion. It is the work of the Spirit. So just as in *Theology of Hope* the Spirit as the life of the new creation arises from the event of the resurrection of Jesus and moves history towards the eschatological transformation of the world, so in *The Crucified God* the Spirit as the reconciling love of God arises from the event of the cross and moves history towards the eschatological unification of the world with God. The structure is the same, but in the second case it is trinitarian – in this sense: that Moltmann identifies the Spirit with the love which unites the Son and the Father on the cross and thereby flows out from the event of the cross to include all reality in the divine love. The Spirit, he says, 'is the unconditioned and therefore boundless love which proceeds from the grief of the Father and the dying of the Son and reaches forsaken men in order to create in them the possibility and the force of new life' (CG 245; cf. TTC 294–5). The language there suggests that Moltmann has in mind not only the Augustinian and Barthian view of the Spirit as the bond of love between the Father and the Son, but also the traditional language about the trinitarian procession of the Spirit from the Father and the Son. He is reinterpreting both with reference to the historical event of the cross in its eschatological openness.

That observation is reinforced by the fact that the Trinity here undoubtedly has a Hegelian dialectical structure (and indeed Moltmann explicitly refers to Hegel: CG 254; cf. FC 82; DGG 175), though this does not mean that the content is entirely Hegelian. The cross is a dialectical event in which God identifies with what contradicts him in order to overcome the contradiction by suffering it in love. The Spirit, as the Spirit of the mutual loving surrender of the Father and the Son, resolves the dialectic, by reconciling the godforsaken to God. The Trinity is therefore a dialectical historical process, inaugurated by the Son's identification with the world in all its negativity on the cross, and taking, through the work of the Spirit, all human history into itself in order to open it to the eschatological future.

It seems as though in *The Crucified God* Moltmann meant to say that the Trinity is actually constituted by the event of the cross. If so, he quickly retreated from that position to the view that God is eternally Trinity. But he has never abandoned the claim that the cross was internal to God's own trinitarian experience, and it is this claim, with its implications, which gives Moltmann's trinitarian doctrine its distinctiveness. If it is the cross as the event of God's suffering love for the world which necessitates trinitarian language, it also necessitates a doctrine of divine passibility, not only in the narrow sense that God can suffer pain, but also in the broader sense that he can be affected by his creation. His love-relationship with the world is a genuinely two-way one in which he not only affects the objects of his love but is himself affected by them. Yet the two-way image is a little misleading because it neglects the trinitarian dimension. What really happens on the cross, according to Moltmann, is that the relationships between the Persons of the Trinity are opened to include the world within them, in such a way that those relationships change and thereby change the world. It is as *Trinity* that God not only affects but is affected by the world.

From his starting-point in the cross there was never any possibility that Moltmann could preserve the traditional distinction between the immanent and the economic trinities. On that view the immanent trinitarian relationships are the eternally unchanging basis for the divine *opera ad extra* in which the economic Trinity acts in human history. But if we perceive the cross as an event of divine suffering we are obliged to speak, however cautiously, of God's experience of the world, and if we perceive the cross as an event of suffering between the trinitarian Persons, we are obliged to speak of a trinitarian experience in which God experiences himself differently in the act of experiencing the world. In other words, what God is for us he is for himself, in his trinitarian self-relation. For Moltmann, this is what it means to say that God is love.

Moltmann therefore follows Rahner in rejecting the distinction between the immanent and the economic Trinities (CG 239–40), but his meaning is more radical than Rahner's. He is attributing to God a real experience of historical becoming in which his trinitarian relationships change as they encompass, experience and affect human history. From the key standpoint of the cross he is envisaging the Trinity as a trinitarian history of God with the world. In other words, the doctrine of the Trinity is not an extrapolation from the history of Jesus and the Spirit; it actually is the history of Jesus and the Spirit in its strictly theological interpretation. It can really only take narrative form as a history of God's trinitarian relationships in himself and with the world. In such a doctrine, the notion of an immanent Trinity might survive in a different form, or rather there are two different forms it might take. It could be conceived as God's trinitarian being as it was in eternity before God entered relationship with the world: this is how Moltmann in *The Church in the Power of the Spirit* treats it as what he calls 'the Trinity in the origin'. Or it could be conceived as what remains unchanging in the changing trinitarian relationships of God's history. It seems to me we do need such a notion if we are to say that God *is* Trinity (as Moltmann certainly wants to say) and in his history remains himself. Moltmann comes close to recognizing this when he reverts to talking about an immanent Trinity in *The Trinity and the Kingdom of God*, but fails to do so explicitly. Instead, he appears to revert to something more like the traditional distinction between the economic and the immanent trinities, but qualified by the assertion that the latter is affected by the former. His reason for adopting this confusing notion is difficult to comprehend, unless it be that it allows him to speculate about aspects of the immanent

Trinity which cannot be directly perceived in God's trinitarian history. I shall have occasion later to criticize this speculative tendency in Moltmann's later work, which seems to me a betrayal of the insight with which his trinitarian thinking began: that the doctrine of the Trinity is the theological interpretation of the history of Jesus and the Spirit.

So far we have seen how Moltmann's trinitarian thinking, starting from the cross, opens out into the concept of God's trinitarian history. Within this concept, the Spirit continues to mediate between the history of Jesus and the eschatological future, the particular and the universal, but he does so now as the trinitarian Person whose role is to integrate creation into the trinitarian life of God. Both this role and the sense in which he is a Person in the Trinity receive much more exposition in Moltmann's work after *The Crucified God*. Not only in *The Church in the Power of the Spirit,* but also in *The Trinity and the Kingdom of God* and *God in Creation* Moltmann's theology becomes fully trinitarian, giving now as much attention to pneumatology as he had previously given to Christology. Even when, in *The Way of Jesus Christ,* he again devotes a book to Christology, he stresses the pneumatological dimension of Christology.

2. The Spirit in the trinitarian history of God

In Moltmann's work from *The Church in the Power of the Spirit* onwards, there are several somewhat differing attempts to summarize the trinitarian history of God. The most complex occurs in *The Trinity and the Kingdom of God* (94–5), but here we shall discuss an earlier and a later scheme: the earlier in *The Church in the Power of the Spirit* (1975), the later in a 1984 article (FHS; cf. HTG 57–69), which incorporates the major developments of *The Trinity and the Kingdom of God* in a usefully simplified form.[2]

The earlier scheme, in *The Church in the Power of the Spirit* (50–65), forms the context for Moltmann's major discussion of ecclesiology. Understanding the trinitarian history of God starts from the history of Jesus and the church's experience

[2] For the latest version of the scheme, see SL 289–301.

of the Spirit, and tries to understand these in two directions: by an inference backwards to what Moltmann calls 'the Trinity in the origin', and by an inference forwards to the eschatological goal of God's trinitarian history, which Moltmann calls 'the Trinity in the glorification'.

The inference backwards is made by way of the sending of the Son and the Spirit into the world from God. This is the inference made in the traditional theological move back from the economic to the immanent Trinity, and Moltmann here criticizes it only as being one-sided. He accepts the traditional view that the missions of the Son and the Spirit into the world must be based on a trinitarian order in the Trinity in the origin: the sending of the Son from the Father corresponds to his eternal generation by the Father, the sending of the Spirit from the Father corresponds to his eternal procession from the Father (or: from the Father and the Son, since Moltmann at this stage refuses to adjudicate the *Filioque* issue).[3]

But the inference backwards to the origin of God's trinitarian history has to be complemented by an inference forwards to its goal: 'the trinity in the glorification'. In eschatological perspective the history of Jesus and the history of the Spirit are movements of the glorification of God: of the Father by the Son, and of the Father and the Son by the Spirit. But since God is glorified in the liberation of his creation, the goal of God's glorification is at the same time the glorification of the world by its inclusion in the divine life.

The overall pattern is therefore this: from eternity the Trinity in the origin is open in love for the world and its history. God's being trinitarian means that he is open in love for the union of his creation with himself. In the missions of the Son and the Spirit God opens himself in seeking love and then in gathering love gathers creation into union with himself. His final unity is then one which includes the whole of his creation in an eschatological, trinitarian 'panentheism'.

In this pattern the work of the Spirit can be seen in two ways, according to the two directions of thought. From one

---

[3] See SL 290–5 for his later critique of the *Filioque* in the context of a restatement of this part of his trinitarian thinking.

point of view the experience of the Spirit is experience of Jesus and the influence of his history: the mission of the Spirit follows from that of Christ as its effect. But from another point of view experience of the Spirit is experience of the powers of the new creation: the Spirit anticipates the future. In this way Moltmann claims to transcend the subordination of pneumatology to Christology in the Protestant tradition of theology. The Spirit does reveal Christ, but he also creates the future. It should be noticed, however, that the Spirit still maintains his historical place between the history of Jesus and the eschatological future.[4]

Finally, the Spirit's particular activities of glorification and unification should be noted, as these are to become increasingly important in Moltmann's pneumatology. How this is so we shall see as we now move to the second schema of the trinitarian history of God, from 1984 (FHS 298–300; cf. HTG 68–9). Here there are three forms in which we know the Trinity. The first Moltmann calls the monarchical form, because it is characterized by the descending order: Father–Son–Spirit. It is the scheme to be found in the Cappadocian Fathers, according to which all the activity of God in the world derives from the Father, is mediated by the Son and is brought to completion in the Spirit. It characterizes all God's works, from creation to salvation, since unlike the earlier schema and in line with his growing emphasis on a doctrine of creation, Moltmann now includes creation in the trinitarian history of God and applies to it the trinitarian order which is discerned in the work of salvation. The Father creates, as he redeems, *through* the Son *in the power of* the Spirit.

In this monarchical form of the Trinity the Spirit, according to Moltmann, does nothing of his own but implements the work of the Father and the Son. Though all the divine activity is pneumatological at its point of completion, it scarcely seems necessary to see the Spirit as a Person, by which Moltmann here means a subject of activity. In this form

---

[4] Only when Moltmann developed the role of the Spirit in creation did his understanding of the Spirit transcend this salvation–historical location, which still remains important.

of the Trinity the Spirit might as well be the power or influence of the Father or the Son.

But the Spirit, so to speak, comes into his own in the second form of the Trinity, which Moltmann calls the eucharistic. These two forms are meant to correspond to the two movements of divine love in the earlier scheme: the seeking love in which the Trinity opens itself to the world and the gathering love in which the world is united to God. Therefore the Spirit's work of glorification features in the eucharistic form of the Trinity. This is the form in which we give praise to God for his work of salvation, thereby moving from our experience of God's activity towards its goal, which is creation's worship and enjoyment of God in the new creation. In our praise of God the Spirit is glorifying the Son and through the Son the Father. The trinitarian order is Spirit–Son–Father, and here the Spirit is the real subject of an activity in relation to the Son and the Father.

Here we see what Moltmann had come to make of the idea of the Spirit's glorification of the Father and the Son in the period since *The Church in the Power of the Spirit*. As an activity of the Spirit which does not complete the initiative of the Father and the mediation of the Son, but is the Spirit's own activity towards the Father and the Son, it enabled Moltmann to attribute real subjecthood to the Spirit and so to develop a fully social doctrine of the Trinity in which the Persons are three subjects in relation to each other.

Two further points about this development are worth noticing. In the first place, it is not in relation to us that the Spirit can be discerned to be a Person, but in relation to the Father and the Son. Moltmann implicitly acknowledges that the Spirit is not a subject over against us.[5] As a subject he is not distinguishable from ourselves as subjects, but acts in our activity. This is so in both forms of the Trinity. In the monarchical form the mission of the church to the world continues the divine activity in the order Father–Son–Spirit. The Spirit

---

[5] But in SL 11 Moltmann distinguishes the Spirit's 'subjectivity' as 'the effector of a work', which can be discerned in our experience of the Spirit, and the Spirit's 'personhood', which is comprehensible only in relation to the Father and the Son.

is here the subject of the church's mission in that he inspires it. In the eucharistic form of the Trinity it is we who make the Son and the Father the objects of our praise, but our praise is inspired by the Spirit, who thereby glorifies the Father and the Son. Moltmann can conclude from this that the Spirit is a subject in a divine community of three persons because of his principle for knowing the Trinity: that our experience of the Trinity is also experience of God's experience (TKG 4). We experience not only God's threefold activity towards us, but also his threefold experience of himself in our history.

Secondly, since the monarchical and eucharistic forms of the Trinity have different orders (Father–Son–Spirit; Spirit–Son–Father), we can see that Moltmann has abandoned the idea that an original trinitarian order is reproduced in God's history with the world. The latter is a history of changing trinitarian relationships, in which no one order has priority. The orders given here, in fact, simplify the more complex picture given in *The Trinity and the Kingdom of God,* but in any case we can see why Moltmann now moves on to a third form of the Trinity which has no order. This is the Trinity as acknowledged in the trinitarian doxology (and reflected in the Nicene Creed) which gives worship and glory to Father, Son and Spirit together. In this doxology we move from praise of God for his works to adoration of God for his own sake. In an anticipation of the beatific vision we contemplate the eternal being of the Trinity itself, in which the Spirit is seen in his eternal fellowship with the Father and the Son (TKG 152–4, 174–6; SL 301–6).

3. The Spirit in the social Trinity

So we come to that concept of the Trinity which dominates Moltmann's later work – the social Trinity – and to a major problem it raises for his understanding of the Spirit. More fundamental than the changing relationships between the Persons of the Trinity is their enduring fellowship of love, in which they are one by virtue of their existence for and in each other in *perichoresis*. Here the Spirit is not merely the love between Father and Son, but himself a subject and object of the mutual love of the three. This trinitarian fellowship Moltmann then frequently treats as the model for true human community, which is both to reflect and to participate in God's own trinitarian life. Relationships of rule and subjection have no final validity either within the Trinity or in God's relationship to the world, since in himself God is a fellowship of love and in his relationship to the world it is not in the last resort his lordship so much as loving fellowship which he seeks. Therefore neither in church nor state should relationships of rule be justified as reflecting the divine monarchy. In the kingdom of the triune God it is relationships of free friendship which most adequately reflect and participate in the trinitarian life (TKG VI).

This concept links clearly enough with the Spirit's work of unification which we have noted as increasingly important to Moltmann:

> The perichoretic unity of the triune God is . . . an open, inviting unity that unites with itself. It is not confined to God in order to define him exclusively as the one over against the many, but is inclusively open for all creation, whose misery consists in isolation from the living God and whose salvation is thus to be found in being graciously taken up into the community of God (IU 56; cf. HTG 87).

Because Moltmann understands the unity of God not in terms of rule, as monarchy, but in terms of love, as *perichoresis,* it is a unity which can open itself to the inclusion of creation and have as its goal the uniting of all things with God and in God, 'that perfect union of which it can be said that in it "God is all in all"' (IU 55). That panentheistic text, 'God will be all in all' (1 Corinthians 15:24), has always been Moltmann's favourite eschatological text: his perichoretic doctrine of the social Trinity then enabled him to give it a trinitarian sense. But how does this doctrine relate to the fact that the unification of all things in and with God is, according to Moltmann, the special activity of the Holy Spirit?

Consideration of this role of the Spirit highlights a problem in Moltmann's doctrine of the Trinity. On the one hand, we seem to be asked to see the Spirit as one of the divine community of three whose fellowship we seek to reflect. It is difficult to do this, because whereas the terms Father and Son refer to mutual relationship and derive for us from the fellowship of Jesus with his Father, the Spirit as a subject in relation to the Father and the Son can only be conceived as a bare, colourless subject. And whereas Moltmann warns us that the Persons are different from each other, both in their relationships to each other and in their character as persons (TKG 189; HTG 88–9; SL 12), it is difficult to give any content whatever to the distinctiveness of the Spirit in his personal relations to the other two,[6] since all the biblical and traditional language about the Spirit characterize him impersonally: as power, water, breath, fire, and so on. The representation of the Spirit as feminine, to which Moltmann does refer, is no help at this point, since he does not suggest that we think of the Spirit as a feminine person in relation to the Father and the Son. When he refers to the Cappadocians' use of a human family of father, mother and child as an image of the Trinity (TKG 199; FHS 290–1; HTG 60; GC 235–41), he does not mean that we think of a divine family in which the Spirit relates as Mother to the Father and the Son. In so far as it has occurred in the tradition, the motherhood of the Spirit has been motherhood in relation to us. The same goes for all the impersonal language which Scripture and tradition use of the Spirit: it characterizes the Spirit's relation to ourselves. The only way in which, from the resources of Scripture and tradition, we can conceive the Spirit's personal relation to the Father and the Son is by bringing *ourselves* into the picture: the Spirit inspires *our* relationship to the Father and the Son. We cannot stand outside the trinitarian fellowship and see it as a model for our own relationships. We can only enter it and experience the Spirit's relationship to the Father and the Son as our own relationship to the Father and the Son.

Moltmann's mistake here has been to abstract the Trinity in itself from God's trinitarian history with the world, not

[6] Moltmann's attempt to characterize the Spirit's specific personhood in SL 285–309 proceeds by claiming that *we* experience the distinctive personhood of the Spirit as 'presence and counterpart'. But since this combination of 'presence and counterpart' is, according to Moltmann, characteristic of the experience of love between persons (SL 262–3), it is hard to see how it distinguishes the Spirit from the Father or the Son.

simply to provide a conceptual basis for the latter, as in his earlier account of 'the Trinity in the origin', but in order to make the Trinity in itself a model for human life. He has been trapped into this by an insufficiently critical appropriation of the tradition's idea of the trinitarian image of God in humanity. But it is inconsistent with his fundamental insight that the doctrine of the Trinity is the theological interpretation of the history of Jesus and the Spirit. The remedy is simple and at hand in Moltmann's own work. The relationships of the Persons as we know them and as they are relevant to us are the relationships of the Persons *in their relationships with the world*. In this context the distinctiveness of the Spirit is not obscure: it is, as Moltmann himself claims, his indwelling of creation:

> God does not simply confront his creation as creator. He is not merely, as the incarnate One, the representative and advocate for men and women. In the Spirit God dwells in man himself (TKG 104).

This is why unification is the special activity of the Holy Spirit. The perichoretic unity of the Trinity is open to us and can include us because one of the three, the Spirit, relates to the Father and the Son in such a way as to be able to be our relationship to the Father and the Son. The Spirit *is* God's ability to be an open fellowship in which his creation can be included, just as the Son is God's ability to be incarnate as a human person. Just as it is dangerously speculative to think of the Son without reference to his incarnation, so it is dangerously speculative to think of the Spirit without reference to his indwelling.

Thus, the human fellowship which the Spirit, through his indwelling, creates cannot be an image of the Trinity as it is in itself apart from us, but it is a participation in the Trinity's history with us. It is the fellowship of sisters and brothers of Jesus, who with Jesus know his Father in the Spirit – and also, Moltmann would add, of the friends of Jesus who share with Jesus his friendship with the Father in the Spirit. Only in this differentiated relationship with the Trinity can we in any sense 'reflect' the Trinity. We do so as the Spirit conforms us to the image of the incarnate Son, in both his loving obedience to the Father and his loving openness to all people. (This last point is made by Moltmann himself in GC 242–3.)

My critique of Moltmann in this section could be accused of neglecting his particular understanding of our *doxological* relationship to the immanent Trinity. It is in doxology, praise of God as he is in himself for his own sake, that we contemplate the social Trinity in its eternal *perichoresis*. In this doxological contemplation Moltmann does seem to understand us to stand in a different relationship to the Trinity from the relationships constituted by salvation-history (see SL 304). In his latest treatment of the theme, he claims that we here know the Spirit both as 'presence' (*Gegenwart*) and 'counterpart' (*Gegenüber*, i.e. person in 'face to face' relationship). In the Spirit's presence we direct the trinitarian doxology to the Spirit as counterpart, along with the Father and the Son, in his eternal fellowship with them. In this adoration we are then drawn into the trinitarian life in a new way: 'into the circular movement of the divine relationships' (SL 305). Moltmann seems to claim that the differentiated relationship to the Trinity which is characteristic of our experience of salvation gives way, in doxology, to a different form of relationship in which we know each of the three Persons in a 'face to face' way, as they know each other.

If this argument, which is clear only in the final pages of his latest work (SL 301–9), could be sustained, it could provide the basis for the social analogy between the Trinity and human community (SL 309). But it hangs a great deal on the trinitarian doxology, as though from the act of glorifying the Spirit together with the Father and the Son can be deduced a different and superior relationship to the Trinity from that in which we stand when, in the Spirit, we glorify the Father through the Son. As the Cappadocian Fathers argued, the trinitarian doxology (which is not, of course, scriptural) expresses recognition of the coequal deity of the three Persons, but the Cappadocians used it, in this way, to support a doctrine they held to be implied in Scripture, not to establish a doctrine without scriptural support. In the trinitarian doxology we recognize the subjectivity and coequal deity of the Spirit, but it is precisely as the indwelling Spirit who enables our relationship with the Father and the Son that we glorify him in his co-equal deity.

Is it really true that in stepping beyond the differentiated relationship in which we know the Father through the Son in the Spirit into contemplation of the three Persons in their *perichoresis* we come 'in sight' of God's eternal being? On the contrary it could be maintained that in the former relationship we know God as Trinity, whereas in the latter we contemplate an abstract idea of God.[7]

4. Further trinitarian speculation

In my view Moltmann in his earlier theology was on the right theological track in working with the principle that the doctrine of the Trinity is the theological interpretation of the history of Jesus in its eschatological openness through the Spirit. If this is the history not just of God's action on history but also of his involvement in history, if God in this history is perceived as suffering love, then it is necessary to speak not only of our threefold relation to God in this history but also of his threefold relation to himself in this history. It is necessary to see the history of Jesus, and with it the history of the world, as internal to God's own trinitarian experience. Because he is love, what he is for us he is also for himself. If we go on to try to say what he is for himself apart from us, what his trinitarian being is in itself apart from his trinitarian history with the world, we must limit ourselves strictly to what is necessary in order to guarantee that in his history with us he is himself.

In his work from *The Trinity and the Kingdom of God* onwards Moltmann does not observe this limit. We have already noticed how he fails to do so in the form which his central notion of the social Trinity takes. But in my view, there are worse examples. Some of them, in chapter 5 of *The Trinity and*

---

[7] Further discussion of this issue could involve the mystics' experiences of the Trinity. See, e.g. G. H. Tavard, *The Vision of the Trinity* (Washington, D.C.: University Press of America, 1981), pp. 104–6.

the Kingdom of God, he attempts to justify by reference to the doxological nature of theology: the claim, which has become increasingly important to him in his recent work, that theology is in the service not only of soteriology and praxis, but also of contemplation and praise of God as he is in himself. While I have no quarrel with this claim, it is no excuse, as Moltmann realizes (TKG 153), for unfounded speculation, which in any case usually proves doxologically arid.

With the tendency of some of Moltmann's later work towards undisciplined speculation is closely linked a degree of hermeneutical irresponsibility. Unable to find a real basis in the biblical history for the kind of speculation in which he engages, Moltmann freely employs inferences from biblical phrases and metaphors which he sometimes admits (e.g. GC 218) cannot be warranted by historical–critical exegesis. In contrast to his earlier work, which was usually soundly rooted in current studies of biblical theology, in his later work Moltmann too often falls back on the mere citation of texts in a pre-critical manner.

I shall instance two examples, both related to the Spirit, of this lack of discipline, as it seems to me, in Moltmann's later work:

(1) The first example relates to the *Filioque.* Since there is no fixed order in the economic Trinity, according to Moltmann, but only a history of changing trinitarian relationships, he cannot argue from the order of the economic Trinity to a corresponding order in the immanent Trinity. Indeed, there is no order in the mutual perichoretic relationships of Moltmann's social Trinity. Nevertheless, he retains the so-called relations of origin in the Trinity, including the monarchy of the Father, as what he calls the constitution of the Trinity. This order of origin can be hermeneutically based solely on the names of the Father, the Son (or the Word) and the Spirit. The extent to which these biblical metaphors are made the source of inferences quite alien to their biblical usage can be seen, for example, when Moltmann seeks to connect the origins of the Son and the Spirit from the Father by observing that speaking and

breathing, the uttering of the Word and the breathing of the Spirit, are complementary, indissoluble activities (TKG 169–70; cf. SL 293, 307). I do not understand what sort of status Moltmann intends us to give to such a statement, which depends on connecting two metaphors which entered the development of trinitarian doctrine quite independently of each other.

When it comes to the *Filioque* Moltmann cannot, of course, employ the Western principle that the relations of origin in the immanent Trinity must correspond to the relations of sending in the economic Trinity. Instead, he falls back on the traditional Greek patristic and Orthodox reliance on the *text* John 15:26, with no reference to the fact that all modern exegesis sees in that text no reference to the pre-temporal origin of the Spirit from the Father, but only to his temporal mission from the Father. Clearly Moltmann is here the victim of his too respectful immersion in the tradition: he cannot envisage the possibility that there might be no way of answering a question to which the tradition has given so much attention. But in drawing unwarranted inferences from John 15:26 Moltmann, in fact, goes even further than the tradition. In his attempt to arrive at a compromise formula acceptable to both sides in the *Filioque* dispute, he begins by insisting that 'proceeds from the Father' in John 15:26 must mean 'proceeds from the Father precisely as the Father of the Son'. This is hermeneutical irresponsibility in the service of speculation which, whatever its value for ecumenical politics, surely lacks any real theological interest.

(2) My second example has much more real theological interest, since it is Moltmann's response to the difficult issue of the appropriate way to use female images of God. Moltmann, in fact, has two quite different proposals. He began, in *The Trinity and the Kingdom of God* (see also MF = HTG 19–25), with the proposal that the Father be thought of as 'the motherly Father', and only later (FHS) took up the image of the Holy Spirit as Mother (see also HTG 64–5; GHH 33–8; SL 157–60). Since he repeated both proposals, in different contexts, in a series of lectures he gave with his wife

Elisabeth Moltmann-Wendel in 1984 (HG 89, 101, 103, 106, 117), he presumably regards them as compatible (cf. also HTG xiv–xv).

One might expect that the proposal that the Father should be understood as motherly Father would focus on Jesus' experience of his Father as tender, nurturing love as well as authority. This is the way in which the proposal might be justified as part of a trinitarian interpretation of the history of Jesus. For Moltmann, however, the main point[8] is a pseudo-biological one, about the trinitarian order of origin, which surely has no basis in New Testament use of the terms Father and Son with reference to God. If the Son originates from the Father alone, then the Father must be both the Father who begets and the Mother who gives birth (TKG 164–5; MF 53; HTG 22). This is simply pressing a metaphor beyond its intended point, and is no less hermeneutically irresponsible because first done by the Council of Toledo in 675. Moreover, the kind of androgynous nature which is thus attributed to the Father does not help us to see God relating to us in a motherly way, because it concerns something which Moltmann makes clear is quite unique to the Son: his divine origin from the Father.

The proposal that we think of the Spirit as Mother has, of course, some roots in the tradition, to which Moltmann appeals, and has become relatively widespread today. Moltmann's discussion highlights its problems. He argues that its advantages are that it expresses better than other images the personal character of the Spirit and that it makes it possible for us to see the feminine in humanity as reflecting the life of the social Trinity just as much as the masculine. However, the argument overlooks (what Moltmann elsewhere seems to take for granted) the peculiar character of the Spirit as known to us in the trinitarian history: that the Spirit is a Person (subject) in relation to the Father and the Son, but not in relation to us (since we experience the Spirit not in a person-to-person relationship but as our own relationship to the Father and the Son). However, it is not in

---

[8] He does also, in MF 54 = HTG 22, try to see a feminine element in the *suffering* of the Father.

relation to the Father and the Son that the Spirit is Mother (according to the tradition and Moltmann) but in relation to us. Thinking of the Spirit as Mother is therefore bound to have one of two possible and unfortunate results. It might encourage us to do what most of the other biblical and traditional images of the Spirit discourage us from doing: to think of the Spirit as a divine Person to whom we relate in a person-to-person relationship. But this is to reject the whole point of speaking of the Spirit at all: as a *distinctive* form of divine presence by indwelling.[9] The second possibility is that the Mother-image will be assimilated to the general trend of language about the Spirit and become not a genuinely personal image at all but an impersonal image of the mother simply as the biological source of our life. Indeed, I think this is probably how it mainly functioned in Syrian Christian tradition, and it is how Moltmann himself seems to be thinking, when he says:

> God comes to us in Jesus as the Brother *next to us*. We come to *face* him as the Abba–Father of Jesus, and we live *out of* our Mother, the Spirit (HG 106 [my italics]).[10]

Whether the Spirit as an impersonal female principle is a desirable way of introducing feminine language into trinitarian terminology I doubt.

[9] In SL 287–9 Moltmann does seem to want to claim that we experience the Spirit as 'counterpart' as well as 'presence'. This seems to me to obscure the experiential basis for making trinitarian distinctions in talk of experience of God.

[10] In SL 157–9, 271 (cf. also HTG 65), Moltmann extends the image of the Spirit as Mother to 'protecting and consoling, love's empathy and sympathy' (SL 159). He does so primarily by interpreting the role of the Paraclete in John as 'comforter' in the sense of a mother comforting her children (evidently following Pseudo-Macarius: HTG 65; SL 158). Of course, this is not at all what 'Paraclete' (almost certainly a legal image) means in John.

8

The Trinity and Human Freedom*

As its title declares, *The Trinity and the Kingdom of God* is not just a book about the Trinity, but a book about the Trinity in relation to God's kingdom. For, as Moltmann says, 'Theology is never concerned with the actual *existence* of a God. It is interested solely in the *rule* of this God in heaven and on earth' (TKG 191). The central *problem* the book addresses is therefore not the problem of the doctrine of the Trinity, presented as the intellectual conundrum it is sometimes made to appear. Certainly, the major task of the book is 'the task of revising the church's doctrine of the Trinity on the basis of the Bible' (TKG 65). But the doctrine of the Trinity, for Moltmann, is not the problem; properly understood, it is the solution.

The problem is that of the rule of God and human freedom. Succinctly put in the words Moltmann quotes from Ernst Bloch: 'Where the great Lord of the universe reigns, there is no room for liberty' (TKG 203). Actually this is two problems. There is the problem that if God is absolute monarch, we are his slaves: the divine sovereignty leaves no room for human freedom. Of course, this is a classic theological problem, but Moltmann is not concerned here with the soteriological debate about predestination and free will. He is more concerned with the modern perception, at the root of modern atheism, of the incompatibility of human freedom with belief in an almighty, sovereign God (TKG 203). But since the modern rejection of God in the name of human freedom has often coincided with the rejection of

---

* This chapter originated as a paper read to the Fifth Edinburgh Conference on Christian Dogmatics in September 1993.

political autocracies in the name of human freedom, there is a second problem about the rule of God and human freedom. This is that the rule of God, as absolute monarch of the world, has functioned in religious history as the model and legitimation for absolute rule by human monarchs on earth.[1] Divine domination authorizes human domination at the expense of human freedom:

> The notion of a divine monarchy in heaven and on earth . . . generally provides the justification for earthly domination – religious, moral, patriarchal or political domination – and makes it a hierarchy, a 'holy rule'. The idea of an almighty ruler of the universe everywhere requires abject servitude, because it points to complete dependency in all spheres of life (TKG 191–2).

What Moltmann calls 'monotheistic monarchianism' – the one God as sole ruler of the universe – both constitutes the first problem and gives rise to the second. He spells this out in a critique of both 'political monotheism' and 'clerical monotheism' (TKG 192–202).

Moltmann uses the term 'monotheism' as the opposite of trinitarianism. So Karl Barth's claim that the doctrine of the Trinity is 'Christian monotheism' (quoted TKG 63, 140) is by no means a recommendation of Barth's doctrine of the Trinity, in Moltmann's eyes. Moltmann might have been less open to misunderstanding had he used the term 'unitarianism'[2] rather than 'monotheism', but he is rather deliberately contrasting the Christian – fully trinitarian – concept of God with non-Christian monotheistic concepts and with Christian theological views which have allowed such concepts priority over the biblical Christian understanding of God as Trinity. Such Christian monotheism occurs when either the Greek philosophical notion of God as supreme substance or the modern idealistic concept of God as absolute subject is given priority over the trinitarian

---

[1] For some discussion and nuancing of this claim, see D. Nicholls, *Deity and Domination: Images of God and the State in the Nineteenth and Twentieth Centuries* (London/New York: Routledge, 1989), especially pp. 234–8. This book is one of the best studies of the relationship between religious and political ideas in the modern period.

[2] Nicholls, *Deity*, p. 234, suggests coining 'monolithism'.

differentiation in God. But the divine unicity – whether as substance or subject – is closely connected with the divine monarchy. The one God is sole ruler, and so other features of classical theism of which Moltmann has long been critical – divine impassibility and the related view of the God–world relationship as a purely one-way relationship: God affects the world but cannot be affected by the world – are implicated in Christian monotheism. What Moltmann opposes comes to classic expression in his account of Barth's trinitarian doctrine, making his disagreement with Barth pivotal for his whole argument. In Barth the sovereignty of God and the notion of God as absolute subject coincide, and the doctrine of the trinity is understood as an interpretation of this: 'God reveals himself as Lord' (see TKG 63, 140–1). Inevitably the Trinity is collapsed into the threefold repetition of a single subject. It is instructive to observe what Moltmann sees as the mistake here. The sole sovereignty of the one God is given priority over the divine Trinity (TKG 63) – and the result is Barth's alleged 'modalism' (only one divine subject in three modes of being). Divine monarchy entails unitarianism. By contrast Moltmann wants to give priority to the Trinity and to understand the rule of God differently in its light. Social trinitarianism will then entail something other than divine monarchy.

Moltmann's criticism of Christian monotheism is both that it makes the rule of God incompatible with human freedom and also that it is insufficiently Christian, i.e. insufficiently trinitarian. The basis of the doctrine of the Trinity is the history of Jesus Christ, which the New Testament tells as a narrative of relationships between three divine Persons. So the non-negotiable starting-point for trinitarian doctrine is that three divine subjects relate to each other in salvation-history. From this starting-point develops a doctrine of the Trinity which we can briefly summarize, for our present purposes, in five closely related points:

(1) The relationship between God and the world is a two-way relationship, in which God is affected by the world as well as affecting it. Moltmann's understanding of the cross,

from which his trinitarian thought originally developed, is central here, in that it entails divine passibility, though this is by no means the only way in which the God–world relationship is reciprocal. The two-way relationship means, of course, that God himself has a history. As far as technical trinitarian theology goes, it means that, while Moltmann in *The Trinity and the Kingdom of God* no longer denies the distinction between the immanent trinity and the economic trinity, as he had in earlier work, the relation between the two has itself to be two-way, not, as in classical theology, one-way.

(2) Moltmann's social doctrine of the Trinity conceives of God as three divine subjects in interpersonal relationship with each other – a fellowship of love. Their unity does not precede their distinction, but consists in their community together, which Moltmann, in one of the finest sections of the book, describes by an interpretation of the doctrine of the trinitarian perichoresis supplemented by a doctrine of trinitarian manifestations. The life of God is a life of living fellowship and a process of expression of the divine life through mutual manifestation (TKG 174–6).

(3) God's trinitarian history with the world is a history in which the three divine Persons relate both to each other and to the world. It is not a history in which a fixed order of trinitarian relationships appears, but a history of changing trinitarian relationships, in which the relations between the Persons both affect the world and are affected by the world. It is a history in which the world is included within the trinitarian relationships of the three divine Persons.

(4) Thus, the Trinity is a process of living relationships of love between the three Persons and open to the inclusion of the world.

(5) This doctrine of the Trinity makes no use of the notion of rule. It is true that, at one of the points where Moltmann is slavishly and unnecessarily faithful to features of traditional trinitarian theology, he does retain the traditional idea of the Father as sole source of Godhead (the so-called monarchy of the Father). But he diverges from

tradition in limiting this element of subordination to what he calls the 'constitution' of the Trinity, allowing it no place in the perichoretic relations between the three: 'Here the three Persons are equal; they live and are manifested in one another and through one another' (TKG 176). The notion of divine monarchy is not used to explain the Trinity; the Trinity itself must reveal the meaning of the kingdom of God.

Of course, Moltmann's point is not to substitute a divine oligarchy of three for a divine monarchy of one. This would be of no benefit to human freedom. The point is that God is defined as love rather than as lordship. God relates to the world in love – both acting in love and suffering in love – and can do so because God's own being is an open fellowship of love. If God's rule is given priority in the doctrine of God, freedom is eliminated. But if the Trinity is given priority, then God's rule can only be the rule of love, which is compatible with freedom just as love is compatible with freedom (or rather: constitutive of freedom).

So far so good. But the two more specific ways in which Moltmann then proceeds to work out the implications of his doctrine of the Trinity seem more problematic. They are two quite different and distinct lines of argument:

(1) Moltmann proposes the trinitarian fellowship of the three divine Persons as a model for true human community which is both to reflect and to participate in God's own trinitarian life. There are two elements to this argument. First, in a development of the idea of the divine image in humanity, Moltmann finds the image of God not in the human individual in his or her isolated subjectivity reflecting the lone divine Subject, but in human community reflecting the interpersonal life of the social Trinity. Karl Rahner's argument that the modern meaning of person requires that God be conceived as one person, is trenchantly (and with justification) criticized for presupposing the modern bourgeois cultivation of the individual (TKG 145, 155 6):

> It is inescapably obvious that, for the sake of the identity of the self-communicating divine subject, Rahner has to surrender the

interpersonal relations of the triune God. And with this, of course, the prototypical character of the triune God for the personal fellowship of men and women in the church and in society collapses too (TKG 156).

The trinitarian perichoresis, in which the divine Persons are themselves in their distinction from and (equally) at-oneness with each other, provides a pattern of personhood as that of individuals in relationship:

> the image of God must not merely be sought for in human individuality; we must look for it with equal seriousness in human sociality. . . . If we take our bearings from the Christian doctrine of the Trinity, personalism and socialism cease to be antitheses and are seen to be derived from a common foundation. The Christian doctrine of the Trinity compels us to develop social personalism or personal socialism (TKG 199).

However, the argument is not merely against individualism, but also against relationships of inequality and domination. This is the second element in the argument, though Moltmann does not readily distinguish the two elements, since he takes it for granted that the possessive individualism which conceives of the person as a self-disposing centre of action independent of others (TKG 145) is closely akin to the practice of lordship which relates to other persons only by way of power to dispose of them (TKG 198). So here it becomes important that the perichoretic unity of the three divine Persons is a non-hierarchical fellowship of open love:

> If . . . we have to recognize the unity of the triune God in the perichoretic at-oneness of the Father, the Son and the Holy Spirit, then this does not correspond to the solitary human subject in his relationship to himself; nor does it correspond, either, to a human subject in his claim to lordship over the world. It only corresponds to a human fellowship of people without privileges and without subordinances (TKG 157).

Thus, both in the church and in society (TKG 157–8, 198–200), the trinitarian image is found in *community*, which domination destroys but open acceptance of the other and participation in the life of the other creates. So, in place of the concept of God as divine monarch providing the prototype for human domination, at the expense of freedom, the social Trinity provides a model for human community in which people are free for each other and find freedom in relationship with each other.

Attractive as it is (and paralleled in the work of other contemporary theologians), there seem to me to be serious problems with this line of argument. Moltmann is trying to hold together the two rather different ideas: that (*a*) the life of the Trinity is an interpersonal fellowship in which we, by grace, participate, and (*b*) the life of the Trinity provides the prototype on which human life should be modelled (for the combination of the two ideas, see especially TKG 157–8). I doubt whether the combination is really successful. According to the first idea, we experience the trinitarian relationships from the inside, and from the standpoint of a specific, differentiated relationship to each of the three Persons: we know Jesus as God become our fellow-human, brother and friend, we know God the Father as his and our Father, we know the Holy Spirit as indwelling life and power. According to the second idea, however, we are invited to stand outside this participation in the Trinity and our specific relationships to the three Persons, and to view the Trinity as an external model which human relationships should reflect. This view of our relationship to the Trinity has no biblical basis (significantly, the New Testament docs not use the idea of the image of God in this way), and is only artificially combined with the first idea.

The two ideas would be fairly easily compatible were we to think of the Trinity as simply like a group of three friends who include us in their friendship as yet more friends. In that case, it would be natural to think that the kind of relationship (friendship) enjoyed by the original group of three friends is the kind of relationship the new members of the circle have with each other, since what has happened is that the friendship circle has been expanded. But it is misleading to think in that way of the Trinity and our participation in the life of the Trinity. It obscures the fact that we enjoy a highly differentiated relationship to the three divine Persons. We do not relate to Jesus the incarnate Son in the same way as we relate to God the Father, though we can think of both in interpersonal terms, while our mode of relationship to the Spirit is not interpersonal at all. The Spirit, by indwelling us in a uniquely divine way for which human personal relationships do not provide an analogy, enables our personal relationship with the Son and the Father, but is not experienced by us as personal other in interpersonal relationship. This is not to deny the subjectivity of the Spirit, but means that we experience that subjectivity as inspiring our own subjectivity, not as *vis-à-vis* our own subjectivity in personal otherness. The point of Christian talk of the Trinity is to ground precisely this highly differentiated threefold relationship in which Christians come to know God and to participate in the divine life. It means that true human community comes about, not as an image of the trinitarian fellowship, but as the Spirit makes us like Jesus in his community with the Father and with others. The way in which this enables freedom needs developing in a different way from this particular line of Moltmann's argument.[3]

A related problem with the argument is that, just as it neglects the differentiated character of our relationship with the trinitarian Persons, so it neglects the differentiated character of the relationships of the trinitarian Persons themselves, which must be, in a way we cannot begin to comprehend, the basis for their ability to relate in a differentiated way to us. The idea of the social Trinity as a model for human community encourages us to think of the differences in the trinitarian relationships – the different ways in which the Father relates to the Son, the Son to the Father, the Father to the Spirit, the Son to the Spirit, the Spirit to each of the other two Persons – as no more significant than the differences in human relationships within the kind of community Moltmann envisages. Or to put the same point another way: it encourages us to apply the term person as univocally to the three divine Persons as we do to human persons. But this is precisely what Moltmann himself warns

---

[3] Cf. the promising suggestion of Nicholls, *Deity*, pp. 117–18 (following Berdyaev: see pp. 121–2) that it is not the Trinity as such but the Trinity involving the incarnation which is the alternative to divine monarchism.

should not be done in his useful section on 'the trinitarian principle of uniqueness' (TKG 188–90):

> The 'three Persons' are different, not merely in their relations to one another, but also in respect of their character as Persons, even if the person is to be understood in his relations, and not apart from them. If we wanted to remain specific, we should have to use a different concept in each case when applying the word 'person' to the Father, the Son and the Spirit. The Holy Spirit is not a person in the same, identical sense as the Son; and neither of them is a person in the same, identical sense as the Father. Their description as divine Persons in the plural already shows a tendency towards modalism in itself. For the generic term hypostasis or person stresses what is the same and in common, not what is particular and different about them (TKG 189–90).

Essentially, this is a correct and necessary safeguard against the illegitimate anthropomorphism which so easily infects discussions of the Trinity, including Moltmann's. The doctrine of the Trinity means that God is God in three inconceivably different ways. We should certainly not reduce these three to three ways in which a single, identical divine subject repeats or relates to himself: to make this point is the merit of Moltmann's argument for social trinitarianism. But we should also beware of supposing that the subjectivity of each is equally analogous to human subjectivity. Rather, each must transcend human subjectivity in a quite different and distinctive way, which we can glimpse only in observing the consequence that incarnation is appropriate to the Son, not to the Father or the Spirit, while inspiration and indwelling in the world are appropriate to the Spirit, not to the Father or the Son. The concept of the Trinity as a society on which human society can be modelled flattens these trinitarian differences and reduces our sense of the otherness of God which precisely the doctrine of the Trinity should heighten.

(2) Moltmann's second line of argument as to the implications of his doctrine of the Trinity is that pursued in the final section of *The Trinity and the Kingdom of God*: 'The Trinitarian Doctrine of Freedom.' Here Moltmann, inspired

by Joachim of Fiore's trinitarian theology of history, develops a trinitarian understanding of the kingdom of God in which three aspects of the kingdom, appropriated to the Father, the Son and the Spirit, relate to three forms or stages of human freedom. Unlike Joachim, Moltmann does not regard the kingdom of the Father, the kingdom of the Son and the kingdom of the Spirit, with the three forms of freedom that correspond to them, as successive chronological periods, but as 'strata in the concept of freedom' (TKG 223). The three forms of freedom are always all present in Christian experience of freedom, but there is also a trend from the first to the third (TKG 223–4).

In the kingdom of the Father, in which God is Creator and Lord of his creation, people experience the freedom of being God's servants, which liberates them from subjection to anything other than the sole lordship of God (TKG 219). (It is interesting to notice that here – but virtually nowhere else in the book – Moltmann acknowledges that the notion of obedience to God as Lord need not be oppressive but has a liberating aspect.)[4] In the kingdom of the Son, the servants of the Lord become the children of the Father, and enjoy the liberty of personal and intimate relationship to the Father and of participation in his kingdom (TKG 219–20). In the kingdom of the Spirit, the servants and the children become God's friends, a relationship which 'becomes possible when people know themselves in God and God in them' (TKG 220), and which is characterized by boldness and confidence in prayer (220–1).

This scheme, which one could have wished to see developed at greater length, is certainly suggestive with regard to the dimensions of freedom in relation to God, but as a *trinitarian* scheme it is somewhat problematic. The relationship of each 'kingdom' and form of freedom to its respective divine Person is certainly to be understood as a form of 'appropriation' (to use traditional trinitarian terminology). In other words, Moltmann does not mean that each form of freedom is a relationship only to the particular trinitarian Person to whose

[4] See A. J. McKelvey, *The Freedom of God and Human Liberation* (London: SCM Press/Philadelphia: Trinity Press International, 1990).

'kingdom' he assigns it, but he does think of the trinitarian Person in question as distinctively active in creating or enabling the form of freedom in question. Thus, for example, it is obvious that the freedom of sons and daughters of God is relationship with the Father, but it is the Son who opens up this relationship for people. But whether these three appropriations can really be sustained is dubious. For example, in the New Testament Christ's redemptive work liberates people from slavery to sin so that they may be obedient to God, and this obedience is at least as characteristically that of servants of *Christ* the Lord as it is that of servants of God the Father. But most problematic is the role of the Spirit, who in Pauline theology makes possible our participation in Jesus' relationship of sonship to God (Romans 8:15–17; Galatians 4:6–7), whereas in John 15:13–15 (cited by Moltmann: TKG 220) it is Jesus who makes his disciples his friends, and the indwelling of the Spirit is not mentioned, even if implicit. To distinguish, even as a matter of appropriation, the Son as the source of the freedom of children of God and the Spirit as the source of the freedom of friends of God seems unfounded. In both cases, the Spirit, as the enabler of relationship, gives the inner freedom of relating to another divine Person: to the Father as Father, to Jesus as friend. If we are to think of an aspect of freedom which should be associated specifically with the Spirit, it is the freedom of being 'led by the Spirit' (Galatian 5:18), which makes goodness not only conformity to the will of another, but also the inner, spontaneous desire of our own hearts.

Rather than trying to modify Joachim's scheme, it would be better to focus on the differentiated structure of the Christian experience of God, in which – to use one set of metaphors – we know God in three dimensions: as God above us (the Father), alongside us (Jesus, the Son), and within us (the Spirit). The fact that this is the structure of God's *love* for us excludes the domination that eliminates freedom. But also the fact that God's love for us has *this* structure excludes the merely paternalistic care that inhibits freedom. The structure gives Christian freedom three poles between which it takes shape: authority with belonging (the

Father), solidarity (the Son), and spontaneity (the Holy Spirit). The correlation of these three poles with the three trinitarian Persons is not to be pressed too far, but they do indicate a trinitarian shape to the Christian experience of freedom. Each of the three would need careful exposition to explode the myth that God's lordship is incompatible with human freedom and to show how, on the contrary, it enables human freedom.[5]

[5] For some further reflection on the subject, see R. Bauckham, *Freedom to Choose* (Grove Spirituality Series 39; Bramcote, Nottingham: Grove Books, 1991).

9

Creation and Evolution*

Moltmann's *God in Creation* treats the problems of relating a Christian understanding of creation to scientific theories of evolution relatively briefly, but this treatment is significant because of its place within Moltmann's much broader theological exploration of the doctrine of creation. This broad context sets the problems in a fresh perspective and facilitates Moltmann's creative theological interpretation and appropriation of evolution. We must therefore begin by sketching the outlines of Moltmann's doctrine of creation in general, before turning to the specific question of its relationship to evolution.

1. An outline of Moltmann's doctrine of creation

(1) *An ecological doctrine of creation*

This is the subtitle of the work and indicates the contemporary context which guides Moltmann's interest in the doctrine of creation. The ecological crisis is a crisis in the human relationship to nature, in human beings' understanding of themselves in relationship to nature. So it requires, theologically, a renewed understanding of nature and human beings as God's creation, and therefore also a renewed understanding of God's relationship to the world as his creation. Moltmann's doctrine of creation is a doctrine not just about the origin of the world, though that is

* Sections 1 and 2 of this chapter were first published as: 'Evolution and Creation: (9) in Moltmann's Doctrine of Creation,' *Epworth Review* 15 (1988), pp. 74–81. Section 3 has not been previously published.

included, but about God's relationship, as Creator, to his creation, about the world as God's creation, and about human beings as part of God's created world. The result is not, as we might expect from Moltmann, a theology which leads at all explicitly into specific recommendations for ecological *praxis*: in this respect it is disappointingly, sometimes frustratingly, lacking in concreteness. Indeed, at its worst this is a book whose argument takes flight into a kind of pure speculation in which Moltmann in his more recent work seems to have developed a tendency to indulge. But at its best, it achieves an understanding of 'God in creation' which critiques the *attitudes* to the natural world that underlie the ecological crisis and promotes alternative attitudes, from which a different kind of praxis can emerge.

The kind of human relationship to nature which has created the ecological crisis and must be superseded is that of exploitative domination. Related to this is the way of knowing nature which was characteristic of the modern scientific enterprise until recently: that of objectifying, analytical thinking, in which the knowing subject masters the object by analysing it. An ecological theology requires instead a participatory kind of knowledge, in which things are perceived in the totality of their relationships and the human subject perceives itself as a participant in the natural world. The purpose of such knowledge is not to dominate nature, but to restore the human sense of community with nature, respecting its independence and participating in mutual relationships with it.

But since, for Moltmann, anthropology always relates closely to an understanding of God, a reconception of the human relationship to nature requires a reconception of God's relationship to nature. An understanding of God as the monarchical ruler of creation encourages an understanding of humanity, his image on earth, as similarly distinguished from nature in a dominating relationship. In order to ground an emphasis on mutual relationship in nature, rather than hierarchical sovereignty, Moltmann appeals to the kind of doctrine of God which he has developed in his earlier works and further develops it with reference to the divine relationship to creation.

(2) *A trinitarian doctrine of creation*

God in himself is not a divine hierarchy, but a trinitarian community of persons, who relate to each other in a relationship of mutual indwelling (*perichoresis*). God's own life therefore provides a pattern for the life of his creation as an intricate community of reciprocal relationships: 'All living things – each in its own specific way – live in one another and with one another, from one another and for one another' (GC 17). Moltmann's long-standing theological principle of relatedness – understanding things not in themselves but in their relationships to other things – which he applied, for example, to ecclesiology in *The Church and the Power of the Spirit*, as well as to the doctrine of God in *The Trinity and the Kingdom of God*, becomes in the present book a general cosmological principle: 'in reality relationships are just as primal as the things themselves' (GC 11). For this principle he can, of course, claim scientific support, implicit, for example, in his use of the term 'symbiosis', but theologically he grounds the principle in the trinitarian *perichoresis*. Its anthropological implication is that, for all our distinctiveness, humanity's fundamental place in creation is that of a participant in the mutually dependent, ecological community of creation.

However, God's trinitarian life is more than a model for the symbiotic life of his creation: it is also the form of God's own relationship with his creation. Since *The Crucified God*, Moltmann has emphasized the Trinity's openness to the world. The relationships of the three divine Persons do not form a closed circle in heaven, but an open community in which the life of the creation may participate. God has a *trinitarian history* with the world, a history of mutual relationships, in which God not only acts on the world but is affected by the world and the trinitarian relationships themselves change as human history is taken within them. Moreover, this trinitarian history has as its goal the kingdom of God, which Moltmann has long conceived as an eschatological panentheism, in which 'God will be all in all': creation will be glorified through its participation in the divine life and God will be glorified in his indwelling of his creation. Moltmann's stress on the divine involvement in history was originally, in *The Crucified God*, especially christological, but since then has become increasingly also pneumatological. This means that now, as he extends the concept more explicitly to the whole of the natural world, it is the Spirit, among the trinitarian Persons, who takes the centre-stage. The immanence of God in his creation is not, for Moltmann, the cosmic Logos-Son of the early Fathers: Moltmann's divine Son is perhaps too centrally the incarnate, human God, the crucified and risen Jesus, for this to be appropriate. The Son is the mediator of creation,[1] rather than the life-giving divine energy within it. Rather, Moltmann tells us, 'By the title "God in Creation" I mean God the Holy Spirit' (GC xii), and as well as calling his doctrine 'a trinitarian doctrine of creation' (GC 14, 86), he can also call it 'a pneumatological doctrine of creation' (GC xii; cf. 9).

Thus, not only is the trinitarian God a perichoretic community and his creation a perichoretic community, but also God's relationship to his creation is one of mutual indwelling. God is not only, as the Father, creation's transcendent Lord, but also, as the Spirit, an immanent divine presence within it. This is the point at which Moltmann's persistent polemic against 'monotheism' (meaning unitarianism) really impinges on the doctrine of creation. Trinitarian theology requires us to think, not of a simple dichotomy between God and the world, but of a tension within God himself, who is both transcendent beyond the world and pervasively immanent within it:

> The trinitarian concept of creation binds together God's trans-
> cendence and his immanence. The one-sided stress on God's
> transcendence in relation to the world led to deism, as with
> Newton. The one-sided stress on God's immanence in the world

---

[1] Later Moltmann interprets Christ's mediation of creation as having three aspects: he is (1) the ground of the creation of all things; (2) the moving power in the evolution of creation; (3) the redeemer of the whole creation process (WJC 286; CCC 182–3).

led to pantheism, as with Spinoza. The trinitarian concept of creation integrates the elements of truth in monotheism and pantheism. In the panentheistic view, God, having created the world, also dwells in it, and conversely the world which he has created exists in him. This is a concept which can really only be thought and described in trinitarian terms (GC 98).

In other words, because God is transcendent beyond the world, it dwells in him, and because he is immanent within it, he dwells in it. Moreover, because of the trinitarian relationship between the transcendence and the immanence of God, the Spirit in the world not only differentiates and binds together all things in the community of creation, but also keeps the world open in self-transcendence:

> If the cosmic Spirit is the Spirit of God, the universe cannot be viewed as a closed system. It has to be understood as a system that is open – open for God and for his future (GC 103).

(3) *A messianic doctrine of creation*

By this term (GC 4–5) Moltmann intends to designate his doctrine of creation as a specifically Christian doctrine of creation, i.e. creation understood in the light of the Gospel of Jesus the Messiah. As we should expect from Moltmann, this means that creation is given an *eschatological* orientation towards the messianic future opened up by the history of Jesus. The purely protological view of creation, to which the Genesis creation narratives confine themselves, has to be supplemented by the eschatological view of creation, which already developed in the Old Testament but for Christians is defined by Jesus' introduction and anticipation of the eschatological kingdom. Creation understood in the light of the redemptive history which leads towards the coming kingdom is revealed as a not yet completed creation, subject to the power of nothingness from which it requires redemption but open to its future goal of transfiguration in the kingdom of glory. Moltmann is here developing the conviction which can be found in his theology from *Theology of Hope* onwards: that the kingdom of God represents the eschatological goal not only of human history but also of the whole material cosmos. Redemption and eschatology do not, therefore, serve to lift humanity out of the material world, but confirm humanity's solidarity with the rest of God's creation in its longing for eschatological liberation. This thought is, of course, an echo of Romans 8:19–23, which is one of the most fundamental texts for Moltmann's doctrine of creation, since it links the Christian experience of the eschatological Spirit with the bondage and hope of the whole creation.

The effect of this is to turn the doctrine of creation into a *history* of God's relationship to his creation. In the beginning the initial divine act of creation *ex nihilo* produced a *creatio mutabilis,* an 'open system' with its goal beyond itself in the future. Creation is not static, nor is its redemption a mere restoration of a paradisal origin. Rather creation is from the beginning orientated towards a goal which will surpass its origin: the eschatological new creation in the kingdom of glory. Therefore the divine activity of *creatio continua,* which leads from the initial creation to the eschatological consummation of creation, is not only a preservatory activity of sustaining the created world, but also an innovatory history which anticipates and prepares for the new creation. Moreover, whereas the initial creation was an effortless act of divine creativity, the continuing history of creation-redemption is a history in which God suffers his creation as well as acts on it. Moltmann's distinctive emphasis on divine passibility here enters his doctrine of creation: 'The inexhaustible creative power of God in history always makes itself known first of all in the inexhaustibility of the power of his suffering' (GC 210). The immanent Spirit co-suffers with creation in its bondage. The Spirit suffers creation's tendency to close in on itself and die, keeps it open beyond itself to life and to the future, and thereby turns creation's history of suffering into a history of hope.

In all this we can see a fairly thorough fusion between creation and redemption in Moltmann's thought, along with a thorough-going assimilation of the creative and salvific activities of the Spirit. Sin and death have their counterparts in the non-human world: its subjection to transience and the power of nothingness. Hence the history of nature is a tormented struggle in which the Spirit's indwelling is a kenotic presence and redemptive suffering. Just as in the history of the church the Spirit is present as the eschatological Spirit, producing anticipations of the coming kingdom but at the same time suffering the contradictions of the present age and keeping humanity's history open in hope for the kingdom, so in the natural world the immanent Spirit is the eschatological Spirit, filling the natural world with promises of its future transfiguration and keeping it open in self-transcendence towards the future. It is important to note that, in consequence, the present indwelling of God through the Spirit in the world does not make nature a theatre of God's glory, in the manner of a natural theology which sees the world as a simple reflection of the divine nature. The divine immanence in nature is historically situated in the messianic history of God with the world: it is a kenotic, suffering, contradicted presence, which can do no more than point towards the future kingdom of glory. Only then will creation be lifted beyond transience through participation in God's eternal life and God's glory will fill his creation.

(4) *A sabbatical doctrine of creation*

Of the four terms I have used to describe Moltmann's doctrine of creation, this is the only one which is not actually used by Moltmann. But he comes close to it when he claims:

> the doctrine of the sabbath of creation becomes the identifying mark of the biblical doctrine of creation, distinguishing it from the interpretation of the world as nature. It is the sabbath which manifests the world's identity as creation, sanctifies it and blesses it (CG 276; cf. 5–6).

Moltmann's interpretation of the Sabbath as the eschatological goal of creation brings together the messianic orientation of his doctrine, which we have just noticed, and the ecological concern with which we began this account of his doctrine. It does so because it characterizes the world as *theocentric* (and therefore *creation*) rather than *anthropocentric.*

The first Genesis creation account, which has so often been interpreted in such a way as to represent humanity as the crown of creation for whom the rest of creation exists, is only amenable to this interpretation, Moltmann points out, if one confines one's attention to the six days of God's work and neglects the seventh day of God's rest. In fact it is the Sabbath, in which God rests from the work of creation in order to enjoy his creation, which is the crown of creation. The Sabbath is the anticipation of the eschatological goal of all God's creative work, in which he will come to rest in his creation and his creation will participate in his rest. The goal of all his work, beyond doing and making, is the joy in existing which the Sabbath represents. But if it is in this Sabbath rest of God that creation comes to completion, human beings, though holding a special position in creation, as the image of God, must not behave as owners of nature. They belong with nature in a community of creation which has its goal in God. And when human beings anticipate the completion of creation by keeping the Sabbath, not interfering in their environment by labour but simply letting it be itself, then they acknowledge creation to be God's creation, with its own value for God.

2. Creation and evolution

The theological structure which we have so far outlined is not without an input from the natural sciences, but is not determined by them. Its main features result from the theological directions already established in Moltmann's early theology, but sharpened in certain respects under the impact of concern about the ecological crisis. In the latter context, theology has a contribution to make which cannot come from science: 'The sciences have shown us how to understand creation as nature. Now theology must show how nature is to be understood as God's creation' (GC 38). Nevertheless, this theological task presupposes and must seek to integrate scientific findings. It can do so in so far as the latter are not confined to objectifying, analytical thinking, but go on to the ecological thinking which seeks to understand each thing in its relationship to the whole. In the end, theology must relate to scientific theories about the universe and the whole process of nature, recognizing that, in view of accelerating scientific progress, these will never be more than provisional drafts. Consequently, 'a theological theory of nature will also be both variable and provisional' (GC 37), a conclusion not at odds with Moltmann's general view of the nature of theological work.

Moltmann's treatment of scientific theories of evolution is in line with this programme. He seeks a broad interpretation of the whole history of nature as an evolutionary process – an interpretation which tries to do justice both to particular scientific findings and to the broad structures, established on theological grounds, of his doctrine of creation. In order to do so he focuses, inevitably, on the respects in which scientific theory appears most amenable to theological interpretation along the lines he has established. The resulting synthesis of theology and scientific theory is necessarily provisional.

In seeking to overcome the supposed opposition between the Christian belief in creation and the scientific understanding of evolution, Moltmann first confronts the hermeneutical issue. Throughout the book he takes the Genesis creation narratives very seriously as theology. Indeed, he is apt to squeeze theological significance out of them in a way which is too little controlled by historical exegesis. But an interesting hermeneutical observation frees him from any need to take them literally as science. The biblical traditions about creation, he points out, are products, at more than one particular point, of a history of reflection on belief in creation, in which new insights into nature had to be continually integrated into the understanding of creation. Thus, the particular syntheses of belief in creation and knowledge of nature which they represent are in principle revisable and require reformulation in the light of fresh understandings of nature.

Moltmann discerns and responds to three further problems about the relation of creation to evolution. In the first place, evolution seemed opposed to creation because 'creation' was too narrowly understood in terms of the initial creation, after which it was conceived as finished. Moltmann's emphasis on the openness of the original creation, which is only on the way to its completion in the kingdom of glory, plainly leaves room, indeed positively welcomes the scientific understanding of nature as an unfinished process which not only has evolved but continues to evolve.

Secondly, and linked to the view of creation as static, God was understood in relation to creation too exclusively as the transcendent cause of creation. Moltmann's emphasis on God's involvement in his creation in a variety of different kinds of relationship, including relationships of mutuality, makes it much easier to see the immanent creative Spirit at work in the processes of natural evolution. We have already noticed how he distinguishes the kind of divine activity involved in the act of initial creation from the kind with which we are concerned in the subsequent history of continuous creation. Of the latter he says: 'Because it is a fundamentally suffering and enduring creating, the activity of God in history is also a silent and a secret one' (GC 211). The creative activity of the immanent Spirit is not distinguishable, as a supernatural intervention, from the processes of nature, but is an unobtrusive accompaniment of them. It has to be conceived as

> a whole series of relationships: God acts *in* and *through* the activity of his creatures; God acts *with* and *out of* the activity of his creatures; created beings act *out of* the divine potencies and *into* a divine environment; the activity of created beings is made possible by the divine patience; the presence of God in the world is the space free *for* the liberty of created beings; and so on (GC 211).

Moltmann's fundamental model of God as the transcendent environment of the world and the pervasive divine immanence in the world thus proves able to accommodate an appropriately complex account of God's relation to the evolutionary process. Moreover, it proves capable of transcending the opposition of creation and evolution in their religious implications:

When eyes were turned towards the initial contingency of the world, theism always presented itself as the obvious philosophy; for theism distinguishes between God and the world. But when we are thinking about the evolution of the cosmos and of life from the contingency of events, dynamic pantheism seems much more plausible: the matter that organizes itself also transcends itself and produces its own evolution (GC 212).

But the trinitarian doctrine of creation unites the transcendent Creator *ex nihilo* with the immanent Spirit of creation's self-transcendence.

Thirdly, evolutionary theory, which made humanity a link in the evolutionary chain, was resisted as an affront to the modern, *anthropocentric* view of the world. Moltmann, however, finds the evolutionary origins of humanity entirely appropriate to his understanding of creation. They highlight the extent to which human beings, as in the first place a product of nature, are members of the community of creation, having as much in common with the rest of creation as they are distinguished from it – as Genesis 1 itself makes clear. Moreover, the understanding of the world as *theocentric* frees us from the need either to understand the whole evolutionary process as having its goal in humanity, or to understand humanity as purely a means to some further goal of the process. Every product of evolution has its own meaning with reference to God.

This last point should indicate how Moltmann's incorporation of evolution into his doctrine of creation at the same time gives it a creative interpretation in line with the particular features of that doctrine. This emerges more fully in the last topic we shall notice: his attempt at 'a hermeneutical theory of evolution', i.e. of the whole series of evolutionary processes from the evolution of the cosmos through the evolution of life to human history. His proposal that systems of matter and life must be understood as 'open systems', i.e. systems open to a partially undetermined future, leads to the question whether the whole universe itself is an open or a closed system. If, by analogy with its parts, we understand the universe as an open, self-transcending system, then we must assume that the universe itself has a transcendent encompassing milieu, with which it is in communication, and a transcendent future into which it is evolving (GC 204).

In other words, the evolutionary model of the universe coheres with the doctrine of creation as existing in God and towards his future:

> God is [the world's] extra-worldly encompassing *milieu,* from which, and in which, it lives. God is its extra-worldly *forecourt,* into which it is evolving. God is the origin of the new possibilities out of which its realities are won. . . . Theologically, the world is comprehended as an open, participatory and anticipatory system once we grasp the history of creation as an interplay between God's transcendence in relation to the world, and his immanence in that world.

3. Christ the Redeemer of evolution

When Moltmann, in his next major work, *The Way of Jesus Christ,* turned to consider, not the Spirit in nature, but Christ in nature – the cosmic Christ – he took a further step in his theological interpretation of evolution, which at the very least corrects a possible misunderstanding of his treatment in *God in Creation.* In the latter the stress on the continuity between creation and salvation is such that we might have supposed the evolutionary process itself to be salvific, i.e. that it is through the evolutionary process that God brings the whole cosmos to the eschatological goal of his indwelling it in glory. In *The Way of Jesus Christ* Moltmann insists that the evolutionary process itself is creative but not redemptive. This must be so because it is necessarily characterized by transience and death, which define the old creation, not by resurrection and eternal life, which are the characteristics of the new creation.

The point is made through a sharp rejection of Teilhard de Chardin's thorough-going identification of the evolutionary process with salvation history. For Teilhard, the evolutionary process itself, in its progress towards the immensely distant Omega Point in the future, was the process of the 'Christification' of the cosmos, a progressive realization on the cosmic scale of that divinization of humanity which began in Jesus Christ. For Moltmann, the weak point in this vision was that

> in his firm faith in progress Teilhard does seem to have over-looked the ambiguity of evolution itself, and therefore to have paid no attention to evolution's victims. Evolution always means *selection*. Many living things are sacrificed in order that 'the fittest' – which means the most effective and the most adaptable – may survive. In this way higher and increasingly complex life systems, which can react to changed environments, undoubtedly develop. But in the same process milliards of living things fall by the wayside and disappear into evolution's rubbish bin (WJC 294).

To this neglect of the victims of evolution corresponds Teilhard's tendency to justify not only natural but also human catastrophes, such as the First World War and Hiroshima, with a kind of progressivist theodicy, neglecting the victims as the price that must be paid for evolutionary progress. This trend of Teilhard's thought collides head-on with Moltmann's deeply rooted conviction of the crucified Christ's identification with victims and his horror of a kind of theodicy which justifies the sufferings of some for the greater good of others:

> The various processes of evolution in nature and humanity can only be brought into a positive relationship to Christ, the perfecter of creation, if Christ is perceived as a victim among other victims. The crucified One was present in the Spirit, not among the inventors and constructors of the atomic bomb, or those responsible for it. He was present in the Spirit among the dead of Hiroshima. There is no conceivable human evolution in the near or remote future which could give any meaning to the mass deaths of the fallen and the murdered in the two world wars of this century. Nor can a peace secured by way of a universal nuclear deterrent provide any justification for the victims of the dropping of the atomic bomb. Not even the best of all possible stages of evolution justifies acquiescence in evolution's victims, as the unavoidable fertilizers of that future – not even the Omega Point, with its divine fulness (WJC 296–7).

In the last sentence we should probably see an echo of Ivan Karamazov's protest against the justification of the suffering of little children as serving some ultimate divine purpose for the world: 'Why should they, too, be used as dung for someone else's harmony?'[2]

The conclusion is that *Christus evolutor*, Christ at work in the process of continuous creation through evolution, should not be identified with *Christus redemptor*, the redeemer of creation, who is Christ in his eschatological coming. Correspondingly, the *teleology* of the evolutionary process should not be identified with *eschatology*. Evolution, to which transience is intrinsic, leaves the victims behind in its movement towards a goal that cannot include them. Eschatology is the perfecting of *all* created things in the eternal indwelling of God's glory in them:

> What is eschatological is the bringing back of all things out of their past, and the gathering of them into the kingdom of glory. . . . To put it simply: God forgets nothing that he has created. Nothing is lost to him. He will restore all (WJC 303).

Eschatological redemption is therefore a movement running counter to evolution:

> It is the divine tempest of the new creation, which sweeps out of God's future over history's fields of the dead, waking and gathering every last created being (WJC 303).

The ideas Moltmann deploys here in fact go back to his earliest thinking about eschatology, where they emerged from his disagreement, not with Teilhard, but with Ernst Bloch.[3] For all that the world, as Bloch argued, is *open* to a future radically transcending the present, it does not itself contain the potential to produce a future transcending death. The hope of the resurrection of the dead, which for Moltmann then and now is the foundation of Christian eschatology, is the hope of the radical transformation of this world of transience and mortality by God. Fundamental to Moltmann's theology here is an apocalyptic dualism of death

---

[2] F. Dostoyevsky, *The Brothers Karamazov* (Harmondsworth: Penguin, 1982), p. 286. See chapter 4 above.

[3] See R. Bauckham, *Moltmann: Messianic Theology in the Making* (Basingstoke: Marshall Pickering, 1987), pp. 14–22.

and resurrection. This dualism understands the eschatological as a counter-movement which does not develop out of this present, transient reality, but *contradicts* the evil, suffering and transience of the world as it is, transforming it by bringing it out of the nothingness to which it tends into the eternal life of divine indwelling. It speaks of new creation because, while the first creation brings all things out of nothing, the new creation brings all things back out of nothing and secures their eternal life. This eschatological dualism or dialectic also, of course, has always been the key to Moltmann's christological dialectic of the cross and the resurrection: the crucified Christ identified with the victims of the suffering and mortality characteristic of this present reality, in order to communicate to them the new life of his resurrection, as the firstborn of the new creation. In the discussion of evolution we have just followed, essentially all that has happened is that Moltmann's earlier eschatological expectation of the resurrection of all people and, more vaguely, the new creation of all things has, with further attention to the non-human creation, become further specified as the resurrection of every individual creature that has and will have ever existed.[4]

Moltmann's eschatology has never been progressive, i.e. it does not envisage the eschaton as the result of a progressive development of the kingdom of God through history. One reason for this is that the eschaton is marked by the transcendence of death itself, as well as the removal of all evil and suffering, in resurrection and new creation. It is not that a progressive development issues in the kingdom of God's glory. Rather the kingdom is *anticipated* within this world from which evil, suffering and death have not yet disappeared.[5] It is this concept of anticipation which now allows Moltmann to see in the evolutionary process in nature, as well as in human history, 'parables and hints, anticipations and preparations for the coming of the

[4] See chapter 10 for some questions about the cogency and necessity of this development.
[5] For the concept of anticipation in Moltmann's early work, see Bauckham, *Moltmann: Messianic Theology in the Making*, pp. 43–5. See also CPS 189–96.

messianic new creation' (WJC 304; cf. 291). This makes nature's history – the history of the Spirit who both lures and suffers the evolutionary process, the history of Christ who both empowers its creative movement and identifies with its victims – a history of hope. But it is a history of hope only because these anticipations point beyond themselves to a redemptive future which is not emerging out of the process but coming to it.

10

Messianic Christology*

The Way of Jesus Christ is the third volume of Moltmann's systematic theology. Since five volumes in all were projected (before Moltmann decided to add *The Spirit of Life* as the fourth), it would have been the central volume. This is appropriate, since Moltmann's theology has always been strongly christocentric, though by no means christomonistic. *The Way of Jesus Christ* is certainly one of the finest of Moltmann's books – in my judgment the finest since *The Crucified God* – and it is probably the most important work on Christology for a decade at least. Those who have had their fill of hackneyed summaries of the early development of Christology, based on outdated consensus views in biblical and patristic scholarship, and of critiques and reconstructions which seem to assume we still have to catch up with the Enlightenment, could well rediscover an appetite for Christology in reading this book. It gathers up and restates the central christological insights of Moltmann's earlier work, but it combines them with much that is entirely fresh and creates an impressive new synthesis. It is one of the few recent christologies which is capable of reinvigorating christological thinking, expanding its horizons and realigning it with the church's task of witness to the contemporary world.

The ambitious intention of the book is to replace the two major christological paradigms of the past – the cosmological paradigm of the patristic age and the anthropological paradigm of the modern period – by a new christological

* This chapter is a revised version of a review article first published as: 'Moltmann's Messianic Christology,' *Scottish Journal of Theology* 44 (1991), pp. 519–31.

paradigm, which is required by our post-modern context. Such paradigm shifts in Christology occur, Moltmann argues, when changes in the human question about salvation shift the focus of the soteriological relevance of Christology. The methodology he employs to form the new paradigm is characteristic of his whole theological project: Christology must find its authentic Christian identity in a hermeneutic of its biblical origins, and its contemporary relevance in a hermeneutic of the modern context to which it must prove soteriologically relevant. The questions of identity ('Is Jesus really the Christ?') and relevance ('Who is Jesus Christ for us today?')[1] are mutually related in such a way that Christology must take equally seriously the biblical witness and 'the misery of the present' and constantly relate the one to the other. This is not simply to reject the christological tradition of the past: important aspects of both previous paradigms can be taken up into the new one. Characteristically, Moltmann depicts both previous paradigms as one-sided and his proposed new one as more comprehensive, though the latter (by stressing eschatological provisionality) includes the recognition of its own historically conditioned character. The shortcomings of the previous paradigms come to light primarily in their inadequacies in soteriological impact on the contemporary context. It is the comprehensive nature of the contemporary crisis of human civilization, as Moltmann sees it, which demands the contemporary development of the full dimensions of biblical Christology.

The cosmological Christology of the patristic period (WJC II.2) corresponded to the cosmocentric worldview of the ancient world, which saw humanity embedded in the orders of the cosmos. The soteriological question arose out of the contrast between the transience of the finite and the eternity of the divine. It was met by the Christology of the two natures: God became human in order to divinize human nature and the whole cosmos. This doctrine of 'physical redemption' (human nature is immortalized by participation in the divine life) has often been denigrated from the perspective of the

[1] Moltmann's concern with the mutual relationship of Christian identity and the church's relevance to its context in the world goes back to CG I.

anthropological Christology of the modern era, but Moltmann is much more sympathetic to it. His theology has always had a strong sense of transience and death as the fundamental natural evil, and therefore of salvation in its fullest sense as resurrection and the annihilation of death, new creation and God's eschatological indwelling of creation. Similarly, he has always stressed that salvation includes the bodily and the material. These themes become even more prominent in the present book. Moreover, since part of the contemporary context is the ecological crisis, the cosmological breadth of patristic Christology becomes a feature to be retrieved for the new paradigm. What Moltmann criticizes in patristic Christology is primarily its focus on the vertical relation between God and humanity, to the neglect of the horizontal, i.e. the particular history of Jesus and its eschatological directedness. This relates directly to the metaphysic of substance which it presupposes and for which Moltmann wishes to substitute a metaphysic of process and relationship. But the loss of eschatology was also due, in Moltmann's view, to the political *Sitz im Leben:* the developing theocracy of the Christian Empire, which saw the kingdom of Christ as triumphant in the present. In distinction from these aspects of the patristic paradigm, the new paradigm will stress that Christ is still 'on his way' (the metaphor of the book's title), within the trinitarian history of God with the world, towards the eschatological future.

The anthropological Christology of the modern period (WJC II.3) corresponded to the anthropocentric worldview of the Enlightenment, which detached human subjectivity from nature in order to make human beings supreme over nature and the subjects of their own history. Against the background of the technological subjugation of nature and the growth of Western democracies, the soteriological concern was not for the divinization of human beings, but for their humanization as free subjects in search of their true identity. Metaphysical incarnation became irrelevant, and Christology focused on the human historical Jesus as the model of true humanity. Moltmann complains that the result has been a series of Jesuologies which projected their own ideals of true humanity onto Jesus, thus neglecting the unique particularity of Jesus in his historical relation to God and reducing Jesus to the earthly Jesus at the expense of his being on the way to the eschatological future. The real problem is that they meet the identity crisis of human beings in modern society purely as an existential question of the individual subjectivity and not in relation to the external conditions of society which provoke the crisis. Their soteriology corresponds to the modern privatization of religion which leaves the structures of society untouched.

This last point has, of course, been met (though Moltmann does not here say so) in recent political and liberation Christologies (such as Moltmann's own previous christological work). These have seen that Christology must be soteriologically relevant in the first place to the victims of modern society and therefore critical of its structures of domination. But in this book Moltmann takes a further, major step beyond the anthropological paradigm in Christology. That paradigm has coincided with the more general paradigm 'history' (meaning history made by human beings) as the modern period's comprehensive category for interpreting all reality (WJC 227). Theology in the modern period has encountered its major problems in the apparent incompatibility of that paradigm with the notion of acts of God in history, but has nevertheless, on the whole, accepted, aided and abetted the paradigm 'history'. Only the ecological crisis has revealed the dangerous limitations of that paradigm. By considering human beings the sole subject of history and nature as mere object of human domination, it has ignored human history's embeddedness in nature. Thus it has been the ideology of modern technological civilization's violent subjugation and exploitation of nature. Thus, the new general paradigm to which the new christological paradigm needs to relate will be neither the cosmocentricity of the ancient world nor the anthropocentricity of the modern era, but a recognition of the mutual dependence and interplay of human history and the history of nature. Moltmann can even use the term 'mutual perichoresis' (WJC 372) here, revealing – by the borrowing from trinitarian terminology – how far this new paradigm coheres with the prominence which the notion of mutuality in relationship has gained in every area of his recent theology. For a long time he has worked to reconceive the relationship of God to the world as a history of mutual relationships – God's own trinitarian relationships affecting and being affected by the world in a history open to eschatological consummation. More recently (especially in *God in Creation*) he has given the non-human creation its own prominent and rightful place in this perichoretic reality, in mutual relationship with God and in mutual relationship with humanity. It is this new development in his theology generally which probably now makes the most difference to Moltmann's Christology, by comparison with his earlier extensive treatments of Christology (in *Theology of Hope* and *The Crucified God*).

Since the ecological crisis has already loomed in this discussion, the best approach to Moltmann's new christological paradigm itself will be via his analysis of its contemporary context (WJC 63–8). From this perspective he calls it: 'Christology in the contradictions of scientific and technological civilization' (WJC 63). These contradictions are three crises of modern civilization which are no superficial hiccups in an ongoing progress but crises so serious and dangerous as to constitute congenital defects in the whole project of modern civilization. The first is the growing North–South inequality, which demonstrates how the creation of the prosperous first world has produced as its inevitable by-product the poor third world. The 'new poor' of the first world itself also belong to this reverse side of the history of progress. The second crisis is the nuclear threat, which Moltmann rightly continues to take very seriously, even though it has now fallen from the fashionable agenda. He sees it as a literally apocalyptic situation, since the end of human history and of all life on earth will now always be possible at any time, and all future history, however long it continues, will therefore always be in an end-time situation, engaged in an endless struggle for life against the threat of extinction (WJC 159). The nuclear threat is one way in which technological mastery of nature has brought the world into apocalyptic peril. Another – the third crisis – is the threat of ecological catastrophe, which Moltmann sees as the consequence of the values of modern industrial civilization, so that the continued progress of that civilization must now lead to universal ecological death.

These three crises represent the contemporary context to which Christology must have soteriological relevance. Though Moltmann's work has always been in this sense contextual, none of his previous books has analysed the context with such clarity and then retained its relevance to this context so successfully. It is a universal context, rather than a more or less local context, which is more often meant when people speak of contextual theology. But in effect (without using these terms) Moltmann is arguing that for the first time a universal contextual theology is both possible and necessary. For the first time a particular critical situation affects all people. Indeed, it affects all life on earth: 'The End-time condition of world history today requires us to see the real misery of human beings as one with the growing universal misery of the earth' (WJC 45). This rules out any less than comprehensive understanding of the soteriological relevance of Christology: 'In the danger of annihilation that is now hanging over us, God's salvation is the healing and survival of the whole threatened earth and all individual created beings, in their common peril' (WJC 46). This means that the personal dimensions of salvation in modern Jesuology can be included and the cosmological dimensions of patristic Christology can be recovered, but now in an ecological sense and in an apocalyptic situation.

However, the context provides only one pole of the new christological paradigm, the other pole of which must be its biblical origins. These origins lead Moltmann initially to the theme of Israel's messianic hope (chapter I) and thereby to take up in a fresh way the theme of Old Testament promise which Moltmann first made the basis of his eschatological Christology in *Theology of Hope*. One difference is that he now explores the messianic character of Christology in dialogue with modern Jewish theologians, since 'Christian Christology is a particular form of Israel's hope for the messiah, and it is still related to, and dependent on, the Jewish forms of the messianic hope that anteceded Christianity and run parallel to it' (WJC 2). A major concern of this discussion is to understand the Christian confession of Jesus as Messiah in a way that is not anti-Jewish. At the same time, by insisting that this confession is valid only in a sense that takes on board the Jewish objection that the world is still unredeemed, the discussion re-establishes the eschatological character of Moltmann's Christology in its continuity with the Old Testament history of promise. This is expressed in the important metaphor of the book's title: 'the way of Jesus Christ' (for the metaphor, see WJC xiii–xv, 33–4, 55, 138–9, 275). Jesus is on the way to his messianic rule: 'The coming One is in the process of his coming and can be grasped only in that light: as on the road, and walking with us. But for that very reason every confession of Christ in the history of this unredeemed world has to be understood as a reaching out, an anticipation of the new creation in which every tongue will confess him. . . . Every confession of Christ leads to the way, and along the way, and is not yet in itself the goal' (WJC 33).

The image of the way of Jesus conveys both the pro-visionality of every Christology – which confesses Christ while we are on the way with him to his eschatological goal – and also the narrative character of Christology's subject. It describes 'Christ-in-his-becoming, the Christ on the way, the Christ in the movement of God's eschatological history' (WJC 33). Therefore the book is organized not, for example, as a discussion of the humanity and the divinity of Christ, but, after the two preliminary chapters, as five chapters on the five stages of Jesus' way: his earthly mission, his cross, his resurrection, his present cosmic role, and his parousia. In this scheme Christ's present is represented solely by his relation to nature (the cosmic Christ: chapter VI), because, as Moltmann explains (WJC xv), Christ's presence in the church and in the poor were fully discussed in *The Church in the Power of the Spirit*. The chapters on the cross (chapter IV) and the resurrection (chapter V) take up much of

Moltmann's early theology from *Theology of Hope* and *The Crucified God*, with important clarifications and interesting new developments, as well as the major new dimension required by the ecological crisis and the related paradigm shift. Apart from this dimension of relating Christology to nature, the chapter on Jesus' earthly ministry (chapter III) represents the most striking new ingredient in the whole scheme, even though some of its roots can be traced in various parts of Moltmann's work since *The Church in the Power of the Spirit*. The parousia as such is not a new ingredient, but the way it is treated is fresh (chapter VII).[2]

The new christological paradigm really combines the two key concepts of *eschatological process* and *relationality*. It is 'a christology in the eschatological history of God' (WJC 70). This is God's trinitarian history with both humanity and nature, aligned towards the coming redemption of all reality in the new creation. (Moltmann's quite frequent use of the word 'process' with reference to this eschatological history should not suggest any newly found closeness to the conceptuality of process theology. For one thing, despite modifications, the essentially dialectical character of his early eschatology survives: the process of life and resurrection runs counter to the history of transience and death.) Within this eschatological process, Jesus is who he becomes in his trinitarian relationships to God the Father and the Holy Spirit, and also in his social relationships with other people and with nature. Hence Moltmann can also call his new paradigm 'an emphatically social christology' (WJC 71). In each stage of his way Jesus is who he is not merely as divine person or as private human person, but in solidarity with or representation of others. This, of course, creates Christology's essential connexion with soteriology.

Finally, in this account of the general character of Moltmann's Christology, we should notice one further implication of the metaphor of the 'way' of Jesus Christ. It is

---

[2] Rather surprisingly, Moltmann thinks it a limitation of his treatment of Christology in *Theology of Hope* and *The Crucified God* that, although it gave an eschatological direction to Christology, it concentrated solely on the resurrection and the cross and was not eschatological enough (WJC 3–4).

a way on which those who believe in him follow him, i.e. it is also an ethical category. Moltmann attempts to bring out the unity of Christology and 'Christopraxis', rejecting any over-simplified derivation of praxis from theory or theory from praxis, but affirming a complex intertwining of the two. Christ is perceived holistically, in a life of following his way, in community with him, in the church, in its discipleship in the world: 'Christology emerges from Christian living and leads into Christian living' (WJC 43). Each chapter therefore draws out, as part of the soteriological relevance of Christology, the implications for the Christian way of life and christologically grounded ethics.

Only some aspects of the very rich discussions in chapters III–VII can be mentioned here. Chapter III is notable for its relatively full treatment of the earthly ministry of Jesus, often more or less completely neglected in Christology. The overall framework Moltmann uses for this discussion is a Spirit-Christology. He sees this not as an alternative to incar-national Christology nor as leading to a degree Christology (the dangers which the tradition has seen in Spirit-Christology): Jesus is the unique bearer of the Spirit who mediates his unique sonship to the Father. But Moltmann's use of Spirit-Christology enables him to see Jesus' personal identity not in isolation but as formed and discovered in relationships, and not as fixed from eternity but as coming to be in his history (which is still open to the future). Primarily Jesus is who he is in relationship, mediated by the Spirit, to the Father he called Abba, and his history is divine trinitarian history. (The background to this lies in Moltmann's treatment of the changing trinitarian relationships in history in *The Trinity and the Kingdom of God*.) But he is also who he is in relationship with other people. In line with Moltmann's key concept of reciprocity in relationship, and in distinction from the common, but surely docetic, impression of a self-sufficient Jesus who gives himself to but does not himself need others, Moltmann stresses Jesus' social personhood: even in the salvific acts of his ministry he is dependent on others as much as they are dependent on him. Hopefully the chapter also stresses the priority of God's grace sufficiently to head off the expected accusation of Pelagianism (WJC 96).

Eschewing two-natures Christology in favour of Jesus' being-in-relation and being-in-history, Moltmann seems to see Jesus as a human being whose relationship to the Father in the Spirit makes him the unique Son of God. Presumably it is this relationship which constitutes Jesus' identity with the eternal Son, but Moltmann offers only the merest hint of this (WJC 143). At this point Moltmann's focus on pneumatological Christology evidently enables him to side-step a classic christological issue; it is less clear that his own trinitarian theology ought to allow him to evade it.

However, the understanding of Jesus' person in this chapter does very effectively cohere with the exposition of Jesus' mission to proclaim and to anticipate the kingdom of God. Criticizing the moralism that results from identifying the kingdom solely with God's present rule, Moltmann insists that it is also the coming new creation, whose character as holistic salvation – for body and soul, individual and community, humanity and nature – forms a major emphasis of the book. This holistic salvation was anticipated in Jesus' healings and exorcisms, whose bodily and cosmic character points to the new creation of all things. In this treatment of Jesus' miracles as also in the more familiar (to readers of Moltmann) material on Jesus' partisanship for the poor the soteriological agenda set by our contemporary context is certainly in view, but this is even more obvious in the treatment of Jesus' ethical teaching.

If it is unusual for a Christology to pay detailed attention to Jesus' earthly ministry, it is even more unusual for it to focus especially on his ethical teaching, as Moltmann does in this chapter. This is the culmination of a tendency in Moltmann's recent work towards seeing Christian ethics as Christian discipleship in the distinctive way of life that Jesus practised and taught. It amounts to extending the Reformation principle of *solus Christus* from faith in Christ to discipleship of Christ in the whole of life, as the Anabaptists did, and results in Moltmann's new principle of the unity of Christology and Christopraxis. The distinctively Christian ethic is to be lived primarily by the Christian community – not in sectarian withdrawal, but as a 'contrast society' which lives out Jesus' programme of social and ecological reform as an alternative to the world's present system and 'through its existence calls in question the systems of violence and injustice' (WJC 122). It is not an ethic purely for Christians, but is recommended to the world through being lived in Christian community. As contemporary political, social and economic systems are bringing the world to apocalyptic disaster, Jesus' alternative programme, so far from appearing unrealistic, looks increasingly like the only reasonable alternative. Prominent in Moltmann's account of this alternative are the principles of non-violent action and creative love of enemies: 'the centre of the Sermon on the Mount is the liberation from violence' (WJC 127). The theme of violence runs through the whole book. Since it includes violence towards nature and is inseparable from injustice, it is the common denominator in the three contemporary crises. So, in a statement he admits to be unusual by comparison with the traditional doctrine of sin and grace, Moltmann claims 'that humanity's real sin is the violence that leads to death; and that consequently humanity's salvation is to be found in the peace that serves our common life' (WJC 127).

In chapter IV ('The Apocalyptic Sufferings of Christ') and chapter V ('The Eschatological Resurrection of Christ') Moltmann takes up the ideas at the heart of his early theology (in *Theology of Hope* and *The Crucified God*), which depended on seeing the cross and resurrection as the eschatological transition from the old to the new creation. He develops that eschatological perspective in two ways here. First, he sets the cross of Christ within the Jewish apocalyptic expectation of unprecedented suffering in the end-time, which, as the birth-pangs of the new creation, bring to an end the old era and bring to birth the new. Since Jesus' resurrection was the anticipation of the new creation, his passion was a vicarious suffering of the end-time sufferings. In the nuclear and ecological end-time in which we now live – which Moltmann describes as 'the great apocalyptic dying, death of all things' (WJC 157) – this apocalyptic perspective can be re-appropriated and the sufferings of Christ related inclusively and vicariously to the victims of violence and injustice in our own time. But secondly, Moltmann now sees both the end-time sufferings and the new creation of all things as embracing nature as well as humanity. Christ dies in solidarity with victimized nature and rises in anticipation of the new creation of all creatures. The relation of Christ's resurrection to nature is developed at some length.

This might suggest that it is only from the violence inflicted on nature by human beings, resulting in the contemporary threat of ecological death, that Christ's death and resurrection redeems nature. In fact, Moltmann claims that just as Christ died in solidarity with all human beings, to redeem them from death, so he dies the death of all the living, in solidarity with all living things that die. All death in nature Moltmann regards not as natural, but as a tragic destiny, whose reversal at the end is anticipated in Christ's resurrection. At this point one may want to ask questions. Does death really have the same significance for every kind of creature? For elephants, who mourn their dead, it is a tragic destiny, as it is for us. But for this year's marigolds, which die in the annual cycle of death and new life that will produce next year's marigolds, is death tragic? Need we mourn the individual marigold as we certainly would the species, should it become extinct? The apparent implication of Moltmann's view that every individual creature that has ever lived – every marigold, every termite, every smallpox virus – will be resurrected in the new creation may seem bizarre, but this problem is alleviated by the novel concept of resurrection which Moltmann introduces in this book. It is that the whole of *history* (the history of nature and human beings) will be redeemed from evil and death and transformed in the eschatological eternity in which all its times will be simultaneous. So not simply creatures in what they have become in their temporal history, but all creatures as they are diachronically in the process of their history and in all their temporal relationships with other creatures, will be resurrected and transfigured in eternity.

Thus nothing transient is lost, except transience itself. However, this concept itself raises so many problems that we must suspend judgment until the detailed explanation it will presumably receive in the projected fifth volume of the series, on eschatology.

The notion of Christ's solidarity with all mortal creatures in his death and resurrection has far-reaching ethical implications:

> If Christ has died not merely for the reconciliation of human beings, but for the reconciliation of all other creatures too, then every created being enjoys infinite value in God's sight, and has its own right to live. . . . If according to the Christian view the uninfringeable dignity of human beings is based on the fact that 'Christ died for them', then this must also be said of the dignity of other living things. And it is this that provides the foundation for an all-embracing reverence for life (WJC 256, cf. 307–8).

This valuation of all life should satisfy the very darkest greens, but its problem is that it provides no basis for ethical distinctions – between, say, murdering human beings, slaughtering animals with callous cruelty, killing slugs to protect my vegetables, pulling up weeds in my garden or pulling up vegetables to eat. All these are creatures of infinite value with their own right to live. It is notable that when Moltmann turns to the practical matter of the need to codify the rights of nature he stops far short of the notion that each individual plant and animal has the right to live (WJC 307–12). But his theological basis is plainly inadequate for the ethical distinctions that need to be made. By founding the value of all creatures on Christ's solidarity in death with all living creatures, it makes death as such an undifferentiated evil in the face of which all creatures have the right to life. Finally, one might also wonder whether Moltmann's understanding of cosmic redemption does not introduce by the back door the anthropocentric view of creation he has been at pains to reject. For why is it in the human being Jesus Christ that God's solidarity with all other creatures is expressed and their redemption accomplished? Perhaps the more modest claim that Christ redeems, not nature as such but the human relationship to nature, can provide the cosmic dimension to Christology and soteriology which the ecological crisis certainly demands without the problems Moltmann encounters. But this whole area of theological thinking is so unexplored that one must be grateful for Moltmann's pioneering exploration as a stimulus to further thought and debate.

11

Mysticism

I

A common criticism of Moltmann's early theology, especially *Theology of Hope*, was that it denied present experience of God. For example, noting that for Moltmann the word 'epiphany' is a bad word, used to characterize a pattern of religious thought which he rejects, John Macquarrie wrote:

> An entire tradition of Christian theology and spirituality, centring on what John Baillie called 'the sense of the presence of God', is thus summarily dismissed. With me, let me confess, 'epiphany' is a good word. If there were no present epiphanies of God among the ambiguities of the world, how could we have any beliefs about his actions in the past?[1]

In the light of Moltmann's sharp distinction between epiphany religion and the biblical religion of promise, and his central claim in *Theology of Hope* that God reveals himself not in direct self-revelation but in his promises for the future, this interpretation of Moltmann's thought is understandable. Moltmann could be understood as continuing the Barthian disjunction between revelation and experience,[2] interpreting the divine word of revelation consistently as promise for the future but still denying to a theology of

---

[1] J. Macquarrie, *Thinking about God* (London: SCM Press, 1975), p. 230; cf. Macquarrie in F. Herzog ed., *The Future of Hope: Theology as Eschatology* (New York: Herder & Herder, 1970), p. 123.

[2] Cf. G. J. Dorrien, *Reconstructing the Common Good: Theology and the Social Order* (New York : Orbis, 1990), p. 96. For Moltmann's indebtedness to Barth in his theology of hope, see M. D. Meeks, *Origins of the Theology of Hope* (Philadelphia: Fortress, 1974), pp. 16–19; R. Bauckham, *Moltmann: Messianic Theology in the Making* (Basingstoke: Marshall Pickering, 1987), p. 5.

revelation, christologically based on the word of God, any possible grounding in human experience. Moltmann's frequent insistence that the word of promise contradicts present experience of the world could only confirm this impression.

To this interpretation of Moltmann's early work, Moltmann's attention to experience in his latest major work, *The Spirit of Life*, is in striking contrast. Here Moltmann rejects the Barthian antithesis between revelation and experience:

> I cannot see that there is any fundamental alternative between God's revelation to human beings, and human experience of God. How is a man or woman supposed to be able to talk about God if God does not reveal himself? How are men and women supposed to be able to talk about a God of whom there is no human experience? (SL 6)

He therefore begins this book on pneumatology 'with the personal and shared *experience of the Spirit*, instead of with the objective word of the proclamation, and the spiritual institutions of the church' (SL 17), not thereby intending such a theology of experience to be an alternative to a theology of revelation, but a complementary approach, which has the advantage of being 'pre-eminently lay theology', whereas 'theology of revelation is church theology, a theology for pastors and priests' (SL 17).

At first sight this looks like the kind of *volte face* of which critics have often been quick to accuse Moltmann. But we should be very cautious of jumping to such a conclusion. Apparent major changes of direction in Moltmann usually turn out, on closer study of his work, to be deeply rooted in an essentially continuous development of his thought.[3] Another reaction might be to wonder whether, despite Moltmann's attempt to define his position by emphatic contrast with Barth's (SL 6–7) – an attempt which is characteristic of Moltmann's later work and which frequently results in a one-sided highlighting of differences and neglecting of similarities – Moltmann's pneumatology in *The*

---

[3] With reference to Moltmann's work up to 1979, I argued this in my *Moltmann: Messianic Theology in the Making*.

Spirit of Life is so completely different from Barth's basic intention in *both* resisting what he saw as the anthropological reduction in nineteenth-century Liberal Protestantism and twentieth-century Existentialist theology (along with Roman Catholicism) *and also* doing justice to their legitimate concerns and insights by means of a pneumatological interpretation.[4] In any case, it is extremely significant that at this point, in drawing the distinction between Barth's approach and his own, Moltmann reverts to the fundamental distinction he made in *Theology of Hope*. To validate his pneumatological theology of experience he appeals to the eschatological perspective which was the principle of his divergence from Barth in *Theology of Hope*:

> The new foundation of the eschatology which takes its bearings from the future by way of the 'theology of hope', does away with the Platonic time-eternity pattern which Barth and his brother, the philosopher Heinrich Barth, maintained in 1930. The new approach now develops eschatology as the horizon of expectation for the historical experience of the divine Spirit (SL 7).

In other words, Moltmann associates precisely Barth's adherence to the epiphanic pattern of religious thought, with its time-eternity dualism,[5] with his inability to admit real experience of the Spirit, while it is precisely the theology of

---

[4] See especially P. J. Rosato, *The Spirit as Lord: The Pneumatology of Karl Barth* (Edinburgh: T. & T. Clark, 1981), chapters 1–2. In 1968, at the end of his life, Barth 'told of his dream . . . that someone, and perhaps a whole age, might be allowed to develop a "theology of the Holy Spirit", a "theology which now I can only envisage from afar, as Moses once looked on the promised land". He was thinking of a theology which, unlike his own, was not written from the dominant perspective of Christology, but from that of pneumatology, and in which the concerns of the theology of the eighteenth and nineteenth centuries were not so much repeated and continued as understood and developed further' (E. Busch, *Karl Barth: His Life from Letters and Autobiographical Texts* [London: SCM Press, 1977], p. 494). An interpretation of Moltmann's work which stressed his continuities with Barth could see his work, in its development from a strongly christological focus in his early work to a complementary pneumatological focus in his later work and from being a theology of the word of God to a complementary stress on experience of God, as appropriating this dream of Barth's and realizing it in a certain sense. And cf. SL 1.

[5] This accusation goes back to TH 39–40, 50–8. Significantly, in both cases, it is Barth's early work which is the focus of attack.

hope which makes possible a theology of experience which does not reduce God to human experience but finds God immanent in human experience. This should encourage us to look again at the alleged exclusion of experience of God from Moltmann's theology of promise in *Theology of Hope*.

II

Moltmann's early theology was not intended to deny experience of God, but to characterize and to situate the Christian experience of God within the history that leads from the divine promise to its fulfilment in the kingdom of God. This is the function of his typological contrast, which is basic to his thinking in *Theology of Hope*, between epiphany religions and the biblical religion of promise. The crucial feature of epiphany religion, in this typology, is that it is anti-historical: it finds religious meaning not in historical change but in contact with changeless eternity. In *Theology of Hope* Moltmann aligns both nature religions, such as those of ancient Canaan, and Greek philosophy, from Parmenides onwards, with this type of religious thought and experience. The experience of the divine in nature religions corresponds to the ever-recurring cycle of the seasons: the gods 'appear' in the seasonal festivities and guarantee 'the eternal return' in which life is renewed through contact with primal time. Thus the stability of a recurring order is protected against the meaningless chaos of history. The appearance of the divine, in such a context, Moltmann calls 'the epiphany of the eternal present'. Its purpose is to grant correspondence with and participation in the timeless world of the divine. Essentially continuous with such nature religions was the Greek philosophical view of reality, according to which the essence of things is the eternal present of being behind the transitory appearance of history (EH 17). In both cases, history is meaningless transience, while the true divine reality in contact with which people seek their true reality is a timeless presence. Moltmann can therefore use this typology both in his interpretation of Old Testament theology (TH chapter 2), where he characterizes the Israelite faith in the

God of promise by distinguishing it from the epiphanic religions of its context in Canaan, and in his critical account of modern theologies of revelation (TH chapter 1), where he finds, again and again, theological equivalents of epiphany religion, i.e. theologies which interpret eschatology with reference to the eternal in the present, rather than with reference to the temporal future. This notion of a non-temporal manifestation of the eternal in the present Moltmann sees as a continuing influence of Greek philosophical thought on Christian theology. It is a way of thinking that goes back to Plato and ultimately to Parmenides (TH 28–30).[6] Wherever 'the epiphany of the eternal present' is found, we are in the presence of 'the God of Parmenides' rather than 'the God of the exodus and the resurrection' (TH 84, cf. TH 28–31, 58, 141).

The point is: 'The eternal present of being extinguishes the experience of history' (GC 111). By contrast, the Old Testament religion of promise, which takes messianic form in relation to the history of Jesus Christ in the New Testament, is intimately related to the history which God's promises for the future set in motion towards its eschatological goal in his kingdom. Instead of abstracting God from history, it involves God in history. Instead of abstracting believers from history and the historical world, it involves them in history and the world. Instead of the dualism of time and eternity there is the apocalyptic dualism between the present and the future. The promise reveals that the present is not yet the kingdom of God, the promise contradicts present reality, but it also promises the coming transformation of the world into the kingdom of God, sets that process of transformation already underway, and involves believers in it.[7] The consequence of Moltmann's theology of hope for experience of God is not therefore to deny experience of God, but to characterize Christian experience of God as that kind of experience of God which lives out of his promises for the future (especially the cross and

---

[6] For a more precise discussion of Parmenides, see GC 110–11.

[7] For detailed exposition, see Bauckham, *Moltmann: Messianic Theology in the Making*, chapter 2.

resurrection of Jesus as the definitive event of universal divine promise) and towards the eschatological kingdom. Experience of the God of Parmenides is experience of timeless eternity and so abstracts from historical and this-worldly reality. Experience of the God of the exodus and resurrection involves believers in the world whose future is opened up by the promise of God.

Admittedly, the overwhelming emphasis of *Theology of Hope* and Moltmann's earliest work is on the 'not yet' of eschatological hope. Lest the critical impact of Christian hope, in exposing the negativities of the world as it is by contrast with what is promised, be undermined, talk of the *presence* of God tends to be reserved for the new creation in which God will indwell the world from which evil and suffering have been removed. But the potential for speaking of the experience of the presence of God in both the contradictions of life in hope and the anticipations of the kingdom in the present is implicit in the structure of Moltmann's early theology. What made it increasingly explicit, however, was Moltmann's developing understanding of God's involvement in the history of the world, in *The Crucified God* and *The Church in the Power of the Spirit*. More and more Moltmann conceived God as moving the world towards its eschatological transformation, not simply by acting on it in his word of promise, but by his passionate and suffering loving involvement in it – in the incarnation and the cross (CG) and in the presence and power of the Spirit (CPS). There is no need to trace these developments in his theology in detail here, but it is especially important in the present discussion to recall that Moltmann's pneumatology developed in this context. The Spirit mediates historically between the messianic history of Jesus and the coming kingdom. If experience of God is related, as in Christian theology it must be, to pneumatology, then it is *historical* experience of God, which experiences God in his trinitarian history with the world, not in his timeless eternity unrelated to the world.

This is precisely what Moltmann says in *The Spirit of Life*. Explaining his intention, which we have already quoted, to begin with experience of the Spirit, he continues:

I am also choosing the phrase 'experience of the Spirit' as a way of understanding appropriately the intermediate state of every *historical experience* between remembered past and expected future. The experience, life and fellowship of God's Spirit come into being when Christ is made present and when the new creation of all things is anticipated. These things are resonances of Christ, and a prelude to the kingdom of God. The experience of the Spirit is never without the remembrance of Christ, and never without the expectation of his future. But in the harmony between this expectation and this remembrance, experience of the Spirit acquires a stature and a dignity of its own, and so entirely without substitute, that it is rightly called *experience of God*. In this sense pneumatology presupposes christology, and prepares the way for eschatology (SL 17–18).[8]

Accordingly, he follows his theoretical chapter on experience (SL chapter 1) with two biblical theological chapters (SL chapters 2 and 3), called 'Historical Experience of the Spirit' and 'Trinitarian Experience of the Spirit', which discuss experience of the Spirit according to both Old and New Testaments. Here an emphasis on experience of God in the Spirit is thoroughly integrated into the eschatological-historical perspective established in *Theology of Hope* and the trinitarian-historical perspective established in subsequent books. These chapters – and much of the rest of the book – set out an understanding of experience of God which is entirely consistent with the broad contours of Moltmann's theology as they were adumbrated in *Theology of Hope* and developed thereafter.

III

It should therefore be clear that experience of God is not in the least foreign to Moltmann's theology, but integral to it.

---

[8] See also SL 151–2, where Moltmann discusses Barth's christological interpretation of regeneration and Otto Weber's eschatological interpretation, and comments: 'Both really evade the question about the *experience* of the Holy Spirit.' He goes on to argue that expectation is always accompanied by experience. These comments on Weber are especially significant in view of the influence of Weber, one of Moltmann's teachers in Göttingen, on Moltmann's early apprehension of the decisive significance of eschatology for the whole of theology (Meeks, *Origins of the Theology of Hope*, pp. 21–4).

His emphasis on it in his most recent pneumatological work develops a theme which was already deeply rooted in his theology. However, it does not follow that the ways in which experience of God has been understood in the dominant Christian traditions of spirituality and mysticism will be congenial to Moltmann's theological perspective. Although Moltmann's fundamental rejection of the epiphanic type of religious thought by no means, as we have seen, excludes experience of God's presence, it would seem to exclude much of the way in which such experience has been articulated in the Christian mystical tradition. Moltmann himself acknowledges this when, reverting in *The Spirit of Life* to the issue of characterizing Old Testament Israel's experience of God, the issue which had played such an important role in his *Theology of Hope,* Moltmann distinguishes historical experience of God – such as Israel's encounters with God in specific events which were remembered as past events and which generated hope for the future – from two non-historical types of experience of God. One is the cosmic experience of God in 'the eternal return of the same thing in the rhythms and cycles of nature'. The other is mystical experiences of God, in which 'time and hour are forgotten. In the eternal present of Being, life's remembrances and life's expectations vanish' (SL 52; other passages in which Moltmann associates the epiphany of the eternal present with 'mysticism' are TH 30; WJC 318; SL 18; cf. SL 90).

To put schematically the difference between Moltmann's understanding of Christian experience of God and that of the mystical tradition, one might say that in the latter God is experienced in turning inward and upward, while for Moltmann God is experienced in turning outward and forward. The tradition sought God in abstraction from the world – turning away from the exterior world into the interior world of the spirit, and in the same movement abstracting from the transitory world of historical experience in order to be united with God in his timeless eternity. Moltmann's theology, by understanding the history of this temporal, physical world as taking place in God's own history of involvement with it, seeks God in involvement with this world with which God is involved and on the way to its eschatological future in which it will be perfected in the presence of God's glory. This schematic opposition has enough truth in it – and enough support in Moltmann's own statements – to make it surprising that it is possible to trace a tentative and guarded, but real and increasing appreciation of the mystical tradition in Moltmann's work. Explicit references to the mystical tradition or to the great Christian mystics and spiritual writers by name are not common in Moltmann's work, and his acquaintance with and indebtedness to this body of Christian religious literature can certainly not be compared with his debt to the Reformers or the Scholastics or even the Jewish mystical tradition (to which he refers more often and more consistently positively than to the Christian mystical tradition). But the evidence of a real attempt to appreciate and to find a place in his theology for the insights of the Christian mystics is nevertheless unmistakable. This attempt has been possible, on the one hand, because the schematic distinction just made by no means does justice to the rich tradition of mystical experience and theology. But it has also been possible, on the other hand, because, although Moltmann's theology necessarily makes some sharp conceptual distinctions (such as that between epiphany religion and religion of promise) and opts for one side of such distinctions in order to establish its perspectives, nevertheless it is frequently able to go on to appropriate in its own way, from its own perspective, much that one might have thought excluded and left aside on the other side of the distinction. This kind of movement of distinction and reappropriation is not peculiar to Moltmann; it can be observed in the work of many great theologians. It is not necessarily a sign of inconsistent thinking – though it is likely to throw up at least superficial inconsistencies in detailed statements – but is characteristic of attempts to think both systematically and comprehensively, to discriminate without dismissing.

We shall understand Moltmann's attitude to the mystical tradition better if we first survey some features of Moltmann's own developing account of Christian experience of God before turning to his explicit interaction with the mystics.

IV

Moltmann has written eloquently, a number of times, of the experience of God from which his own Christian faith and, ultimately, his theology sprang (e.g. EH 85; EG 7–9; HTG 166).[9] No one who knows of this autobiographical root of Moltmann's theology could be content with the idea that experience of God is not important in his theology. He sees this experience, when he was a prisoner of war in Scotland after the end of the Second World War, as one of those elemental experiences of life, which never become merely past, but continue to shape one's life throughout life as one continually reinterprets them (EG 9; cf. SL 20–1).[10] Common to Moltmann's accounts of this experience of God's presence are the elements of suffering and hope – the experience of God's fellowship in suffering and the experience of God as the power of hope in suffering. It is easy to identify here the experiential roots of his theology of the cross and his theology of hope and of the intimate relationship between the two (which was by no means absent from *Theology of Hope*, even though for most readers it became clear only when re-reading *Theology of Hope* in the light of *The Crucified God*). Indeed, the echoes of this experience and his continuing reflection on it still reverberate in his most recent work (e.g. SL 75–6, where the reflections on freedom as the negation of the negative in the experience of prisoners should be read in conjunction with EG 7 on his own experience in the prison camp; and SL 104–5).

It is significant that Moltmann never recounts this experience so as to imply that he made, at the time, an explicit connexion between it and the history of Jesus Christ on which his later theological reflections on suffering and hope were based. He does not say that the divine fellowship in suffering he experienced he knew to be that of the crucified Christ or that the hope he was given was that messianic,

[9] See also Moltmann's foreword to Meeks, *Origins of the Theology of Hope*, pp. x–xi.

[10] The language in SL 20–21 is general, but echoes the way he reflects on his experience as a prisoner of war in EG 9.

eschatological hope which arises from the resurrection of Christ. Nevertheless, the experience as he describes it has the structure of that historical experience of God within the trinitarian history of God that he develops in his theology. The latter makes explicit that such experience is experience of our own history with Jesus Christ's history (cf. EG 3). It comes to self-understanding and self-expression as experience that lives between remembrance and hope, between remembered past and expected future, between, specifically, the remembrance of Christ and the expectation of his future (EG 4; SL 17). Located thus between the past history of Jesus Christ and the expectation of the messianic kingdom which arises from that history, it is experience of the Spirit who mediates the two and it is characterized by the fellowship of the crucified Christ and the hope of the coming of the kingdom. Moltmann continually recurs to these twin characteristics of Christian experience of God.

They characterize Christian experience of God as participation in God's trinitarian history with the world and so not as flight from the world but as suffering solidarity with the world for the sake of its future. The fellowship of Christ's sufferings means not only the experience by those who suffer of God's suffering presence with them through his trinitarian suffering in the event of the cross; it also means that Christians should themselves enter into loving solidarity with those who suffer, thereby participating in God's fellowsuffering with the suffering (e.g. CPS 288).

There is an instructive passage (CPS 282–8; repeated in a more popular form in OC 40–9) in which Moltmann discusses three 'creative tensions' in the Christian lifestyle, by which he means tensions between two poles which are often polarized as alternatives but should be realized as creative tensions in which to live. They are: prayer and faithfulness to the earth, contemplation and political struggle, transcendental religion and the religion of solidarity. Significantly, it is when these tensions are understood within the trinitarian history of God, i.e. in terms of historical experience of God taking place in the Spirit's historical and eschatological mission, between remembrance of Christ and expectation of his kingdom, that they can be appreciated as creative tensions rather than polarized alternatives.

The discussion of the first of the tensions makes much reference to Bonhoeffer, to whom Moltmann originally owed something of his vision of a worldly spirituality, rejecting the alternative of a godless this-worldliness or an other-worldly piety. The quotation from Bonhoeffer is a favourite of Moltmann's: 'Only the man who loves the earth and God as a single unity can believe in the kingdom of God' (CPS 284). Moltmann's interpretation, while certainly not a distortion of Bonhoeffer, takes a direction thoroughly characteristic of Moltmann himself:

> Bonhoeffer's notion of the profound this-worldliness of the Christian life takes its whole colouring from the present actualization of the crucified and risen Liberator and has as little to do with bourgeois secularization as it has with a religious moderation of the feelings. The more intensely a man loves the earth, the more strongly he feels the injustice done to it, its fatal self-destruction and the way it is forsaken, and the more spontaneously he laments with the suffering and cries out with the wounded – which is to say prays, if praying means crying out to God the lament of the people, the cry of the oppressed and the hunger of those who hope. The more spontaneous and worldly a man's prayer is in this sense, the more deeply he is drawn into the people's suffering and will participate in it as God's suffering over the world. Praying in the Spirit and interest in life drive one another on, *if both are concentrated on the crucified Christ and his messianic kingdom* (CPS 284 [italics mine]).[11]

In the discussion of the second tension, Moltmann develops a point which he will repeat on later occasions: that contemplation and praxis are complementary: 'Just as meditation cannot be a flight from action, so, conversely, action cannot be a flight from meditation. . . . Meditation and liberating practice in the different spheres of life complement one another and deepen one another mutually' (CPS 285–6). This is because Christian contemplation is 'not meditation without any object' but 'at heart *meditatio crucis*'. Since

---

[11] Compare this treatment of prayer with that in SL 76–7, which makes a complementary point about the cries of the suffering themselves as the cries of the indwelling Spirit.

meditation leads to that participatory knowledge in which the knower is transformed, meditation on the passion of Christ draws Christians into Christ's history, turns them not only to Christ but to those for whom Christ died and focuses their life on God's messianic intention for the kingdom of God (CPS 285; cf. EG 62; TKG 8; SL 203). Moreover, by situating them within God's trinitarian history, it gives them the knowledge of who they are and where they belong without which praxis is futile activism:

> In meditating on the history of Christ and in becoming conscious, in the Spirit, of our own history in relation to this history of Christ, we discover ourselves and our tasks in the process of this open history. This can only be the reverse side of the practical life in which we try to realize ourselves and our destiny in the messianic history of God's dealings with the world (CPS 286).

In this way activity requires meditation and meditation liberates for authentic praxis.

The necessary complementarity of praxis and contemplation Moltmann later developed as a major point about theological methodology and types of knowing (TKG 5–9). An exclusive emphasis on praxis, as the end to which all theological reflection is only the means, assimilates theology to the pragmatic thinking of the modern world in which the knowing subject masters its object in order to dominate it. Moltmann insists, by contrast, on the necessity, in theology, of the participatory knowledge – characteristic of meditation, contemplation and doxology – in which the knower opens himself or herself to the other in receptivity, love and wonder, perceives himself or herself in mutual relationship with the other, and so can be transformed (TKG 8–9; cf. TKG 5; OC 44–5; EG 57–9; GC 32; CJF 60–1; SL 73, 199–201). It is obvious how this coheres with his increasing theoretical attention to experience of God. It is also clear how it generates sympathy not only with the more contemplative strands in traditional theology – in the Fathers, for example[12] – but also with mysticism itself.

[12] In TKG it enables Moltmann to appreciate – even rather uncritically! – the doxological character of patristic trinitarian theology, which a purely praxis-orientated theology would regard as merely speculative.

This sympathy began to surface, at a surprisingly early date (1971), in the context of a discussion of 'the vicious circle of the destruction of nature' (EH 184), a concern which appeared in Moltmann's work long before it became an inescapable contemporary theme. He was already arguing that the 'Western values of conquest and control of nature must give way to the ancient values of the joy of living and reverence for the creation', and hazarded

> the conjecture that, if we reorient our society's life-values, we will find a great deal of relevance in the old, meditative, doxological forms of faith and life practised by the ancient church and the monks (EH 184).

By the time this theme is developed in Moltmann's account of mystical theology in *The Spirit of Life* (199–202, material which appeared earlier in EG 57–61) it is no longer a conjecture but a settled conviction utterly characteristic of Moltmann's thinking.

The third 'creative tension' needs no further discussion here, but a further point needs to be made about the concept of participation in the trinitarian history of God which undergirds Moltmann's whole treatment of these issues. We need to remember that Moltmann's development of the theological concept of the trinitarian history of God entailed the reciprocity of God and the world. God is affected by the world – in suffering and joy – as well as affecting the world. This means that experience of God is experience of God's experience – it is the genuinely intersubjective experience of persons in mutual relationship:

> If a person experiences in faith how God has experienced – and still experiences – him, for that person God is not the abstract origin of the world or the unknown source of his feeling of absolute dependency; he is *the living God*. He learns to know himself in the mirror of God's love, suffering and joy. In his experience of God he experiences – fragmentarily, indeed, and certainly 'in a glass, darkly' – something of God's own experience with him (TKG 4).

Although this may seem to be claiming a great deal, it is strictly necessary to, for example, Moltmann's understanding of the sufferer's experience of God's sympathetic fellow-suffering. To know God in suffering as the one who shares one's suffering in loving solidarity one must in some sense experience God's experience of one's suffering. This notion of experiencing God's experience gives depth also to Moltmann's regular insistence on the two sides of the church's experience – suffering with the suffering and over the injustices and unfreedom of the world and rejoicing in the Spirit's anticipations of the kingdom (e.g. SL 74–7).[13] These are experiences of the concrete realities of the world, but they are at the same time experiences of God's experience of those realities. Once more, for Moltmann it is through the most passionate involvement – in suffering and joy – in God's world that the God who is passionately involved in his world can be experienced.

With Moltmann's increasing sense of the mutual co-inherence of God and the world and of God's experience and human experience, such that in both the sufferings and the joys of human life we may experience God's experience of our experience, he has been inspired both by some of the Christian mystics and by the Jewish mystical notion of the divine Shekinah. As an example of discovering 'in one's own pain the pain of God' (WJC 180), he more than once cites Catherine of Sienna's cry, 'My God where were you when my heart was in darkness and the shadow of death?', and the answer she heard: 'My daughter, did you not feel it? I was in your heart' (HTG 29; WJC 180). And in a creative development of the Jewish understanding of the exile and home-coming of the Shekinah, he says: 'We are conscious of God's happiness in us, and are conscious of ourselves in God's bliss' (SL 50).

V

From what has been said in the last section, it will be apparent that the aspects of the Christian mystical tradition which Moltmann will find it easiest to integrate into his theology are those which focus on the history of Jesus,

---

[13] See, in detail, the section 'Suffering and Joy' in chapter 6 above.

meditation on his sufferings, identification with him in his sufferings, and experience of his fellowship in suffering, rather than those which aspire to union with God in abstraction from all historical and worldly reality. In an appreciative treatment of Teresa of Avila (TA), originally published in 1982,[14] he compared her 'mysticism of the cross' with Martin Luther's, finding that, despite differences, 'both lead away from the false route of transcendental mysticism and return to Christ himself, to his humanity, to the crucified God. For Christian mysticism is, in essence, a mysticism of the cross, of meditation on the Passion, of eucharistic experience' (TA 267–8).

Already in *The Crucified God* this theme received significant attention – in two forms. The section (II.3) entitled 'The Mysticism of the Cross' considers the devotional tradition, which flourished in the late middle ages, of devotion to the passion of Christ. Moltmann finds parallel forms of spirituality in Latin America (CG 47), in American black slave spirituals (CG 48) and generally in the Christianity of the poor. In this form of piety people find help in their own sorrows and sufferings through realizing the crucified Christ's identification with them:

> This mysticism of the passion has discovered a truth about Christ which ought not to be suppressed by being understood in a superficial way. It can be summed up by saying that suffering is overcome by suffering, and wounds healed by wounds. For the suffering in suffering is the lack of love, and the wounds in wounds are the abandonment, and the powerlessness in pain is unbelief. And therefore the suffering of abandonment is overcome by love. . . . Through his own abandonment by God, the crucified Christ brings God to those who are abandoned by God. Through his suffering he brings salvation to those who suffer. Through his death he brings eternal life to those who are dying. And therefore the tempted, rejected, suffering and dying Christ came to be the centre of the religion of the oppressed and the piety of the lost (CG 46–7).

---

[14] TA (1984) is the English translation of 'Die Wendung zur Christusmystik bei Teresa von Avila,' in W. Herbstrith (ed.), *Gott allein: Teresa von Avila heute* (Freiburg: Herder, 1982), pp. 184–208.

This 'mysticism of the passion' provides, in fact, a point of entry to the central soteriological theme of *The Crucified God*: God's identification on the cross with the godless and the godforsaken. It is, in a sense, the experiential side of this theme. It illustrates how God's presence in loving fellow-suffering with all who suffer has been experienced by those who through devotion to the crucified Christ find God with them in their sufferings. Moltmann is therefore at pains to show that, although the church has often abused this mysticism of the passion in order to justify suffering in the interests of those who profit from the sufferings of the poor (CG 49), this does not explain the liberating appeal of the crucified Christ to the poor and oppressed.

The late medieval passion mysticism offered a path to fellowship with God through meditation on the passion by which people made the sufferings of Christ their own and achieved a conformity of the soul with the crucified Christ (CG 45). While mentioning this aspect in his introduction to the section (CG II.3), Moltmann's attention in the section soon shifted to the way in which those who were already suffering sufficiently in their daily lives discovered, in passion mysticism, the solidarity of the suffering Christ with them. The aspect he finds valuable is not the contemplative imitation of Christ's sufferings, but the experience of God's suffering love for the forsaken. This 'Lutheran' preference, appropriate in a chapter whose climax is the discussion of Luther's *theologia crucis*, reappears in the lecture on Teresa and Luther (see especially TA 273–5), and indeed remains fundamental to Moltmann's work. The experience of God's gracious love, identifying with us where we are in suffering and alienation, has the primacy. Following Christ, finding fellowship with him through conformity to his sufferings, is consequent.[15]

However, when Moltmann discusses this active following of the crucified Christ, in the following section of *The Crucified God* (II.4: 'Following the Cross'), the models he

---

[15] Cf. SL 249: 'It is surprising how little the mediaeval "theology of love" [in considering our active love for God, for neighbour and for self] takes as its starting point God's love, and the human experience of being loved.'

approves are the apostle and the martyr, who in mission and
testimony to Christ in the world participated in the sufferings
of Christ (CG 56–8). The monastic and mystical movements
then changed the notion of following Christ, by responding
to his mission and suffering persecution, into that of imitat-
ing Christ by self-denial and meditative conformity to his
sufferings. On a tradition whose featured representatives are
Bonaventura, Eckhart, Tauler, Thomas à Kempis and
Ignatius Loyola (CG 59–60), the verdict appears to be: 'This
"mysticism of introversion", an internalization of the
following of Christ, can be considered a departure from the
practical, physical following of Christ' (CG 60). This verdict
has much to do with the thrust of Moltmann's theology
towards active discipleship of Christ in the world for the sake
of the coming kingdom. While this does not replace faith
with ethical activity, it makes following Christ in conformity
with his sufferings especially a matter of loving solidarity with
the marginalized and the oppressed (CG 62–3) and makes a
purely inward conformity with the cross suspect: 'to be
crucified with Christ is no longer a purely private and
spiritualized matter, but develops into a political theology of
the following of the crucified Christ' (CG 63).

Something of this evaluation survives, but is given a rather
different slant, in Moltmann's later treatment of the same
subject, in his essay on 'The Theology of Mystical Experience' (EG 55–80), first published in 1979[16] and later adapted
to form chapter X of *The Spirit of Life*. Here (in section 4:
'Mysticism and Martyrdom') Moltmann describes the mystical
experience of conformity to Christ's cross as primarily and
properly the experience of the martyr, who suffers for his
witness to the truth in public discipleship. Moltmann now
refers, appropriately, to the widespread contemporary
experience of martyrdom:

> God in the cell, God in the interrogation, God in the torture,
> God in the body's agony, God in the darkness that has
> descended on the soul – that is the political mysticism of the
> martyrs. It is not going too far to say that today prison is a very

[16] German original in *Gotteserfahrungen: Hoffnung, Angst, Mystik* (Munich:
Chr. Kaiser, 1979).

special place for the Christian experience of God. In prison, Christ is experienced in the Spirit. In prison the soul finds the *unio mystica* (SL 209; cf. the earlier version in EG 72–3).

Once again Moltmann points out that the mystical and devotional practices of spiritual participation in Christ's sufferings are a kind of substitute for the 'bodily and political discipleship' of the martyr, but he now allows them their place provided they do not become a total substitute:

> It is true that on the way from martyrdom to mysticism, com-munion with Christ is raised to another level; discipleship becomes imitation, the sufferings of humiliation become the virtue of humility, external persecution becomes inner assail-ment, and murder becomes 'spiritual death'. And yet the mysticism that is centred on Christ keeps alive the recollection of Christ's sufferings and the remembrance of the martyrs. This also means a firmly held hope for the future of Christ in history. If we understand the spiritual dying-with-Christ in this sense, then mysticism does not mean estrangement from action; it is a preparation for public discipleship . . .(SL 209; cf. EG 73).

The significance of this more positive evaluation of mystical *conformitas crucis* is that it is achieved by relating this kind of mysticism to the history that happens between the remem-brance of Christ and the expectation of his kingdom. If it is understood, not as a withdrawal from that history into a purely inward experience, but as positively related to discipleship of the crucified Christ in the world in which his kingdom will come, then its value can be understood.

However, at the end of this discussion Moltmann charac-teristically takes a further step: to the 'mysticism of everyday life' (EG 76; SL 211):

> The soul does not merely die with Christ and become 'cruciform' by way of spiritual exercises; nor does it do so only by public martyrdom. It already takes the form of the cross in the daily pains of life and in the sufferings of love. The history of the suffering and forsaken Christ is so open that the sufferings and anxieties of every loving man and woman find a place there (SL 210; cf EG 75).

Here and in the two paragraphs which follow we find a spirituality corresponding to the distinctive christological heart of Moltmann's theology. Because the cross of Christ makes all suffering God's suffering and the resurrection of Christ opens up a new future for all of reality, the whole of life can be lived with Christ, included in his history. We might ask whether in the expression 'the mysticism of everyday life'[17] the word 'mysticism' is not being misused. But Moltmann has defined his usage: 'By "mystical" we do not mean here special supernatural experiences. We mean the intensity of the experience of God in faith, so that in this sense we are talking about the deep dimension of every experience of faith' (SL 198).[18] There is a mysticism of everyday life because everyday life lived in love is not shallow: its experiences are experiences of the crucified and risen Christ. God is in its sufferings and joys, and they are in God.

VI

It is not surprising that the aspects of the Western mystical tradition of which Moltmann is most critical are those which stem from the Platonic influence in Christianity which, at its worst, he considers Gnostic. Throughout his theological work he has been at pains to repudiate the Platonic dualisms of time and eternity, and soul and body, which encourage withdrawal from the world, and to replace them with the apocalyptic dualism of past and future. Instead of the redemption of the soul from the body, the individual from society, and the human from nature, the authentic, biblical Christian expectation is for the redemption of all reality. In his earlier work the emphasis was on opposing a spirituality of withdrawal from the world with a worldly spirituality of political involvement in society for the sake of the coming kingdom. In his later work, he has increasingly added a stress

---

[17] The phrase may well be taken from Ernst Bloch, who in his discussion of 'the darkness of the lived moment' (the phrase explicitly quoted from Bloch in SL 211 = EG 80), refers to 'this inconspicuous everyday mysticism, the only kind which has remained, which is worthy of remaining' (*The Principle of Hope*, p. 295).

[18] These two sentences, not in the earlier version in EG 55, are added in SL. Though the idea of 'the mysticism of everyday life' is already in EG, Moltmann has slightly increased the emphasis on it in SL.

on the body and on non-human nature. Moreover, whereas in his earlier theology it was mainly eschatology which functioned to affirm the bodily, the social, the political and the rest of nature, by the time he wrote *The Spirit of Life* he had developed 'a holistic pneumatology'[19] in which the divine Spirit is the source of the life of all creation and the source of its new creation. The Spirit is not to be associated with the 'spiritual' (in the sense of non-bodily or non-sensuous), the inward, and the detachment of the human spirit from the body, society and nature in its search for God beyond this world. Rather the Spirit is the divine energy of life animating the whole creation, experienced in the body and in society and in nature, resisting the drive to death and destruction in this world, and, as the life of resurrection and new creation, bringing rebirth and renewal to all things (e.g. SL 8–9, 83–98). This understanding of the Spirit leads to a spirituality, a life in the Spirit, which Moltmann calls 'the new vitality of a love for life' (SL 9). Instead of 'the *spirituality* of a not-of-this-world life *in* God' (SL 83), which 'splits life into two, and quenches its vitality' (SL 84), he advocates a return to 'the *vitality* of a creative life *out of* God' (SL 83), which expresses itself above all in love for life: 'The full and unreserved "yes" to life, and the full and unreserved love for the living are the first experiences of God's Spirit' (SL 97).[20] Against all platonizing abstraction from bodily, social and natural life – the 'mysticism of the soul' (SL 94) – this holistic pneumatology requires 'the spirituality of the body', 'the spirituality of sociality or fellowship' (SL 94), and 'the spirituality of the earth' (SL 97). All these dimensions belong to 'the spirituality of life' which battles against 'the mysticism of death' (SL 97).

A result of this way of thinking is to associate the Western mystical tradition, from its roots in Augustinian theology,

[19] The German subtitle of *The Spirit of Life* is: *Eine ganzheitliche Pneumatologie.* Cf. also SL xiii; 37.

[20] Note the continuity between this theme of vitality and affirmation of life, so characteristic of *The Spirit of Life*, with Moltmann's earlier concern with 'the passion for life' (e.g. OC I) in the face of the 'apathy' of modern Western people. The latter was developed primarily christologically, the former is developed pneumatologically.

with the unfortunate influence of the platonizing dualisms of time and eternity, soul and body.[21] The current fashion for deploring Augustine's influence over Western theology sometimes leads to ridiculously summary dismissals of an immensely subtle and complex thinker. Moltmann does not make this mistake. His account of Augustine's understanding of the human desire for God and its fulfilment (SL 90–3) is not without appreciation for some elements of Augustine's thought. But the overall verdict is severe:

> The concentration of his theology on 'God and the soul' led to a devaluation of the body and nature, to a preference for inward, direct self-experience as a way to God, and to a neglect of sensuous experiences of sociality and nature (SL 90).

Moreover, his influence on the Western mystical tradition is required to take the blame for a great deal:

> this mysticism has also led to the repression of the body and to nature's subjection to the dominance of the human mind. It generated Western individualism, for which the values of the human person take precedence over the values of human sociality (SL 93).

As an historical account of the intellectual roots of these features of modernity this is of very dubious value. It vastly exaggerates the influence of mysticism on the general intellectual history of the West, and it commits an error which is oddly common in current attacks on modernity, i.e. it seeks the roots of modernity in medieval theology and bypasses the much more obvious importance of the Renaissance (whose Platonism was not derived from the mystical tradition) in exalting humanity over nature and originating the modern project of domination of nature. In so far as Western mysticism was otherworldly in orientation – one of

---

[21] But this does not entail, as it does in some writers, an undiscriminating rejection of all asceticism. Note SL 95–6: 'If from this standpoint [of the liberation of the body for its true health] we look back self-critically at traditional ascetic practices, such as fasting and meditation, we shall find that many of them are not mortifications hostile to the body at all. They are rather ways of freeing and releasing the body from its exploitation through work, and its nervous tensions.'

Moltmann's chief complaints – it is an implausible source of modern Western humanity's very worldly attempt to exploit the natural world for its very material benefit. Spiritual flight from the world through mysticism and mental domination of the world through technology are very different, and what they do have in common – a sense of the superiority of spirit/ mind over body/nature – is not sufficient to make a genealogy.

Moltmann's account here is useful not as history but as theological–mystical typology. The chapter (SL IV) which includes his critique of Augustine concludes with his own 'Answer' to Augustine's question 'What do I love when I love God?' Augustine himself *(Conf.* 10.6.8) answers this question by distinguishing God from everything physical and temporal in order to experience God in his inward self. Moltmann answers that when he loves God he loves all God's physical creation, for he loves God with all his senses in God's creation:

> For a long time I looked for you within myself, and crept into the shell of my soul. . . . But you were outside – outside myself – and enticed me out of the narrowness of my heart into the broad place of love for life. So I came out of myself and found my soul in my senses, and my own self in others (SL 98).

The typological contrast is very clear: is God found on 'the inward road' (cf. SL 92) or in the love for all of life in which God is present as its source? In the first version of his essay on 'The Theology of Mystical Experience' Moltmann himself had written: 'The longest journey is always the inward one' (EG 57). When he incorporated this essay into *The Spirit of Life,* he evidently recognized that this sentence was inconsistent with his use of the inward/outward image in that book. In its place he spoke of the journey of mystical experience as 'an experience not of the world beyond but of this one, the experience not of a spiritual life but of vital life in the midst of the world in which we live' (SL 199).

However, the contrast Moltmann sets up in his answer to Augustine's question is perhaps too simple. To recognize *God* in all of his creation, to find *God* in all experience, to love not merely the creation but God in it, requires a distinguishing of God *from* all things at the same time as his presence *in* all things is perceived. Moltmann touches on this issue in his section on 'The Theology of the Social Experience of God' (SL 248–67), in which he seeks to correct the inward-looking individualism of the mystical tradition with a developed spirituality of sociality.[22] The aim is 'to discover God's love *in* the love between human beings, and the love between human beings *in* God's love' (SL 248). But illuminating as the section is, it is more an analysis of forms of human loving relationship than an account of the way in which divine love can be discerned in human love. The need to distinguish the one from the other is acknowledged (SL 260: 'To find experiences of God *in* the experiences of love does not mean divinizing the experience of love. . . . To perceive the one *in* the other means being able to connect and to distinguish'),[23] but the point is not explored.

The mystical tradition frequently emphasizes the need for detachment from creatures (including the self) in order to love God for his own sake. Properly understood, this is not a matter of devaluing God's creation, but of learning to distinguish God from his creation. God, as the highest Good and the source of all value, must be loved uniquely, above all else. God would not be God if this were not so. In the end, he must be loved not for his gifts but for himself. But the aim of the process of detachment from creatures is not that they should not be loved, but that they should be loved rightly. Freed from the desire for God which, misdirected to the creatures, seeks from them what they can never give, they

[22] This section (XI.3) seems intended as a counterpart to chapter X ('Theology of Mystical Experience'). The latter deals largely with the teaching of the Western mystical tradition. Moltmann has placed it in Part 2 of the book, because that Part provides Moltmann's version of the traditional Protestant *ordo salutis*, which traditionally featured the mystical union as one of its topics (SL 81; cf. TA 268). Part 2 follows the tradition in dealing with the process of salvation rather individualistically, but breaks out of this in chapter IX. So it is not clear why chapter XI is excluded from Part 2 and made one of the two chapters of Part 3. Its place in the otherwise fairly clear structure of the book is obscure.

[23] Cf. also SL 280: 'Human love and divine love are not identical, but the one can happen and confront us in the other.'

may be loved appropriately, precisely as creatures, whose value derives from and reflects their Creator. Even if the tradition does not always draw this conclusion, 'detachment' from creatures can be seen as the way in which it becomes possible to love them in God and to love God in them.

Moltmann's attitude to this Augustinian-mystical way of relating the love of God and the love of creatures seems highly ambivalent (see SL 91–2, 206–8, 248–9). Especially interesting is the way that it is treated in the essay on 'The Theology of Mystical Experience' (EG 55–80 = SL X). In the earlier version of this essay, the process of detachment from the world and the self in order to love God for his own sake is expounded, apparently sympathetically, as the way to the mystical union itself, according to the mystics (EG 68–71), though the account gives prominence to the extreme version of the tradition to be found in Meister Eckhart. But the section ends:

> The road from contemplation to the mystical moment leads (as Eckhart makes plain) to the abolition of man's likeness to God for God's sake, and ultimately to the abolition of God for God's sake. Then the soul has found its way home; then love has found bliss; then passion ends in infinite enjoyment; then like is with like. But is this really the goal of union with Christ? I believe not. I believe we must look in a completely different direction and take an entirely different path (EG 71).

There follows the section we have already discussed (in section V above) on martyrdom, passion mysticism and the mysticism of everyday life. Moltmann seems to be saying that this – the way of union with the crucified and risen Christ, whether in the extremes of suffering discipleship or in the 'secret mysticism' and 'quiet martyrdom' of everyday life – is the true way to the true mystical union, rather than the path of transcendental detachment. So of the martyr he says: 'In prison the soul finds the *unio mystica*' (EG 72–3); and the mysticism of everyday life he says is probably 'the profoundest mysticism of all' (EG 76). This coheres well with his lecture on Teresa of Avila and Luther, where he contrasts 'the false route of transcendental mysticism', rejected by both, with the truly Christian mysticism that is 'in essence, a mysticism of the cross' (TA 267–8). In other words, when he wrote the first version of 'The Theology of Mystical Experience', Moltmann apparently saw in the mystical path of detachment from creatures in order to love God alone for his own sake a route of abstraction from worldly reality, which led in 'a completely different direction' from that involvement with God in God's own passionate involvement in the world which is participation in the history of Jesus Christ.

In *The Spirit of Life*, where a slightly adapted version of the essay on 'The Theology of Mystical Experience' is incorporated as chapter X of the book, these two sections are substantially reproduced, but, remarkably, the negative evaluation of the path from contemplation to the mystical moment disappears. The last three sentences of the quotation above (EG 71: 'But is this really union with Christ? I believe not. I believe we must look in a completely different direction and take an entirely different path') are omitted. Nothing is put in their place. Nothing now explains the relation between these two sections, which seem now to constitute a sequence, where before they were alternative routes to the mystical union. The result is somewhat incoherent, but the reason for the change can be discerned. By the time he wrote *The Spirit of Life*, Moltmann had come to a very positive view of the experience of 'timeless' mystical ecstasy in which God is loved and worshipped purely for his own sake and in himself.[24] We consider this development in the next section.

VII

Probably the most remarkable instance of Moltmann's subsequent appropriation for his own theological use of a concept he had previously repudiated is the idea of the epiphany of the eternal present. As we saw (in section II above) Moltmann established his eschatological approach to

---

[24] Note that the sentences, 'In moments such as these the experience of God becomes so intensive that there is no more remembrance and no more expectation. God is pure present' (SL 206), are an addition to the earlier text found in EG 68.

theology by contrasting, as opposed types of religion, the epiphany of the eternal present and the biblical religion of promise. The former is non-temporal, non-historical, while the latter enables the historical experience of God characteristic of Israel and Christianity. But Moltmann remained fascinated with the idea of the eternal present as a kind of experience of eternity interrupting the experience of time. He returns to it at various points in his work (e.g. GC 109–12, 303; WJC 318). Might it be possible for him to appropriate it, understanding it not anti-eschatologically as dissolving the illusion of the temporal in the reality of the eternal, but rather eschatologically as anticipation of the eschatological future? The possibility is suggested by his treatment of the Sabbath, not precisely as eternal present, but certainly as the weekly interruption of God's history by the anticipation of that history's goal: God's presence (GC XI).

In *The Spirit of Life* he avails himself of this possibility, in a way that brings together experience, Blochian philosophy, mystical theology, and his own doxological understanding of the Trinity. Very early in the book he indicates that justice will be done to experiences of God only if account is taken, not only of the historical experience that takes place between remembrance and expectation, but also of moments of eternal present:

> But the experience of life can also be so intensive that remembrances and expectations are forgotten, and all there is is pure present. We then talk about life's ecstasies. Experiences of God can be so intensive that, as Parmenides said, 'the beginnings are obliterated and the ending vanishes' and the eternal present fills everything. Then we talk about mystical or 'eschatological' moments (SL 18).

The language here typically relates 'ordinary' experience to experience of God. It is closely echoed several times later in the book (SL 52, 206, 303; cf. 39–40, 211).

There is some evidence that in trying to do justice to this kind of experience of a non-temporal moment, Moltmann reverted to the work of his long-familiar philosophical dialogue partner, Ernst Bloch,[25] who cited Plato, Parmenides and Meister Eckhart as having rightly recognized 'a real Now',[26] the non-temporal moment out of which time arises. In it 'the beginning and the end are both present', as Moltmann writes, summarizing Bloch (EG 76 = SL 211[27]). For Bloch, the 'lived moment' always remains 'dark', 'essentially invisible';[28] it can be experienced only as past or expected. 'As immediately being there, it lies in the darkness of the moment.'[29] But although it cannot be experienced, contact with it occurs especially in intense experiences and experiences of 'absolute astonishment'.[30] Could the content of the Now be extracted and retained, the eschatological goal of the world process would be reached.[31] Moltmann's understanding of the mystical or eschatological moment of pure presence by no means corresponds entirely to Bloch's. For one thing, Moltmann's eternal moment seems not nearly so dark as Bloch's. But it does draw inspiration from Bloch. Bloch's discussion would have shown Moltmann how a world-view for which eschatologically orientated temporal process is constitutive, can accommodate and even give remarkable

[25] There is explicit reference to Bloch at EG 76 = SL 211. The other passages in *The Spirit of Life* which refer to this experience have resemblances to Bloch's language in E. Bloch, *Geist der Utopie* (Frankfurt am Main: Suhrkamp, 3rd edition, 1980), pp. 237–56; idem, *The Principle of Hope* (tr. N. Plaice, S. Plaice and P. Knight; Oxford: Blackwell, 1986), pp. 287–300, though Bloch is not the only source of the categories Moltmann uses in these passages. Cf. also SL 157 ('The heart of the lived moment always remains dark. . . .'), where the dependence on Bloch is obvious: Bloch's idea is here used for a quite different purpose, but the passage shows that it was in Moltmann's mind when writing *The Spirit of Life*. For the way in which Moltmann developed his theology of hope in dialogue with Bloch's philosophy of hope, see Bauckham, *Moltmann: Messianic Theology in the Making*, chapter 1. For Moltmann's continuing recourse to Bloch's ideas and dialogue with them, see GC 42–5, 178–81; HTG 143–55.

[26] Bloch, *The Principle of Hope*, p. 292.

[27] Cf. Bloch, *The Principle of Hope*, p. 308.

[28] Bloch, *The Principle of Hope*, p. 291.

[29] Bloch, *The Principle of Hope*, p. 287.

[30] Cf. Bloch, *The Principle of Hope*, pp. 292–5; and cf. Moltmann's reference to this in HTG 143.

[31] Bloch, *The Principle of Hope*, p. 290. On Bloch's idea of the moment, see W. Hudson, *The Marxist Philosophy of Ernst Bloch* (London: Macmillan, 1982), pp. 96–8.

significance to the non-temporal moment which in some sense already contains the goal of the whole process.

In chapter X ('Theology of Mystical Experience') Moltmann makes clear that the mystical union sought by the mystics in forgetting all else in contemplation of God in himself and for his own sake is this kind of intensive experience of pure present. The same language finally recurs in section XII.3.4 (SL 301–6: 'The Trinitarian Doxology'). Here Moltmann takes up a point he made long ago in relation to trinitarian theology (TKG 151–4): that statements about the immanent Trinity (God in himself) are doxological. They arise in that adoring, wondering perception of God which goes beyond thanksgiving for the salvation experienced to praise of God for himself. In *The Spirit of Life* Moltmann expands on the experience implicit in this doxological perception of God as immanent Trinity. The trinitarian doxology in the liturgy, with its evocation of God's eternal being ('Glory be to the Father and to the Son and to the Holy Spirit, as it was in the beginning, is now and ever shall be, world without end'), '*interrupts* the liturgy . . . because it directs the senses to *the eternal present* in which we no longer remember the past and no longer wait for any other future'. As such it is the liturgical equivalent of those exceptional, ecstatic experiences of life, in which the present is so intensively experienced as to be 'a momentary awareness of eternity' (SL 303). But it also corresponds to the way the mystic, climbing the ladder of love, forgets even God's gifts and his own relation to God in selfless contemplation of God as God is in himself (SL 302). Moltmann goes so far (further in this respect than the Orthodox tradition) as to define this doxological, mystical perception of God in the eternal moment of ecstasy as seeing God face to face (SL 304–5; cf. 302–3).[32] This, of course, defines it as precisely a momentary

[32] Contrast this passage with EG 80: 'Suppose there were a ladder up to heaven, and that we were at last able to see God face to face. Whom should we find there? We should find ourselves standing before the Man on the cross. *Ecce Deus* – there is God. And whoever wants to find him must look for him in the fellowship of Jesus Christ. He will find God at the foot of the cross on Golgotha.' The preceding paragraph, the quotation from Buber, reappears in

anticipation of the eschatological presence of God (cf. SL 205).

In this development we seem to have a revaluation of an element of the mystical tradition due to its coherence with the way Moltmann's trinitarian theology has developed. It is a remarkable development in both its trinitarian and its mystical aspects, because it envisages moments in which we step out of the temporal process, our consciousness abstracted from that messianic and trinitarian history in which God is, according to Moltmann's theology, so very deeply involved. But it is the notion of eschatological anticipation which enables such a development not to subvert completely the major thrust of Moltmann's theological project. The epiphany of the eternal present, which first featured in Moltmann's theology only as an alternative to the biblical religion of promise, is finally integrated into a theological structure derived from the notion of promise.

VIII

The mystical moment is exceptional, not only in its non-temporal quality, but also in that it is apparently an experience of God in himself, unrelated to the world. (In this respect it differs significantly from the Sabbath, with which, as anticipation of God's eschatological presence, we compared it above. The Sabbath 'points to the Creator's immanence in his creation' [GC 280].) By contrast, the kind of experience of God of which Moltmann speaks through the rest of *The Spirit of Life* is quite different: it is experience of God in all things and of all things in God.

This way of speaking of experience of God depends on that view of the relationship of God and the world which could be called Moltmann's version of panentheism and which is highly developed in his work by this stage. The

---

The Spirit of Life (250–1) but not this. Has Moltmann adopted the position of 'transcendental mysticism,' repudiated earlier (TA), that all mediations of God, including the humanity of Christ, must be left behind in the attainment of immediate, 'face to face' experience of God?

term panentheism, which Moltmann uses (e.g. CG 277; GC 98), he does not regard as fully adequate, because it does not express the trinitarian nature of the relationship as Moltmann envisages it (GC 103). In any case, it needs defining. For Moltmann the key concept is reciprocal indwelling, most simply and commonly expressed as: 'God *in* the world, and the world *in* God' (GC 17; cf., e.g. SL 34, 195, 282). Though this way of putting it becomes a developed principle in Moltmann's later work, there are significant examples in his earlier work (e.g. CG 277–8, cf. 255) which show that it develops a fundamental tendency of his whole theological project. It is way of expressing an intimacy of relationship between God and his creation, which does justice both to the divine immanence in creation and to the divine transcendence beyond creation. God is transcendent not only as the source of creation's being and life, but also as able to keep creation open in self-transcendence towards its goal, which is a divine indwelling in rest, joy and glory, not yet attained. 'God in the world' expresses his immanence in it, 'the world in God' expresses his transcendence beyond it and its openness to this transcendence. The concept is trinitarian because the Spirit as trinitarian Person is the immanent side of God's presence to the world. Finally, it should be noted that the concept is an integrating, holistic one, which does not divide reality but finds the presence of God in all things and sees all things being taken up into the new creation which God will indwell in glory. On the other hand, this universal presence of God is not undifferentiated, as though evil were divine or as though God were present in the same way in all things.

Two important aspects help to secure the necessary differentiation. One is the role of the cross. It is highly significant that the language of mutual indwelling first featured centrally in Moltmann's work in the section of *The Crucified God* in which he expounded in the strongest terms the claim that in the crucified Christ God made all suffering his own and took all evil and suffering into his own trinitarian history with the world. But the claim that the 'incarnate God is present, and can be experienced, in the humanity of every man' (CG 276), and that 'in communion with Christ it can truly be said that men live *in God* and *from God*' (CG 277) may not be 'understood in pantheistic terms'. If it were, it

> would be a dream which would have to ignore the negative element in the world. But a trinitarian theology of the cross perceives God in the negative element and therefore the negative element in God, and in this dialectical way is panentheistic. For in the hidden mode of humiliation to the point of the cross, all being and all that annihilates has already been taken up in God and God begins to become 'all in all' [1 Corinthians 15:28]. To recognize God in the cross of Christ, conversely, means to recognize the cross, inextricable suffering, death and hopeless rejection in God (CG 277).

Significantly, the same point is made at the end of his essay on 'The Theology of Mystical Experience', where he explains that the mystics' 'vision of the world in God, and God in the world' (called 'pantheistic' in EG 77, corrected to 'panentheistic' in SL 211) would, without the cross of Christ,

> be pure optimistic illusion. The suffering of one, single child would prove it to be so. Without the recognition of the suffering of God's inexhaustible love no 'pantheism' [SL 213 adds: 'and no panentheism'] can endure in this world of death. It would soon become pannihilism (EG 79; cf. SL 213).

Hence passion mysticism, in its various forms, must complement and be integrated into the mysticism of the panentheistic vision of the world in God. Suffering is suffering, evil is evil, and God's presence in the crucified Christ and the sighings of the Spirit suffers them, in order to overcome them in his eschatological indwelling in joy and glory and Sabbath rest.

The role of the cross is therefore closely connected with the second aspect of Moltmann's panentheism which ensures that it does not identify created reality and experience with God in an undifferentiated, homogenizing way. Panentheism in Moltmann's understanding is a movement towards the goal of the future in which 'God *will* be all in all' (1 Corinthians 15:28: Moltmann's favourite eschatological text, which he calls in EG 78 'pantheistic-sounding', corrected in SL 212 to 'panentheistic-sounding'). The presence of God now is the presence of his suffering and creative love moving his world towards its goal. His presence is therefore discernible in a way which itself differentiates. For example:

> The crucified One was present in the Spirit, not among the inventors and constructors of the atomic bomb, or those responsible for it. He was present in the Spirit among the dead of Hiroshima (CG 296).

The extent to which Moltmann's panentheistic understanding of experience of God was already clearly adumbrated in *The Crucified God* can also be seen in a passage which speaks of 'the conception of reality as a *sacrament,* that is, as a reality qualified by God's word and made the bearer of his presence'. Liberation theology, he argues here, requires 'materializations of the presence of God', which are (as in Luther's sacramental theology) 'real presences of his coming omnipresence' (CG 337; cf. HD 110–11). Much of Moltmann's later thought is presaged in the description of these anticipatory presences of God – in forms of liberation which point forward to his eschatological presence in all things – 'as the history of the Shekinah wandering through the dust, as the history of the spirit [*sic*] which comes upon all flesh' (CG 338; cf., e.g., EG 78 = SL 212: the 'history of the Spirit which will be poured out on all flesh'). But the Lutheran sacramental language itself recurs in *The Spirit of Life*, where panentheism means that it 'is possible to experience God *in, with and beneath* each everyday experience of the world' (SL 34; cf. also SL 17).

Another way of describing the implications of panentheism, which Moltmann uses in *The Spirit of Life*, is the phrase 'immanent transcendence' (SL 31, etc.). Because of the immanence of the transcendent God in all things, every experience can have 'a transcendent, inward side' (SL 34), while in every one of God's creatures he is present and 'is himself their innermost mystery' (SL 50). It is worth noticing how this both parallels and transcends the Augustinian notion that the human spirit is the location of immanent transcendence. Because, in Augustine's conception, it is the inner spiritual being of the individual which reflects God and is closest to God on the scale of being, the individual experiences God by turning inwards. The inward route is the upward route to God. By identifying immanent transcendence as the inner (but not 'spiritual' in the sense of 'non-physical') reality of all creatures and all experience, Moltmann makes experience of God, not a matter of individual introspection, but of encounter with God in all things and in all experience. Hence: 'We expect the mystical union of the Shekinah with God in every true encounter. . . . We encounter every other created being in the expectation of meeting God' (SL 51; cf. SL 36). 'Immanent transcendence' certainly does not exclude the experience of God in one's self (SL 35), but it includes experience of God in bodily experience, in sociality, and in nature. For the last he appeals to the tradition of Christian nature mysticism (CJF 75–6).

To experience God in all things and all things in God is not to lose sight of the individuality of things in a homogenizing pantheism. Rather, it involves ceasing to view things solely in terms of their value for us, perceiving them in their value for God, in what they mean for him as he experiences them in his love for his creation in all its variety, recognizing the creatures in the sharp contours of their distinctive being as they appear in the context of God's embracing love for them (SL 35–6). Moltmann is articulating a way of experiencing creation and God which neither confuses nor separates the two, which does not overload creation with the value *of* God, but promotes reverence for its own created reality through perception of its value *for* God. This is an important variation on the way in which the Christian mystical and devotional tradition has, at its best, viewed creation religiously. The emphasis has usually been on creation reflecting its Creator and so pointing us to God. Moltmann supplements this with a perception of the relationship of the creatures and God which points us to their value for God.

As well as the simple language of mutual indwelling – 'God in the world and the world in God' – Moltmann can also express panentheism in terms of reciprocal movement out of and into. For example, in the eschaton 'the triune God is at home *in* his world, and his world exists *out of* his inexhaustible glory' (TKG 128). He sees an appropriate expression of 'immanent transcendence' also in the Neoplatonic language of emanation and return used in the mystical tradition (EG 77 = SL 212) to express, in a sense, the continuity of the divine and the human life which is lived out of its source in the divine life. He warms to the images of the Spirit as flowing light (Mechthild of Magdeburg), water welling up from underground (Meister Eckhart) and fertility (Hildegard of Bingen) (SL 281–5; cf. 212, 275; EG 77):

> In the mystical metaphors, the distance between a transcendent subject and its immanent work is ended. The distinctions between causes and effects disappear. In the metaphors of light, water and fertility, the divine and the human are joined in an organic cohesion. The result is a perichoretic interpenetration: you in me – I in you. The divine becomes the all-embracing presence in which what is human can fruitfully unfold.

In the end, what is distinctive of Moltmann's appropriation of aspects of the mystical tradition is his determination to speak of an intimacy with God which excludes no aspect of God's creation.

A Moltmann Bibliography

This bibliography is not merely a listing of literature used in the preparation of this book, but is intended as a resource for English-speaking students of Moltmann's work. Emphasis is given to Moltmann's works in English translation in section B and to secondary literature in English in section C.

A. ABBREVIATIONS

In the text and notes the following abbreviations are used for Moltmann's works. Full bibliographical details will be found in section B of the Bibliography.

AH   'L'Absolu et l'Historique dans la doctrine de la Trinité.'
CCC   'Christ in Cosmic Context.'
CCR   'The Cross and Civil Religion.'
CG   *The Crucified God.*
CJC   'The Confession of Jesus Christ: A Biblical Theological Consideration.'
CJF   *Creating a Just Future.*
CPS   *The Church in the Power of the Spirit.*
CR   'The Challenge of Religion in the 1980s.'
DGG M. Welker (ed.), *Diskussion über Jürgen Moltmanns Buch »Der gekreuzigte Gott«.* Munich: Chr. Kaiser, 1979. (This includes J. Moltmann, '»Dialectik, die umschlägt in Identität« – was ist das? Zu Befürchtungen Walter Kaspers'; and 'Antwort auf die Kritik an »Der gekreuzigte Gott«.')

DTH	W.-D. Marsch (ed.), *Diskussion über die »Theologie der Hoffnung« von Jürgen Moltmann*. Munich: Chr. Kaiser, 1967. (This includes J. Moltmann, 'Antwort auf die Kritik der »Theologie der Hoffnung«.')
EC	'The Expectation of His Coming.'
EG	*Experiences of God.*
EH	*The Experiment Hope.*
FC	*The Future of Creation.*
FH	F. Herzog (ed.), *The Future of Hope: Theology as Eschatology*. New York: Herder & Herder, 1970. (This includes J. Moltmann, 'Theology as Eschatology'; and 'Towards the Next Step in the Dialogue.')
FHS	'The Fellowship of the Holy Spirit – Trinitarian Pneumatology.'
FTO	'The Future As Threat and As Opportunity.'
GC	*God in Creation.*
GEB	*Im Gespräch mit Ernst Bloch.*
GHH	*God – His and Hers.*
GK	'God's Kingdom as the Meaning of Life and of the World.'
GTT	'The "Crucified God": God and the Trinity Today.'
HC	T. Runyon (ed.), *Hope for the Church: Moltmann in Dialogue with Practical Theology*. Nashville: Abingdon, 1979. (This includes J. Moltmann, 'The Diaconal Church in the Context of the Kingdom of God'; and 'Response'.)
HD	*On Human Dignity.*
HFM	E. H. Cousins (ed.), *Hope and the Future of Man*. London: Teilhard Centre for the Future of Man, 1973. (This includes J. Moltmann, 'Response to the Opening Presentations'; and 'Hope and the Biomedical Future of Man'.)
HG	*Humanity in God.*
HP	*Hope and Planning.*
HTG	*History and the Triune God.*
IU	'The Inviting Unity of the Triune God.'
JM	*Jewish Monotheism and Christian Trinitarian Doctrine.*
LF	'The Liberating Feast.'
M	*Man.*

MF	'The Motherly Father: Is Trinitarian Patripassianism Replacing Theological Patriarchalism?'
MSM	'Man and the Son of Man.'
OC	*The Open Church.*
PPL	*The Power of the Powerless.*
PR	'Die politische Relevanz der christlichen Hoffnung.'
PT	*Perspektiven der Theologie.*
RP	'A Response to my Pentecostal Dialogue Partners.'
RRF	*Religion, Revolution, and the Future.*
SB	*Die Sprache der Befreiung.*
SL	*The Spirit of Life.*
T	'Theodicy.'
TA	'Teresa of Avila and Martin Luther: The turn to the mysticism of the cross.'
TC	'Cross, Theology of the.'
TGT	'Theology in Germany Today.'
TH	*Theology of Hope.*
TJ	*Theology and Joy.*
TKG	*The Trinity and the Kingdom of God.*
TT	*Theology Today.*
TTC	'The "Crucified God": A Trinitarian Theology of the Cross.'
UZ	*Umkehr zur Zukunft.*
VZ	'Verschränkte Zeiten der Geschichte: Notwendige Differenzierungen und Begrenzungen des Geschichtsbegriffs.'
WJC	*The Way of Jesus Christ.*

B. MOLTMANN'S WORKS

The following bibliography attempts a relatively complete listing of Moltmann's work in English translation, though it is not exhaustive. Works in German (and occasionally in French) are included only in the case of important works, consulted in the preparation of this book, which are not available in English. Articles which have been subsequently reprinted in the volumes of Moltmann's collected essays are not usually listed separately, and in the case of articles published in more than one journal or book, only one place is usually given.

The compilation of a complete and fully accurate bibliography of Moltmann's work in English would be a difficult task. There are many publications of minor articles in minor journals, magazines and as pamphlets. Moltmann quite frequently recycles the same material in somewhat different forms. Translations of his articles often fail to give the publication details of the German originals. Occasionally more than one English translation of the same German article has been published. The following bibliography is intended merely as the best guide yet available to Moltmann's work in English.

A fairly complete bibliography of Moltmann's works (including translations) up to 1974 appears in R. Gibellini, *La teologia di Jürgen Moltmann* (Brescia: Queriniana, 1975), pp. 343–76; while the bibliography (confined to works in German) in P. F. Momose, *Kreuzestheologie: Ein Auseinandersetzung mit Jürgen Moltmann* (Freiburg: Herder, 1978), pp. 186–90, goes up to 1976. But these are now largely superseded by the very full bibliography (528 items) up to 1987 in D. Ising (with G. Geisthardt and A. Schloz), *Bibliographie Jürgen Moltmann* (Munich: Chr. Kaiser, 1987). This includes translations in all languages, but is not fully exhaustive in its coverage of Moltmann's work in English.

'A Christian Declaration on Human Rights.' *Reformed World* 34 (1976), pp. 58–72.

'A Conversation with Jürgen Moltmann.' In T. Cabestrero, *Faith: Conversations with Contemporary Theologians* (tr. D. D. Walsh; Maryknoll, New York: Orbis, 1980), pp. 121–38.

'All Things New: Invited to God's Future.' *Asbury Theological Journal* 48 (1993), pp. 29–38.

'Antwort auf die Kritik an »Der gekreuzigte Gott«.' In *Diskussion über Jürgen Moltmanns Buch »Der gekreuzigte Gott«*, (ed.) M. Welker (Munich: Chr. Kaiser, 1979), pp. 165–90.

'Antwort auf die Kritik der »Theologie der Hoffnung«.' In *Diskussion über die »Theologie der Hoffnung« von Jürgen Moltmann*, (ed.) W.-D. Marsch (Munich: Chr. Kaiser, 1967), pp. 201–37.

'A Response to my Pentecostal Dialogue Partners.' *Journal of Pentecostal Theology* 4 (1994), pp. 59–70.

'"Behold, I make all things new": The Category of the New in Christian Theology.' In M. Muchenhirn (ed.), *The Future as the Presence of Shared Hope* (New York: Sheed & Ward, 1968), pp. 9–33.

'Christian Discipleship in a Nuclear World.' In B. McSweeney (ed.), *Ireland and the Threat of Nuclear War* (Dublin: Dominican Publications, 1985), pp. 104–18.

'Christian Theology and Political Religion.' In L. S. Rouner (ed.), *Civil Religion and Political Theology* (Boston University Studies in Philosophy and Religion 8; Notre Dame, Indiana: University of Notre Dame Press, 1986), pp. 41–58.

'Christ in Cosmic Context.' In H. D. Regan and A. J. Torrance (eds), *Christ and Context: The Confrontation between Gospel and Culture* (Edinburgh: T. & T. Clark, 1993), pp. 180–91, 205–9.

'Christliche Hoffnung: Messianisch oder transzendent? Ein theologisches Gespräch mit Joachim von Fiore und Thomas von Aquin.' *Münchener Theologischer Zeitschrift* 33 (1982), pp. 241–60.

'Christologie – die paulinische Mitte: Bemerkungen zu Georg Eichholz' Paulus interpretation.' *Evangelische Theologie* 34 (1974), pp. 196–200.

Communities of Faith and Radical Discipleship. By J. Moltmann *et al.* Macon: Mercer University Press, 1986.

'Covenant or Leviathan? Political Theology for Modern Times.' *Scottish Journal of Theology* 47 (1994), pp. 19–41.

Creating a Just Future: The Politics of Peace and the Ethics of Creation in a Threatened World. Tr. J. Bowden. London: SCM Press/Philadelphia: Trinity Press International, 1989.

'Cross, Theology of the.' In *A New Dictionary of Christian Theology*, (eds) A. Richardson and J. Bowden (London: SCM Press, 1983), pp. 135–7.

'Commentary on "To Bear Arms".' In R. A. Evans and A. F. Evans, *Human Rights: A Dialogue between the First and Third Worlds* (Maryknoll, New York: Orbis Books/Guildford: Lutterworth Press, 1983), pp. 48–52.

'Communities of Faith and Radical Discipleship; An Interview with Jürgen Moltmann.' (Interview by M. Volf.) *Christian Century* 100 (1983), pp. 240–9.

'Descent into Hell.' *Duke Divinity School Review* 33 (1968), pp. 115–19.

'»Dialektik, die umschlägt in Identität« – was ist das? Zu Befürchtungen Walter Kaspers.' In *Diskussion über Jürgen Moltmanns Buch »Der gekreuzigte Gott«'*, (ed.) M. Welker (Munich: Chr. Kaiser, 1979), pp. 149–56.

'Die Bibel und das Patriarchat: Offene Fragen zur Diskussion über "Feministische Theologie".' *Evangelische Theologie* 42 (1982), pp. 480–4.

'Die Entdeckung der Anderen: Zur Theorie des kommunikativen Erkennens.' *Evangelische Theologie* 50 (1990), pp. 400–14.

'Die politische Relevanz der christlichen Hoffnung.' In *Christliche Freiheit im Dienst am Menschen* (Martin Niemöller Festschrift), (ed.) K. Herbert (Frankfurt am Main: Otto Lembeck, 1972), pp. 153–62.

Die Sprache der Befreiung: Predigten und Besinnungen. Munich: Chr. Kaiser, 1972.

'Dostoyevsky and the Theology of Hope.' In J. Armenti (ed.), *The Papin Festschrift: Essays in Honour of Joseph Papin*, vol. 2 (Villanova: Villanova University Press, 1976), pp. 399–407.

'Editorial: Can there be an Ecumenical Mariology?' *Concilium* 168 (1983) = *Mary in the Churches*, (eds) H. Küng and J. Moltmann (Edinburgh: T. & T. Clark, 1983), pp. xii–xv.

Experiences of God. Tr. M. Kohl. London: SCM Press, 1980.

'Fellowship in a Divided World.' *Ecumenical Review* 24 (1972), pp. 436–6.

'Foreword.' In A. J. Conyers, *God, Hope, and History: Jürgen Moltmann and the Christian Concept of History* (Macon: Mercer University Press, 1988), pp. vii–ix.

'Foreword.' In M. D. Meeks, *Origins of the Theology of Hope* (Philadelphia: Fortress, 1974), pp. ix–xii.

'Foreword.' In R. J. Bauckham, *Moltmann: Messianic Theology in the Making* (Basingstoke: Marshall Pickering, 1987), pp. vii–x.

'Foreword.' In W. H. Capps, *Time Invades the Cathedral: Tensions in the School of Hope* (Philadelphia: Fortress, 1972), pp. xi–xv.

'God and the Nuclear Catastrophe.' *Pacifica* 1 (1988), pp. 157–70.

God – His and Hers. By E. Moltmann-Wendel and J. Moltmann. Tr. J. Bowden. London: SCM Press, 1991.

God in Creation: An Ecological Doctrine of Creation. Tr. M. Kohl. London: SCM Press, 1985.

God Means Freedom. Nairobi: Association of Theological Institutions in Eastern Africa, n.d.

'God Means Freedom.' In H. J. Young (ed.), *God and Human Freedom* (Howard Thurman Festschrift; Richmond, Indiana, 1983), pp. 10–22.

'God's Kingdom as the Meaning of Life and of the World.' *Concilium* 117 (8/1977) = *Why did God make me?*, (eds) H. Küng and J. Moltmann (New York: Seabury Press, 1978), pp. 97–103.

'God's Protest Against Death.' In F. Thatcher (ed.), *The Miracle of Easter* (Waco, Texas: Word Books, 1980), pp. 69–77.

'Has Modern Society any Future?' *Concilium* (1/1990) = *On the Threshold of the Third Millennium* (London: SCM Press, 1990), pp. 54–65.

'Hope Beyond Time.' *Duke Divinity School Review* 33 (1968), pp. 109–14.

'Hope in the Struggle of the People.' *Christianity and Crisis* 37 (1977), pp. 49–55.

History and the Triune God: Contributions to Trinitarian Theology. Tr. J. Bowden. London: SCM Press, 1991.

'Hope.' In *A New Dictionary of Christian Theology*, (eds.) A. Richardson and J. Bowden (London: SCM Press, 1983), pp. 270–2.

Hope and Planning. Tr. M. Clarkson. London: SCM Press, 1971.

'Hope and the Biological Future of Man.' In *Hope and the Future of Man*, (ed.) E. H. Cousins (London: Teilhard Centre for the Future of Man, 1973), pp. 89–105.

Human Identity in Christian Faith. (Raymond Fred West Memorial Lectures on Immortality.) Stanford: Stanford University Press, 1974.

Humanity in God. By E. Moltmann-Wendel and J. Moltmann. London: SCM Press, 1984.

'Human Rights, the Rights of Humanity and the Rights of Nature.' *Concilium* (2/1990) = *The Ethics of World Religions and Human Rights*, (eds) H. Küng and J. Moltmann (London: SCM Press, 1990), pp. 120–35.

'Ich glaube an Gott den Vater: Patriarchalische oder nichtpatriarchalische Rede von Gott?' *Evangelische Theologie* 43 (1983), pp. 397–415.

Im Gespräch mit Ernst Bloch: Eine theologische Wegbegleitung. (Kaiser Traktate 18.) Munich: Chr. Kaiser, 1976.

'In Search for an Equilibrium of "Equilibrium" and "Progress".' *Ching Feng* 30 (1987), pp. 5–17.

'Introduction.' In E. Bloch, *Man on his Own: Essays in the Philosophy of Religion,* tr. E. B. Ashton (New York: Herder & Herder, 1970), pp. 19–29.

'Jesus and the Kingdom of God.' *Asbury Theological Journal* 48 (1993), pp. 5–18.

Jesus Christ for Today's World. Tr. M. Kohl. London: SCM Press, 1994.

Jewish Monotheism and Christian Trinitarian Doctrine. A Dialogue by Pinchas Lapide and Jürgen Moltmann. Tr. L. Swidler. Philadelphia: Fortress Press, 1981.

'L'Absolu et l'Historique dans la doctrine de la Trinité.' In L. Rumpf *et al., Hegel et la théologie contemporaine: L'absolu dans l'histoire?* (Neuchatel/Paris: Delachaux & Niestlé, 1977), pp. 190–204.

'Liberation in the Light of Hope.' *Ecumenical Review* 26 (1974), pp. 413–29.

'Liberation through Reconciliation.' In J. W. Cox (ed.), *The Twentieth Century Pulpit,* vol. 2 (Nashville: Abingdon Press, 1981), pp. 118–36.

'Man and the Son of Man.' In *No Man is Alien: Essays on the Unity of Mankind,* (ed.) J. R. Nelson (W. A. Visser't Hooft Festschrift; Leiden: E. J. Brill, 1971), pp. 203–24.

Man: Christian Anthropology in the Conflicts of the Present. Tr. J. Sturdy. London: SPCK, 1974.

Meditations on the Passion: Two Meditations on Mark 8:31–38. By J.-B. Metz and J. Moltmann. New York: Paulist Press, 1979.

'Messianic Atheism.' In L. S. Rouner (ed.), *Knowing Religiously* (Notre Dame, Indiana: University of Notre Dame Press, 1985), pp. 192–206.

'Messianic Hope: 2. In Christianity.' *Concilium* 8/10 (1974) = *Ecumenism: Christians and Jews,* (eds) H. Küng and W. Jasper (London: Concilium, 1974), pp. 155–61.

'Messianic Lifestyle.' In D. Snowden (ed.), *Vessels for New Wine: Papers for Christian Living Today* (Bath: National Student Christian Congress and Resource Centre, n.d.), pp. 6–12.

'Messianismus und Marxismus.' In *Über Ernst Bloch: Mit Beiträgen von Martin Walser, Ivo Frenzel, Jürgen Moltmann, Jürgen Habermas, Fritz Vilmar, Iring Fetscher und Werner Maihofer* (Frankfurt am Main: Suhrkamp, 1968), pp. 42–60.

'Nachwort.' In P. F. Momose, *Kreuzestheologie: Eine auseinandersetzung mit Jürgen Moltmann* (Freiburg/Basel/Vienna: Herder, 1978), pp. 174–83.

On Human Dignity: Political Theology and Ethics. Tr. M. D. Meeks. London: SCM Press, 1984.

'On Latin American Liberation Theology: An Open Letter to José Miguez Bonino.' *Christianity and Crisis* 36 (1976), pp. 57–63.

'Peace: The Fruit of Justice.' *Concilium* 195 (1988) = *A Council for Peace,* (eds) H. Küng and J. Moltmann (Edinburgh: T. & T. Clark, 1988), pp. 109–20.

'Perseverance.' In *A New Dictionary of Christian Theology,* (eds) A. Richardson and J. Bowden (London: SCM Press, 1983), pp. 441–2.

Perspektiven der Theologie: Gesammelte Aufsätze. Munich: Chr. Kaiser/Mainz: Matthias Grünewald, 1968.

'Politics and the Practice of Hope.' *Christian Century* 87 (1970), pp. 288–91.

Prädestination und Perseveranz: Geschichte und Bedeutung der reformierten Lehre 'de perseverantia sanctorum'. (Beiträge zur Geschichte und Lehre der Reformierten Kirche 12.) Neukirchen: Neuchirchener Verlag, 1961.

'Protest and Celebration.' *One World* 15 (1976), pp. 14–17.

'Reformation and Revolution.' In M. Hoffman (ed.), *Martin Luther and the Modern Mind* (Toronto Studies in Theology 22; Toronto, 1985), pp. 163–90.

'Religion and Politics in Germany.' In J. A Cooney, G. A. Craig *et al.* (eds), *The Federal Republic of Germany and the United States* (Boulder/London: Westview Press), pp. 98–108.

'Religion and State in Germany – West and East.' *Annals of the American Academy of Political and Social Science* 483 (1986), pp. 110–18.

Religion, Revolution, and the Future. Tr. M. D. Meeks. New York: Charles Scribner's, 1969.

'Response.' In J. Moltmann with M. D. Meeks, R. J. Hunter, J. W. Fowler, N. L. Erskine, *Hope for the Church: Moltmann in Dialogue with Practical Theology*, ed. and tr. T. Runyon (Nashville: Abingdon, 1979), pp. 128–36.

'Response to the Opening Presentations.' In *Hope and the Future of Man*, (ed.) E. H. Cousins (London: Teilhard Centre for the Future of Man, 1973), pp. 55–9.

'Revolution, Religion and the Future: German Reactions.' *Concilium* 201 (1/1989) = *1789: The French Revolution and the Church*, (eds) C. Geffré and J.-P. Jossua (Edinburgh: T. & T. Clark, 1989), pp. 43–50.

'Schöpfung, Bund und Herrlichkeit: Zur Diskussion über Karl Barths Schöpfungslehre.' *Evamgelische Theologie* 48 (1988), pp. 108–27.

'Teresa of Avila and Martin Luther: The turn to the mysticism of the cross.' *Studies in Religion/Sciences Religieuses* 13 (1984), pp. 265–78.

'The Alienation and Liberation of Nature.' In L. Rouner (ed.), *On Nature* (Indiana: University of Notre Dame Press, 1984), pp. 133–44.

'The Challenge of Religion in the 1980s.' In *Theologians in Transition: The Christian Century "How My Mind Has Changed" Series*, (ed.) J. M. Wall (New York: Crossroad, 1981), pp. 107–12.

'The Christian Theology of Hope and its Bearing on Development.' In *In Search of a Theology of Development: A SODEPAX Report* (Geneva: WCC, 1969), pp. 93–100.

The Church in the Power of the Spirit: A Contribution to Messianic Ecclesiology. Tr. M. Kohl. London: SCM Press, 1977.

'The Confession of Jesus Christ: A Biblical Theological Consideration.' *Concilium* 118 (8/1978) = *An Ecumenical Confession of Faith?*, (eds) H. Küng and J. Moltmann (New York: Seabury Press, 1979), pp. 13–19.

'The Cosmic Community: A New Ecological Concept of Reality in Science and Religion.' *Ching Feng* 29 (1986), pp. 93–105.

'The Cross and Civil Religion.' In J. Moltmann, H. W. Richardson, J. B. Metz, W. Oelmüller, M. D. Bryant, *Religion and Political Society*, ed. and tr. in the Institute of Christian Thought (New York: Harper & Row, 1974), pp. 9–47.

'The "Crucified God": A Trinitarian Theology of the Cross.' *Interpretation* 26 (1972), pp. 278–99.

'The "Crucified God": God and the Trinity Today.' *Concilium* 8/6 (1972), pp. 26–37.

The Crucified God: The Cross as the Foundation and Criticism of Christian Theology. Tr. R. A. Wilson and J. Bowden. London: SCM Press, 1974.

'The Diaconal Church in the Context of the Kingdom of God.' In J. Moltmann with M. D. Meeks, R. J. Hunter, J. W. Fowler, N. L. Erskine, *Hope for the Church: Moltmann in Dialogue with Practical Theology*, ed. and tr. T. Runyon (Nashville: Abingdon, 1979), pp. 21–36.

'The Ecological Crisis: Peace with Nature?' *Colloquium* 20 (1988), pp. 1–11.

'The Ecological Crisis: Peace with Nature?' *Scottish Journal of Religious Studies* 9 (1988), pp. 5–18.

'The Ecumenical Church under the Cross.' *Theology Digest* 24 (1976), pp. 380–9.

'The Ethics of Biomedical Research and the Newer Biomedical Technologies.' In S. Blesh (ed.), *Recent Progess in Biology and Medicine: Its Social and Ethical Implications* (UNESCO House, Paris: Council for International Organizations of Medical Sciences, 1972), pp. 68–72.

'The Expectation of His Coming.' *Theology* 88 (1985), pp. 425–8.

The Experiment Hope. Ed. and tr. M. D. Meeks. London: SCM Press, 1975.

'The Fellowship of the Holy Spirit – Trinitarian Pneumatology.' *Scottish Journal of Theology* 3 (1984), pp. 287–300.

'The Future As Threat and As Opportunity.' In *Contemporary Religion and Social Responsibility*, (eds) N. Brockman and N. Piediscalzi (New York: Alba House, 1973), pp. 103–17.

The Future of Creation. Tr. M. Kohl. London: SCM Press, 1979.

The Gospel of Liberation. Waco, Texas: Word Books, 1973.

'The Inviting Unity of the Triune God.' *Concilium* 177 (1/1985) = *Monotheism*, (eds) C. Geffré and J.-P. Jossua (Edinburgh: T. & T. Clark), pp. 50–8.

'The Liberating Feast.' *Concilium* 2/10 (1974) = *Politics and Liturgy*, (eds) H. Schmidt and D. Power (London: Concilium, 1974), pp. 74–84.

'The Liberation of Oppressors.' *Christianity and Crisis* 38 (1978), pp. 310–17, and also *Journal of Theology for Southern Africa* 26 (1979), pp. 24–38.

'The Life Signs of the Spirit in the Fellowship Community of Christ.' In J. Moltmann with M. D. Meeks, R. J. Hunter, J. W. Fowler, N. L. Erskine, *Hope for the Church: Moltmann in Dialogue with Practical Theology*, ed. and tr. T. Runyon (Nashville: Abingdon, 1979), pp. 37–56.

'The Lordship of Christ and Human Society.' In J. Moltmann and J. Weissbach, *Two Studies in the Theology of Bonhoeffer* (New York: Charles Scribner's, 1967), pp. 19–94.

'The Motherly Father: Is Trinitarian Patripassianism Replacing Theological Patriarchalism?' *Concilium* 143 (1981) = *God as Father?*, (eds) E. Schillebeeckx and J. B. Metz (Edinburgh: T. & T. Clark, 1981), pp. 51–6.

'Theodicy.' In *A New Dictionary of Christian Theology*, (eds) A. Richardson and J. Bowden (London: SCM Press, 1983), pp. 564–6.

'Theological Proposals Towards the Resolution of the Filioque Controversy.' In L. Vischer (ed.), *Spirit of God, Spirit of Christ: Ecumenical Reflections on the Filioque Controversy* (Faith and Order Paper 103; Geneva: WCC, 1981), pp. 164–73.

'Théologie et droits de l'homme.' *Revue des Sciences Religieuses* 52 (1978), pp. 299–314.

Theology and Joy. Tr. R. Ulrich. London: SCM Press, 1973.

'Theology as Eschatology.' In *The Future of Hope: Theology as Eschatology*, (ed.) F. Herzog (New York: Herder & Herder, 1970), pp. 1–50.

'Theology in Germany Today.' In *Observations on "The Spiritual Situation of the Age": Contemporary German Perspectives*, (ed.) J. Habermas, tr. and intro. A. Buchwalter (Cambridge, Mass./London: MIT Press, 1984), pp. 181–205.

Theology of Hope: On the Ground and the Implications of a Christian Eschatology. Tr. J. W. Leitch. London: SCM Press, 1967.

Theology Today: Two contributions towards making theology present. Tr. J. Bowden. London: SCM Press, 1988.

The Open Church: Invitation to a Messianic Lifestyle. Tr. M. D. Meeks. London: SCM Press, 1978. American edition: *The Passion for Life: A Messianic Lifestyle.* Philadelphia: Fortress Press, 1978.

'The Passion for Life.' *Currents in Theology and Mission* 4 (1977), pp. 3–10.

'The Passion of Christ and the Suffering of God.' *Asbury Theological Journal* 48 (1993), pp. 19–28.

'The Possible Nuclear Catastrophe and Where is God?' *Scottish Journal of Religious Studies* 9 (1988), pp. 71–83.

The Power of the Powerless. Tr. M. Kohl. London: SCM Press, 1983.

'The Realism of Hope: The Feast of the Resurrection and the Transformation of Present Reality.' *Concordia Theological Monthly* 40 (1969), pp. 149–55.

'The Revolution of Freedom: The Christian and Marxist Struggle.' In T. W. Ogletree (ed.), *Openings for Marxist–Christian Dialogue* (Nashville: Abingdon Press, 1969), pp. 47–71.

'The Right to Bear Arms.' In R. Evans (ed.), *Human Rights: A Dialogue Between the First and Third World* (New York, 1983), pp. 48–53.

The Spirit of Life: A universal affirmation. Tr. M. Kohl. London: SCM Press, 1992.

The Trinity and the Kingdom of God: The doctrine of God. Tr. M. Kohl. London: SCM Press, 1981.

'The Unity of the Triune God: Comprehensibility of the Trinity and its Foundation in the History of Salvation.' *St Valdimir's Theological Quarterly* 28 (1984), pp. 157–71.

The Way of Jesus Christ: Christology in messianic dimensions. Tr. M. Kohl. London: SCM Press, 1990.

'Towards the Next Step in the Dialogue.' In *The Future of Hope: Theology as Eschatology,* (ed.) F. Herzog (New York: Herder & Herder, 1970), pp. 154–64.

Umkehr zur Zukunft. Munich: Chr. Kaiser, 1970/Gütersloh: Gerd Mohn, 1977.

'Verschränkte Zeiten der Geschichte: Notwendige Differenzierungen und Begrenzungen des Geschichtsbegriffs.' *Evangelische Theologie* 44 (1984), pp. 213–27.

'Warum "Schwarze Theologie"? Einführung.' *Evangelische Theologie* 34 (1974), pp. 1–3.

'What Kind of Unity? The Dialogue Between the Traditions of East and West.' In L. Vischer *et al.* (eds), *Lausanne 77: Fifty Years of Faith and Order* (Faith and Order Paper 82; Geneva: WCC, 1977), pp. 38–47.

'Zum Gespräch mit Christian Link.' *Evangelische Theologie* 47 (1987), pp. 93–5.

C. STUDIES OF MOLTMANN'S THEOLOGY

The following bibliography of secondary literature on Moltmann's work gives special attention to works in English, though it is not limited to these. D. Ising (with G. Geisthardt and A. Schloz), *Bibliographie Jürgen Moltmann* (Munich: Chr. Kaiser, 1987), pp. 71–7, gives a (not complete) list of monographs (books and dissertations) on Moltmann's theology up to 1987. Some dissertations not listed below will be found there.

Abbott, D. 'Divine Participation and Eschatology in the Theodicies of Paul Tillich and Jürgen Moltmann.' Ph.D. thesis, University of Virginia, 1987.

Alves, R. A. *A Theology of Human Hope.* New York: Corpus, 1969. (Pages 56–68 on Moltmann.)

Arts, H. *Moltmann and Tillich: Les fondements de l'espérance chrétienne.* Gembloux: J. Duculot, 1973.

Attfield, D. G. 'Can God be Crucified? A Discussion of J. Moltmann.' *Scottish Journal of Theology* 30 (1977), pp. 47–57.

Balthasar, H. Urs von. 'Zu einer christlichen Theologie der Hoffnung.' *Münchener Theologische Zeitschrift* 32 (1981), pp. 81–102.

Basset, J.-C. 'Croix et dialogue des religions.' *Revue d'histoire et de philosophie religieuses* 56 (1976), pp. 545–58.

Bauckham, R. J. 'Bibliography: Jürgen Moltmann.' *Modern Churchman* 28 (1986), pp. 55–60.

— 'Evolution and Creation: (9) in Moltmann's Doctrine of Creation.' *Epworth Review* 15 (1988), pp. 74–81.

— 'In Defence of *The Crucified God.*' In N. M. de S. Cameron (ed.), *The Power and Weakness of God: Impassibility and Orthodoxy* (*Scottish Bulletin of Evangelical Theology* Special Study 4; Edinburgh: Rutherford House Books, 1990), pp. 93–118.

— 'Jürgen Moltmann.' In *One God in Trinity*, (eds) P. Toon and J. D. Spiceland (London: Bagster, 1980), pp. 111–32.

— 'Jürgen Moltmann.' In D. F. Ford (ed.), *The Modern Theologians: An Introduction to Christian Theology of the Twentieth Century*, vol. 1 (Oxford: Blackwell, 1989), pp. 293–310. (German translation in D. Ford (ed.), *Theologen der Gegenwart* [Paderborn: F. Schöningh, 1993], pp. 272–87.)

— 'Moltmann's Eschatology of the Cross.' *Scottish Journal of Theology* 30 (1977), pp. 301–11. (German translation in *Diskussion Über Jürgen Moltmanns Buch »Der gekreuzigte Gott«,* (ed.) Michael Welker [Munich: Chr. Kaiser, 1979], pp. 43–53.)

— 'Moltmann, Jürgen.' In A. E. MacGrath (ed.), *The Blackwell Encyclopaedia of Modern Christian Thought* (Oxford: Blackwell, 1993), pp. 385–8.

— *Moltmann: Messianic Theology in the Making.* Basingstoke: Marshall Pickering, 1987.

— 'Moltmann's Messianic Christology.' *Scottish Journal of Theology* 44 (1991), pp. 519–31.

— 'Moltmann's *Theology of Hope* Revisited.' *Scottish Journal of Theology* 42 (1989) pp. 199–214.

— '"Only the suffering God can help": divine passibility in modern theology.' *Themelios* 9/3 (1984), pp. 6–12.

— 'Theodicy from Ivan Karamazov to Moltmann.' *Modern Theology* 4 (1987), pp. 83–97.

Bergin, H. F. 'The Death of Jesus and its Impact on God – Jürgen Moltmann and Edward Schillebeeckx.' *Irish Theological Quarterly* 52 (1986), pp. 193–211.

Blancy, A. 'Lire Moltmann.' *Etudes théologiques et religieuses* 46 (1971), pp. 355–83.

Blancy, A. '"Le Dieu crucifié" de Jürgen Moltmann.' *Etudes théologiques et religieuses* 50 (1975), pp. 321–33.

— 'Théologie trinitaire et éthique sociale chez J. Moltmann.' *Etudes théologiques et religieuses* 2 (1982), pp. 245–54.

Blaser, K. 'Les enjeux d'une doctrine trinitaire sociale: A propos du dernier livre de Jürgen Moltmann.' *Revue de théologie et de philosophie* 113 (1981), pp. 155–66.

Borowitz, E. B. *Contemporary Christologies: A Jewish Response.* New York: Paulist Press, 1980.

Braaten, C. E. 'A Trinitarian Theology of the Cross.' *Journal of Religion* 56 (1976), pp. 113–21.

— 'Toward a Theology of Hope.' In *New Theology No. 5*, (eds) M. E. Marty and D. G. Pearman (New York: Macmillan/ London: Collier-Macmillan, 1968), pp. 90–111.

Bringle, M. 'Leaving the Cocoon: Moltmann's Anthropology and Feminist Theology.' *Andover Newton Quarterly* 20 (1980), pp. 153–61.

Brinkman, B. R. *To the Lengths of God.* London: Sheed & Ward, 1988. (Chapter 4 on Moltmann.)

Bühler, P. 'Existence et histoire: Quelques éléments de réponse à Jean-Pierre Thévenaz.' *Revue de théologie et de philosophie* 115 (1983), pp. 209–14.

— *Kreuz und Eschatologie: Eine Auseinandersetzung mit der politischen Theologie, im Anschluss an Luthers theologia crucis.* (Hermeneutische Untersuchungen zur Theologie 17.) Tübingen: Mohr (Siebeck), 1981.

Bush, R. B. *Recent Ideas of Divine Conflict: The Influences of Psychological and Sociological Theories of Conflict upon the Trinitarian Theology of Paul Tillich and Jürgen Moltmann.* San Francisco: Mellen Research University Press, 1991.

Capps, W. H. *Hope Against Hope: Moltmann to Merton in One Theological Decade.* Philadelphia: Fortress, 1976.

— *Time Invades the Cathedral: Tensions in the School of Hope.* Philadelphia: Fortress, 1972.

Chan, S. K. H. 'An Asian Review' [of *The Spirit of Life*]. *Journal of Pentecostal Theology* 4 (1994), pp. 35–40.

Chapman, G. C., Jr. 'Black Theology and Theology of Hope: What Have They To Say To Each Other?' *Union Seminary Quarterly Review* 29 (1974), pp. 107–29.

Chapman, G. C., Jr. 'Hope and the ethics of formation: Moltmann as an interpreter of Bonhoeffer.' *Studies in Religion/Sciences religieuses* 12 (1983), pp. 449–60.

— 'Jürgen Moltmann and the Christian Dialogue with Marxism.' *Journal of Ecumenical Studies* 18 (1981), pp. 435–50.

— 'Moltmann's Vision of Man.' *Anglican Theological Review* 56 (1974), pp. 310–30.

Chiba, S. 'Transcendence and the Political: A Critical Comparison of Reinhold Niebuhr and Jürgen Moltmann.' Ph.D. thesis, Princeton Theological Seminary, 1983.

Chopp, R. S. *The Praxis of Suffering: An Interpretation of Liberation and Political Theologies.* Maryknoll: Orbis, 1986. (Chapter 6 on Moltmann.)

Claybrook, D. A. 'The Emerging Doctrine of the Holy Spirit in the Writings of Jürgen Moltmann.' Ph.D. thesis, Southern Baptist Theological Seminary, 1983.

Cobb, J. B., Jr. 'Reply to Jürgen Moltmann's "The Unity of the Triune God".' *St Vladimir's Theological Quarterly* 28 (1984), pp. 173–8.

Cole-Turner, R. S. 'God's Experience: The Trinitarian Theology of Jürgen Moltmann in Conversation with Charles Hartshorne.' Ph.D. thesis, Princeton Theological Seminary, 1983.

Conyers, A. J. *God, Hope, and History: Jürgen Moltmann and the Christian Concept of History.* Macon: Mercer University Press, 1988.

Cook, M. L. *The Jesus of Faith: A Study in Christology.* New York: Paulist Press, 1981.

Dabney, D. L. 'The Advent of the Spirit: The Turn to Pneumatology in the Theology of Jürgen Moltmann.' *Asbury Theological Journal* 48 (1993), pp. 81–108.

Deane-Drummond, C. 'A Critique of Jürgen Moltmann's Green Theology.' *New Blackfriars* 73 (1992), pp. 554–65.

— 'Moltmann's Ecological Theology: A Manifesto for the Greens?,' *Theology in Green* 1 (1992), pp. 21–7.

— 'Towards a Green Theology Through Analysis of the Ecological Motif in Jürgen Moltmann's Doctrine of Creation.' Ph.D. thesis, University of Manchester, 1992.

Deuser, H., Martin, G. M., Stock, K., Welker, M. (eds), *Gottes Zukunft – Zukunft der Welt: Festschrift für Jürgen Moltmann zum 60. Geburtstag.* Munich: Chr. Kaiser, 1986.

Dillistone, F. W. 'The Theology of Jürgen Moltmann.' *Modern Churchman* 18 (1974–5), pp. 145–50.

Dorrien, G. J. *Reconstructing the Common Good: Theology and the Social Order.* Maryknoll, New York: Orbis, 1990. (Chapter 4 on Moltmann.)

Dumas, A. *Political Theology and the Life of the Church.* Tr. J. Bowden. London: SCM Press, 1978. (Chapter 5 on Moltmann.)

Eckardt, A. R. 'Jürgen Moltmann, the Jewish People, and the Holocaust.' *Journal of the American Academy of Religion* 44 (1976), pp. 675–91.

Eckardt, A. R. and A. *Long Night's Journey into Day: Life and Faith after the Holocaust.* Wayne State University Press, 1982.

Eyt, P. 'La réévaluation de l'espérance selon J. Moltmann.' *Bulletin de littérature ecclésiastique* 72 (1971), pp. 161–86.

Fiddes, P. S. *The Creative Suffering of God.* Oxford: Clarendon Press, 1988. (Pages 5–14, 80–6, 135–43 on Moltmann.)

Ford, J. C. 'Towards an Anthropology of Mutuality: A Critique of Karl Barth's Doctrine of the Male–Female Order as A and B with a Comparison of the Panentheistic Theology of Jürgen Moltmann.' Ph.D. thesis, Northwestern University (Evanston, Ill.), 1984.

Fiorenza, F. P. 'Dialectical Theology and Hope.' *Heythrop Journal* 9 (1968), pp. 143–63, 384–99; 10 (1969), pp. 26–42.

French, W. 'Returning to Creation: Moltmann's Eschatology Naturalized.' *Journal of Religion* 68 (1988), pp. 78–86.

Gibellini, R. *La Teologia di Jürgen Moltmann.* (Giornale di Teologia 89.) Brescia: Queriniana, 1975.

Gilkey, L. *Reaping the Whirlwind: A Christian Interpretation of History.* New York: Seabury, 1976. (Pages 226–38 on Moltmann.)

— 'Reinhold Niebuhr's Theology of History.' In *The Legacy of Reinhold Niebuhr,* (ed.) N. A. Scott (Chicago: University of Chicago Press, 1975), pp. 63ff. (= *Journal of Religion* 54/4, 1974).

Grässer, E. '»Der politisch gekreuzigte Christus«: Kritische Anmerkungen zu einer politischen Hermeneutik des Evangeliums.' *Zeitschrift für die neutestamentliche Wissenschaft* 62 (1971), pp. 260–94.

Gunneman, J. P. *The Moral Meaning of Revolution.* New Haven: Yale University Press, 1979.

Gutiérrez, G. 'Response to Jürgen Moltmann.' In H. D. Regan and A. J. Torrance (eds), *Christ and Context: The Confrontation between Gospel and Culture* (Edinburgh: T. & T. Clark, 1993), pp. 201–4.

Hafstad, K. 'Gott in der Natur: Zur Schöpfungslehre Jürgen Moltmanns.' *Evangelische Theologie* 47 (1987), pp. 460–6.

Havrilak, G. 'Eastern Christian Elements in the Christology of Karl Rahner and Jürgen Moltmann: Contemporary Trends in Catholic and Protestant Thought from an Orthodox Perspective.' Ph.D. thesis, Fordham University, 1986.

Hedinger, U. 'Glaube und Hoffnung bei Ernst Fuchs und Jürgen Moltmann.' *Evangelische Theologie* 27 (1967), pp. 36–51.

Henke, P. *Gewissheit vor dem Nichts: Eine Antithese zu den theologischen Entwürfen Wolfhart Pannenbergs und Jürgen Moltmanns.* Berlin/New York: de Gruyter, 1978.

Herman, W. R. 'Moltmann's Christology.' *Studia Biblica et Theologica* 17 (1989), pp. 3–31.

Herzog, F. (ed.) *The Future of Hope: Theology as Eschatology.* New York: Herder & Herder, 1970.

Hill, W. J. *The Three-Personed God: The Trinity as a Mystery of Salvation.* Washington, D.C.: Catholic University Press of America, 1982. (Pages 166–75 on Moltmann.)

Hodgson, P. C. *Jesus – Word and Presence: An Essay in Christology.* Philadelphia: Fortress, 1971. (Pages 9–20, 220–41 on Moltmann.)

Hryniewicz, W. 'Le Dieu souffrant? Réflexions sur la notion chrétienne de Dieu.' *Eglise et théologie* 12 (1981), pp. 333–56.

Hunsinger, G. 'The Crucified God and the Political Theology of Violence.' *Heythrop Journal* 14 (1973), pp. 266–79, 379–95.

Irish, J. A. 'Moltmann's Theology of Contradiction.' *Theology Today* 32 (1975–6), pp. 21–31.

Jantzen, G. M. 'Christian Hope and Jesus' Despair.' *King's Theological Review* 5 (1982), pp. 1–7.

Johnston, R. K. *The Christian at Play*. Grand Rapids: Eerdmans, 1983. (Pages 64–71 on Moltmann.)

Kerstiens, F. 'The Theology of Hope in Germany Today.' *Concilium* 9/6 (1970), pp. 101–11.

King, A. 'The Question of "Person" and "Subject" in Trinitarian Theology: Moltmann's Challenge to Rahner and its Implications.' Ph.D. thesis, Fordham University, 1986.

Küng, H. 'Die Religionen als Frage an die Theologie des Kreuzes.' *Evangelische Theologie* 33 (1973), pp. 401–23.

Kuschel, K.-J. *Born Before All Time? The Dispute over Christ's Origin.* Tr. J. Bowden. London: SCM Press, 992. (Pages 440–51 on Moltmann.)

Kuzmic, P. 'A Croatian War-Time Reading' [of *The Spirit of Life*]. *Journal of Pentecostal Theology* 4 (1994), pp. 17–24.

Lapoorta, J. J. 'An African Response' [to *The Spirit of Life*]. *Journal of Pentecostal Theology* 4 (1994), pp. 51–8.

Lavalette, H. de. 'Ambiguïtés de la théologie politique.' *Recherches de science religieuse* 59 (1971), pp. 545–62.

Link, C. 'Schöpfung im messianischen Licht.' *Evangelische Theologie* 47 (1987), pp. 83–92.

Lønning, P. 'Die Schöpfungstheologie Jürgen Moltmanns – eine nordische Perspektive.' *Kerygma und Dogma* 33 (1987), pp. 207–23.

Lunn, A. J. 'The Doctrine of Atonement: (3) The Significance of the Cross for Moltmann and Dillistone.' *Epworth Review* 19/1 (1992), pp. 26–34.

Macchia, F. D. 'A North American Response' [to *The Spirit of Life*]. *Journal of Pentecostal Theology* 4 (1994), pp. 25–33.

MacDade, J. 'The Trinity and the Paschal Mystery.' *Heythrop Journal* 29 (1988), pp. 175–91.

McGrath, A. E. *The Making of Modern German Christology: From the Enlightenment to Pannenberg.* Oxford: Blackwell, 1986. (Chapter 8 on Moltmann.)

Mackey, J. P. *The Christian Experience of God as Trinity.* London: SCM Press, 1983. (Pages 202–9 on Moltmann.)

MacPherson, J. 'Life, the Universe and Everything: Jürgen Moltmann's *God in Creation.' St Mark's Review* 128 (1986), pp. 34–46.

Macquarrie, J. *Christian Hope.* London/Oxford: Mowbrays, 1978. (Pages 47–9, 101–3 on Moltmann.)

— 'Theologies of Hope: A Critical Examination.' In *Thinking about God* (London: SCM Press, 1975), pp. 221–32.

— 'Today's Word for Today: I. Jürgen Moltmann.' *Expository Times* 92 (1980), pp. 4–7.

McWilliams, W. 'Divine Suffering in Contemporary Theology.' *Scottish Journal of Theology* 33 (1980), pp. 35–53.

— *The Passion of God: Divine Suffering in Contemporary Protestant Theology.* Macon: Mercer University Press, 1985. (Chapter 2 on Moltmann.)

Marsch, W.-D. (ed.) *Diskussion über die »Theologie der Hoffnung« von Jürgen Moltmann.* Munich: Chr. Kaiser, 1967.

Mason, G. 'God's Freedom as Faithfulness: A Critique of Jürgen Moltmann's Social Trinitarianism.' Ph.D. thesis, Southwestern Baptist Theological Seminary, 1987.

Matic, M. *Jürgen Moltmanns Theologie in Auseinandersetzung mit Ernst Bloch.* (Europäische Hochschulschriften 23/209.) Frankfurt am Main: P. Lang, 1983.

Meeks, M. D. *Origins of the Theology of Hope.* Philadelphia: Fortress, 1974.

— 'Trinitarian Theology: A Review Article.' *Theology Today* 38 (1981–2), pp. 472–7.

Meyendorff, J. 'Reply to Jürgen Moltmann's "The Unity of the Triune God".' *St Vladimir's Theological Quarterly* 28 (1984), pp. 183–8.

Migliore, D. L. 'Biblical Eschatology and Political Hermeneutics.' *Theology Today* 26 (1969–70), pp. 116–32.

Miguez Bonino, J. *Revolutionary Theology Comes of Age.* London: SPCK, 1975. (Pages 144–50 on Moltmann.)

Molnar, P. 'The Function of the Trinity in Moltmann's Ecological Doctrine of Creation.' *Theological Studies* 51 (1990), pp. 673–97.

Momose, P. F. *Kreuzestheologie: Eine Auseinandersetzung mit Jürgen Moltmann. Mit einem Nachwort von Jürgen Moltmann.* Freiburg/Basel/Vienna: Herder, 1978.

Mondin, B. 'Theology of Hope and the Christian Message.' *Biblical Theology Bulletin* 2 (1972), pp. 43–63.

Morse, C. *The Logic of Promise in Moltmann's Theology.* Philadelphia: Fortress, 1979.

Mottu, H. 'L'espérance chrétienne dans la pensée de Jürgen Moltmann.' *Revue de théologie et de philosophie* 17 (1967), pp. 242–58.

Müller, D. 'Résumé des débats.' In L. Rumpf *et al.*, *Hegel et la théologie contemporaine: L'absolu dans l'histoire?* (Neuchatel/Paris: Delachaux & Niestlé, 1977), pp. 219–25.

Muller, R. A. 'Christ in the Eschaton: Calvin and Moltmann on the Duration of the Munus Regium.' *Harvard Theological Review* 74 (1981), pp. 31–59.

Neuhaus, R. J. 'Moltmann vs. Monotheism.' *Dialog* 20 (1981), pp. 239–43.

Niewiadomski, J. *Die Zweideutigkeit von Gott und Welt in J. Moltmanns Theologien.* (Innsbrucker theologische Studien 9.) Innsbruck/Vienna/Munich: Tyrolia, 1982.

O'Collins, G. 'Spes Quaerens Intellectum.' *Interpretation* 22 (1968), pp. 36–52.

— 'The Principle and Theology of Hope.' *Scottish Journal of Theology* 21 (1968), pp. 129–44.

O'Donnell, J. J. 'The Doctrine of the Trinity in Recent German Theology.' *Heythrop Journal* 23 (1982), pp. 153–67.

— 'The Trinity as Divine Community: A Critical Reflection upon Recent Theological Developments.' *Gregorianum* 69 (1988), pp. 5–34.

— *Trinity and Temporality: The Christian Doctrine of God in the Light of Process Theology and the Theology of Hope.* Oxford: Oxford University Press, 1983.

Olson, R. 'Trinity and Eschatology: The Historical Being of God in Jürgen Moltmann and Wolfhart Pannenberg.' *Scottish Journal of Theology* 36 (1983), pp. 213–27.

Pannenberg, W. *Christian Spirituality and Sacramental Community.* London: Darton, Longman & Todd, 1984. (Chapter 3 on Moltmann.)

Pawlikowski, J. 'The Holocaust and Contemporary Christology.' *Concilium* 175 (5/1984) = *The Holocaust as Interruption,* (eds) E. S. Fiorenza and D. Tracy (Edinburgh: T. & T. Clark, 1984), pp. 43–9.

Peters, T. 'Trinity Talk: Part I.' *Dialog* 26 (1987), pp. 44–7.

— 'Moltmann and the Way of the Trinity.' *Dialog* 31 (1992), pp. 272–9.

Preston, R. H. 'Reflections on Theologies of Social Change.' In *Theology and Change: Essays in Memory of Alan Richardson*, (ed.) R. H. Preston (London: SCM Press, 1975), pp. 143–66 = R. H. Preston, *Religion and the Persistence of Capitalism* (London: SCM Press, 1979), pp. 135–61.

Primavesi, A. 'The Cross and the Rose: The Interaction of Lutheran Paradox and Hegelian Dialectic Exemplified in the Theology of Jürgen Moltmann.' Ph.D. thesis, Heythrop College, University of London, 1987.

Ricoeur, P. 'Freedom in the Light of Hope.' In Ricoeur, *Essays on Biblical Interpretation*, (ed.) L. S. Mudge (London: SPCK, 1981), pp. 155–82.

Ritschl, D. 'Die vier Reiche der drei göttlichen Subjekte: Bemerkungen zu Jürgen Moltmanns Trinitätslehre.' *Evangelische Theologie* 41 (1981), pp. 463–71.

Runia, K. *The present-day Christological debate.* Leicester: Inter-Varsity Press, 1984. (Pages 38–46 on Moltmann.)

Sauter, G. '"Exodus" and "Liberation" as Theological Metaphors: A Critical Case-Study of the Use of Allegory and Misunderstood Analogies in Ethics.' *Scottish Journal of Theology* 34 (1981), pp. 481–507.

Schuurman, D. 'Creation, Eschaton and Ethics: An Analysis of Theology and Ethics in Jürgen Moltmann.' *Calvin Theological Journal* 22 (1987), pp. 42–67.

Schweitzer, D. 'The consistency of Jürgen Moltmann's Theology.' *Studies in Religion/Sciences religieuses* 22 (1993), pp. 197–208.

Sepúlveda, J. 'The Perspective of Chilean Pentecostalism' [on *The Spirit of Life*]. *Journal of Pentecostal Theology* 4 (1994), pp. 41–9.

Simpson, G. M. '*Theologia Crucis* and the Forensically Fraught World: Engaging Helmut Peukert and Jürgen Habermas.' *Journal of Religion* 57 (1989), pp. 509–42.

Sobrino, J. *Christology at the Crossroads: A Latin American Approach.* Tr. J. Drury. London: SCM Press, 1978. (Pages 28–33 on Moltmann.)

Steen, M. 'Jürgen Moltmann's Critical Reception of K. Barth's Theopaschitism.' *Ephemerides Theologiae Lovanienses* 67 (1991), pp. 276–311.

Stibbe, M. W. G. 'A British Appraisal' [of *The Spirit of Life*]. *Journal of Pentecostal Theology* 4 (1994), pp. 5–16.

Strunk, R. 'Diskussion über "Der gekreuzigte Gott".' *Evangelische Theologie* 41 (1981), pp. 89–94.

Surin, K. *Theology and the Problem of Evil.* Oxford: Blackwell, 1986. (Pages 124–32 on Moltmann.)

Sykes, S. W. 'Life After Death: the Christian Doctrine of Heaven.' In *Creation Christ and Culture: Studies in Honour of T. F. Torrance,* (ed.) R. W. A. McKinney (Edinburgh: T. & T. Clark, 1976), pp. 250–71.

Tang, S.-K. 'God's History in the Theology of Jürgen Moltmann.' Ph.D. thesis, University of St Andrews, 1994.

Thévenaz, J.-P. 'Le Dieu crucifié n'a-t-il plus d'histoire?' *Revue de théologie et de philosophie* 115 (1983), pp. 199–208.

— 'Passion de Dieu, passions humaines et sympathie des choses: Ethique et messianisme chez J. Moltmann.' *Revue de théologie et de philosophie* 119 (1987), pp. 303–21.

— 'Vérité d'espérance ou vérité de connaissance? Les enjeux théoriques et politiques de la théologie de Jürgen Moltmann.' *Etudes théologiques et religieuses* 49 (1974), pp. 225–47.

Thils, G. '»Soyez riches d'espérance par la vertu du Saint-Esprit« (Romans 15,13): La théologie d'éspérance de J. Moltmann.' *Ephemerides Theologicae Lovanienses* 47 (1971), pp. 495–503.

Thistlethwaite, S. B. 'Comments on Jürgen Moltmann's "The Unity of the Triune God".' *St Vladimir's Theological Quarterly* 28 (1984), pp. 179–82.

Timm, H. 'Evangelische Weltweisheit: Zur der ökotheologischen Apokalyptik.' *Zeitschrift für Theologie und Kirche* 84 (1987), pp. 340–70.

Torrance, A. J. 'Response to Jürgen Moltmann.' In H. D. Regan and A. J. Torrance (eds), *Christ and Context: The Confrontation between Gospel and Culture* (Edinburgh: T. & T. Clark, 1993), pp. 192–200.

Tripole, M. R. 'A Church for the Poor and the World: At Issue with Moltmann's Ecclesiology.' *Theological Studies* 42 (1981), pp. 645–59.

— 'Ecclesiological developments in Moltmann's Theology of Hope.' *Theological Studies* 34 (1973), pp. 19–35.

Vignaux, P. 'Conditions d'une théologie d'espérance.' In J. Daniélou *et al.*, *Espérance chrétienne et avenir humaine* (Les quatres Fleuves 2) (Paris: Editions du Seuil, 1974), pp. 82–96.

Walsh, B. J. 'Theology of Hope and the Doctrine of Creation: An Appraisal of Jürgen Moltmann.' *Evangelical Quarterly* 59 (1987), pp. 53–76.

Webster, J. B. 'Jürgen Moltmann: Trinity and Suffering.' *Evangel* 3/2 (1985), pp. 4–6.

Welker, M. (ed.), *Diskussion über Jürgen Moltmanns Buch »Der gekreuzigte Gott«*. Munich: Chr. Kaiser, 1979.

West, P. 'Cruciform Labour? The Cross in Two Recent Theologies of Work.' *Modern Churchman* 28/4 (1986), pp. 9–15.

Widmer, G.-P. 'Le nouveau et le possible: Notes sur les théologies de l'espérance.' *Revue d'histoire et de philosophie religieuses* 55 (1975), pp. 165–75.

— 'L'essence trinitaire et l'histoire trinitaire de Dieu.' *Revue d'histoire et de philosophie religieuses* 56 (1976), pp. 495–508.

Wiebe, B. 'Interpretation and Historical Criticism: Jürgen Moltmann.' *Restoration Quarterly* 24 (1981), pp. 155–66.

— 'Revolution as an Issue in Theology: Jürgen Moltmann.' *Restoration Quarterly* 26 (1983), pp. 105–20.

Wiederkehr, D. 'Neue Interpretation der Kreuzestodes Jesu: Zu J. Moltmanns Buch »Der gekreuzigte Gott«.' *Freiburger Zeitschrift für Philosophie und Theologie* 20 (1973), pp. 441–63.

Williams, S. N. *Jürgen Moltmann: A Critical Introduction*. Leicester: Theological Students Fellowship, 1987.

Williams, S. N. 'Reformed Perspective on Mission and Hope.' *Reformed World* 39 (1986), pp. 625–31.

Willis, W. W., Jr. *Theism, Atheism and the Doctrine of God: The Trinitarian Theologies of Karl Barth and Jürgen Moltmann in Response to Protest Atheism.* Atlanta: Scholars Press, 1987.

Winling, R. 'Futur et Avenir: à propos d'une mise au point de J. Moltmann.' *Recherches de science religieuse* 53 (1979), pp. 180–4.

Witvliet, T. *The Way of the Black Messiah.* Tr. J. Bowden. London: SCM Press, 1987. (Pages 51–9 on Moltmann.)

Wood, L. W. 'From Barth's Trinitarian Christology to Moltmann's Trinitarian Pneumatology.' *Asbury Theological Journal* 48 (1993), pp. 49–80.

Young, N. *Creator, Creation and Faith.* London: Collins, 1976. (Chapter 8 on Moltmann.)

Zimany, R. D. 'Moltmann's Crucified God.' *Dialog* 16 (1977), pp. 49–56.

Index